AF515856

Words Confused & Misused

English words that almost everyone confuses and misuses...

Words Confused & Misused

English words that almost everyone confuses and misuses...

Raman D'Souza

arihant
ARIHANT PUBLICATIONS (INDIA) LIMITED

arihant

ARIHANT PUBLICATIONS (INDIA) LIMITED
All Rights Reserved

© Publisher

No part of this publication may be re-produced, stored in a retrieval system or by any means, electronic, mechanical, photocopying, recording, scanning, web or otherwise without the written permission of the publisher. Arihant has obtained all the information in this book from the sources believed to be reliable and true. However, Arihant or its editors or authors or illustrators don't take any responsibility for the absolute accuracy of any information published and the damage or loss suffered thereupon.

All disputes subject to Meerut (UP) jurisdiction only.
Administrative & Production Offices

Regd. Office

'Ramchhaya' 4577/15, Agarwal Road, Darya Ganj, New Delhi -110002
Tele: 011- 47630600, 43518550

Head Office

Kalindi, TP Nagar, Meerut (UP) - 250002
Tel: 0121-7156203, 7156204

Sales & Support Offices

Agra, Ahmedabad, Bengaluru, Bareilly, Chennai, Delhi, Guwahati, Hyderabad, Jaipur, Jhansi, Kolkata, Lucknow, Nagpur & Pune.

ISBN 978-93-27198-81-2

PRICE ₹185.00

PO No. : TXT-59-T050993-12-22

Published by Arihant Publications (India) Ltd.

For further information about the books published by Arihant, log on to www.arihantbooks.com or e-mail at info@arihantbooks.com

Follow us on

CONTENTS

1

First Word of Each Group Beginning with-A

1. ABANDON/DESERT

abandon : (a) go away from a thing, place or person not intending to return :
The crew *abandoned* the sinking ship.
(b) leave sth/sb to be taken by sb :
('sth' stands for 'something', 'sb' stands for 'somebody')
They *abandoned* their lands and property to the invading forces.
(c) give up completely :
The match was *abandoned* because of bad weather.
(d) yield completely to an emotion or impulse :
He *abandoned* himself to despair.

desert : (a) leave sb without help or support :
He *deserted* his young wife and went abroad.
(b) leave service in the armed forces :
Ten soldiers *deserted* from the army.
(c) fail sb :
His coverage *deserted* him.

2. ABATE/ABET

abate : (a) become less :
I left home when the storm had *abated*.
(b) make less :
People are campaigning to *abate* the noise in the cities.

abet : (a) help or encourage sb to commit an offence or do sth wrong :
He was abetted in these illegal activities by his wife.
(b) encourage a crime, etc :
You are *abetting* theft.

3. ABDICATE/RESIGN/RELINQUISH

abdicate : (a) resign from or formally renounce the throne :
The king of Egypt *abdicated* about forty years ago.
(b) formally give up power, a high official position, etc :
He has *abdicated* all responsibility in the affair.

resign : give up a job, position, etc :
She *resigned* her directorship and left the firm.
I *resigned* my post as chairman of the company.

relinquish :
(a) give up or cease to feel, practise, etc, sth :
You should *relinquish* bad habits.
They *relinquished* the struggle for power.
(b) give up or renounce a claim, etc; surrender sth :
I *relinquished* the possession of the house in favour of my brother.

4. ABILITY/CAPACITY

ability : (a) power to do sth physical or mental :
Mohini has the *ability* to do the work.
(b) cleverness; intelligence :
He is a man of great *ability*.
(c) talent :
He has a great musical ability.

capacity : (a) ability to hold or contain sth :
This hall has a seating *capacity* of 6000.
The cinema is filled to *capacity*.
(b) power to produce sth :
Our factory is working at full *capacity*.
(c) ability to produce, experience, understand or learn sth:
I have an enormous *capacity* for hard work.
This book is within the *capacity* of (i.e. can be understood by) younger readers.

5. ABJECT/OBJECT: *ALSO REFER TO P. 148.*

abject : (a) hopeless; wretched:
They are living in *abject* poverty.
(b) despicable; contemptible:
He is an *abject* devil.

object : (a) purpose; intention; thing aimed at :
What is your *object* in life?
(b) person or thing to which sth is done or some feeling or thought is directed :
This building is the main *object* of his interest.
Her indomitable courage is an *object* of great admiration.

6. ABLE/CAPABLE

able : (a) have the power, means or opportunity to do sth :
The child is not yet *able* to write.
(b) competent; having knowledge or skill :
He is an *able* worker.

capable : (a) having the ability or power necessary for sth :
I am *capable* of better work than this.
She is *capable* of running a mile in five minutes.
(b) having ability :
She is a very *capable* woman.
(c) have the character or inclination to do sth :
He is quite *capable* of lying to get out of trouble.
(d) open to or allowing sth :
Our position is *capable* of improvement.

7. ABNORMAL/SUBNORMAL

abnormal : different, in an undesirable way, from what is normal, ordinary or expected : is he mentally *abnormal*?

subnormal :
(a) below normal; less than normal :
Subnormal temperature does not suit my health.
(b) below the normal level of intelligence :
He has a *subnormal* child.

8. ABSTAIN/REFRAIN

abstain : (a) keep oneself from doing or enjoying sth' especially taking alcoholic drinks :
He *abstains* from drinks and drugs.
(b) decline to use one's vote :
At the last election, I *abstained* from voting.

refrain : keep oneself from doing sth :
You should *refrain* from smoking.
I hope she will *refrain* from hostile action.

9. ACCEDE/EXCEED

accede : (a) agree to request, proposal, and so on :
She *acceded* to my earnest request.
(b) take office :
I *acceded* to the chancellorship of the university last year.
(c) become monarch :
When did Akbar, the Great, *accede* to the throne?

exceed : (a) go beyond what is allowed, necessary or advisable :
Don't *exceed* the speed limit.
Your expenses should not *exceed* your income.
(b) be greater or more numerous than sth :
Her success *exceeded* all expectations.
The price will not *exceed* two hundred rupees.

10. ACCEPT/EXCEPT

accept : (a) take sth offered willingly :
She accepted my invitation to dinner.
I *accepted* your apology.
(b) to say 'yes' to an offer :
She offered me a lift and I *accepted* it.
I proposed marriage and she *accepted* my proposal.
(c) receive sb/sth as suitable or adequate :
Will you accept a cheque?
The college I applied to has *accepted* me.
(d) be willing or agree to sth :
He *accepted* the magistrate's decision.
I *accept* the proposed changes.
(e) take upon oneself a responsibility, etc :
He *accepts* blame for the accident.
You must *accept* the consequences of your action.
(f) take sth as true; believe sth :
I do not *accept* your explanation.
(g) treat sb/sth as welcome :
He was never really *accepted* by his colleagues.

except : not including sb/sth; but not :
The restaurant is open everyday *except* Monday.
Everyone *except* me got an invitation.
I answered all the questions *except* for the last.

Note : *Except*, as a verb, means exclude sb/sth; leave sb/sth out :
Only children under five are *excepted* from this survey.
We all had to take part in the training run, with nobody *excepted*.

11. ACCESS/EXCESS

access : (a) means of approaching or entering a place; way in :
Where is the *access* to the airport?
His farmhouse is easy to *access*.
(b) opportunity or right to use sth or approach sb :
Only high officials have *access* to the Prime Minister.
Students must have *access* to a good library.

excess : (a) more than the reasonable, expected or moderate degree or amount of sth :
Excess of anything is bad.
An *excess* of fat in your diet can lead to heart disease.
(b) going beyond the normal or accepted limit :
Don't carry your anger to *excess*.
Do you drink to *excess*?

12. ACCESSARY/ACCESSORY

accessary : (a) person who helps another in a crime :
He was charged with being an accessary to murder.
She was made an *accessary* to the crime.

accessory : (a) sth extra, helpful, useful, but not an essential part of :
What are the *accessories* of a scooter?
(b) small articles of a woman's dress :
Can you name the *accessories* of a woman's dress?

13. ACCIDENT/INCIDENT

accident : (a) event that happens unexpectedly and causes damage, injury, and so forth :
Five persons were killed in a road *accident*.
(b) chance; fortune :
By *accident* of birth, he is entitled to British citizenship.

incident : (a) event or happening, often of minor importance :
He narrated every trivial *incident* in great detail.
(b) hostile military activity between countries, opposing forces, etc:
There were border *incidents* in the recent past.
(c) public disturbance, *accident* or violence :
The demonstration proceeded without incident.

14. ACE/ACHE

ace : person who is an expert at some activity :
He is an *ace* pilot.

ache : continuous dull pain :
She has an *ache* in her chest.

15. ACKNOWLEDGE/ADMIT/CONFESS

acknowledge :
(a) accept the truth, reality or existence of sth :
We *acknowledge* the need for social reform.
He *acknowledged* it to be true.
They refused to *acknowledge* defeat.
(b) report that one has received sth :
I *acknowledged* receipt of her letter.

(c) express thanks for sth :
He *acknowledged* my help.
His services to the country were never officially *acknowledged*.

(d) show by a smile, nod of the head, greeting, etc. that one has noticed or recognised sb :
I was standing right next to her, but she did not even *acknowledge* my presence.

(e) accept sb as sth :
I *acknowledged* him as my heir.
He was generally *acknowledged* to be the greatest historian in the country.

(f) accept or recognise sth :
The country *acknowledged* his claim to the throne.

admit : (a) allow sb /sth to enter :
Each ticket *admits* two presons to the party.

(b) accept sb into a hospital as a patient, or into a school, etc. as a pupil :
He was *admitted* to hospital with minor burns.
Our school admits seventy new boys and girls every year.

(c) have room for sb/sth :
The theatre admits only 400 persons.

(d) to recognise sth as true, often reluctantly :
He *admitted* his mistake.

(e) leave room for sth; allow the possibility of sth:
Your conduct *admits* of no excuse.
The plan does not admit of improvement.

confess : (a) say formally that one has committed a crime. etc :
The prisoner *confessed* that he had murdered her.

16. ACME/ACNE

acme : point of perfection; highest stage of development:
He is eager to reach the *acme* of success.

acne : inflammation of the oil-glands of the skin, producing red pimples on the face and neck :
Many adolescents suffer from *acne*.

17. ACT/ACTION

act : (a) thing done; deed :
It is an *act* of kindness to help a blind man cross the street.

(b) any of the main divisions of a play or an opera :
This is a play in five *acts*.

(c) any of a series of short performances in a programme; piece of entertainment :
There was a song and dance *act* in the programme.

(d) decree or law made by a legislative body :
Parliament has passed an *Act* which makes such sports illegal.

(e) way of behaving which is not genuine, but adopted for the effect it will have on others; pretence :
Don't take him seriously-it is all an *act*.
She is just putting on an *act*.

Note : *Act*, as a verb, means :

1. do sth :
His life was saved because the doctors *acted* very promptly.

2. do what is expected of one as a professional or an official person :
The police refused to *act* without more evidence.
3. Perform a part in a play or film; be an actor or actress :
She *acts* well.
Have you ever *acted*?
4. take the part of a character in a play or film :
Who is *acting* the part of Sita ?
5. pretend by one's behaviour to be a certain person or type of person :
He is not really angry— he is just *acting*.

action : (a) process of doing sth; activity; using energy or influence :
The time has come for *action*.
He is a man of *action*.
(b) events in a story or play :
The *action* of the play is set in Kolkata.
(c) fighting in battle between troops, warships, and so on :
Hundreds of people were killed in *action* during the Iraq- U.S.A. war.
He saw *action* during the last Indo-Pak war.
(d) legal process; lawsuit :
He brought an *action* against her.
(e) way of functioning, especially of a part of the body :
Study the *action* of his liver.

18. ADAPT/ADEPT/ADOPT

adapt : (a) make sth suitable for a new use, situation, etc; modify sth :
The styles can be *adapted* to suit individual tastes.
(b) alter or modify a text to suit television, stage, etc :
This story has been *adapted* for radio from the English original.
(c) become adjusted to new conditions, etc :
I *adapted* myself quickly to the new climate.

adept : expert or skilful in sth :
You are *adept* in telling lies.

Note : *Adept*, as a noun, means person who is skilful in something :
He is an *adept* in carpentry.

adopt : (a) take sb into one's family, especially as one's child or heir :
As he has no child of his own, he decided to *adopt* an orphan.
(b) choose sb as a candidate or representative :
He has been *adopted* as congress candidate from New Delhi.
(c) take over and have or use sth as one's own :
They *adopted* our production methods.
Have you *adopted* a new style of dress?
(d) approve; accept a report, recommendation, etc :
The government has *adopted* the committee's suggestions to root out corruption.

19. ADDICTED/DEVOTED

addicted : (a) unable to stop taking or using sth due to habit :
He has become *addicted* to drugs.
(b) strongly interested in sth, being a hobby or pastime :
Are you *addicted* to T.V. soap operas?

devoted : very loving or loyal :
I am *devoted* to my friends.
Are you *devoted* to your wife?

20. ADDITION/EDITION

addition : (a) adding, especially calculating the total of two or more numbers :
The sign + stands for *addition*.
(b) person or thing added :
She will be a very useful *addition* to our team.

edition : (a) form in which a book is published :
It is a paperback *edition* of the book.
(b) total number of copies of a book, newspaper, etc. issued atone time :
This is a revised *edition* of the book, titled-Interview Manual.
This is the morning *edition* of the newspaper.

21. ADMISSION/ADMITTANCE

admission : entering or being allowed to enter a building, society, club, school, college, and so on :
Admission to the club is restricted to its members only.
Admission to universities depends on examination results .
How does one gain *admission* to a medical college?

admittance : allowing sb or being allowed to enter, especially a private place; right of entry :
He was refused admittance to the house.
No *admittance*-keep out.

22. ADVERSE/AVERSE

adverse : (a) not favourable; contrary :
He is living in *adverse* circumstances.
(b) opposing; hostile:
Your *adverse* criticism has hurt her feelings.
There was an *adverse* reaction to your proposals.
(c) harmful:
There are *adverse* effects of this medicine.

averse : opposed to sth; not liking sth :
He seems to be *averse* to hard work.

23. ADVICE/ADVISE

advice : (a) opinion given about what to do or how to behave :
She acted on my *advice*.
(b) formal note giving information about a transaction, etc :
We have received the *advice* that the goods had been dispatched.

advise : (a) recommend; give advice to sb :
The doctor *advised* me to take complete rest.
I *advise* the government on economic affairs.
I *advised* her against marrying early.
(b) inform or notify sb :
please *advise* us of the dispatch of the goods.

24. AFFECTION/AFFECTATION

affection : love; feeling of fondness :
He felt great *affection* for his sister.

He tried to win her *affection*.
Have you *affection* for your children?

affectation : (a) unnatural behaviour, manner of speaking, etc, intended to impress others:
I detest all *affectation*.
His little *affectations* irritated her.
(b) pretence; deliberate display of gestures etc. that are not truly felt :
His *affectation*, while singing, really gets on my nerves.

25. AFFECT/EFFECT

affect : (a) have an influence on sb/sth; produce an effect on :
Their opinion will not affect my decision.
The change in climate may *affect* your health.
The tax increases have *affected* us all.
Alcohol *affects* the driver's concentration.
(b) infect; attack sb/sth :
Cancer *affected* his lungs.
(c) cause sb to have feelings of sadness or sympathy; touch :
We were deeply *affected* by the news of her sad and sudden demise.

Note : There is another *affect* having the following meanings :
1. make an obvious show of using, wearing or liking sth :
He *affects* a pretentious use of the English language.
2. pretend to have or feel sth :
He *affected* a foreign accent.
3. pose as; pretend to be sth :
She *affects* the helpless female.

effect : (a) bring sth about; cause to occur; accomplish :
They *effected* their escape in the middle of the night.
The government has *effected* many an economic reform.

Note : *Effect*, as a noun, means :
1. change produced by an action or cause; result or outcome :
What are the *effects* of heat on metal?
Did the medicine have any *effect*?
My advice had no *effect* on him.
2. impression produced on the mind of the listener, spectator, reader, etc :
The general effect of the painting was over-whelming.
The stage lighting gives the *effect* of a moonlight scene.
She dresses like that only for the *effect* it creates.
3. personal property; possessions :
Where are your household *effects*?

Note : In the sense as (c) above, *effects*, plural form of *effect*, must be used :

26. AFFECTING/AFFECTED

affecting : moving or touching:
The Prime Minister made an *affecting* appeal for help.

affected : artificial; pretended; not natural or genuine.
He has a highly *affected* style of writing.
Do try not to be so *affected*.

27. AFFLICT/INFLICT

afflict : cause trouble, pain or distress to sb/sth :
She is *afflicted* with arthritis.
Severe drought has *afflicted* many rural areas.

inflict : (a) cause a blow, penalty, etc. to be suffered by sb :
We *inflicted* crushing defeat on the enemy.
I *inflicted* a severe wound on the thief.
(b) force sb to accept one's unwelcome presence :
He apologized for *inflicting* his company on us.
My uncle is *inflicting* himself on (i.e. visiting) us again this weekend.

28. AFT/APT

aft : near or towards the stem of a ship, or the tail of an aircraft :
The security guard asked us not to go *aft*.

apt : (a) suitable; appropriate; to the point :
That was an *apt* quotation.
(b) quick at learning :
She is one of my *aptest* students.
He is very *apt* at picking up a new subject.
(c) likely or having a tendency to do sth :
As he is very old and feeble, he is *apt* to be forgetful.
My pen is rather *apt* to leak.

29. AGO/BEFORE

ago : used to indicate time measured back to a point in the past. It is always placed after the word or words it modifies and used with the simple past tense :
The train left a few minutes *ago*.
His brother died five years *ago*.
How long *ago* was it that you last saw her?

before : already; at an earlier time :
I have seen that film *before*.
You should have told me so *before*.

Note : Here, *before* has been used as an adverb.

30. AID/AIDE

aid : (a) help :
She came quickly to my *aid*.
I finished the work with the *aid* of a friend.
(b) thing or person that helps :
Do you need a hearing *aid*?
(c) food, money, etc. sent to the needy to help it :
How much foreign *aid* does India get?

aide : assistant :
She is one of the chief *aides* to the President.

31. A1U/ALE

ail : trouble sb in body or mind :
Let me know what *ails* you.

ale : a type of strong beer :
They sell a wide range of *ales*.

32. AIR/HEIR

air : (a) mixture of gases surrounding the earth and breathed by all land animals and plants :
Let us go out for some fresh *air*.
(b) the earth's atmosphere; open space :
He likes to be in the open *air*.
(c) the earth's atmosphere is the space where aircrafts fly :
Send the goods by *air*.
I always travel by *air*.
The site of the old fort is clearly visible from the *air*.
(d) impression given; appearance or manner :
He smiled with a triumphant *air*.
That place has an *air* of mystery.

heir : person with the legal right to receive property, etc. when the owner dies :
Are you the *heir* to the throne?
He is the *heir* to a large fortune.
He made her his *heir*.

33. ALIGN/ALIEN

align : (a) place or arrange a thing or things in a straight line:
There is a row of trees *aligned* with the edge of the road.
(b) put parts of a machine into the correct position in relation to each other:
Let him *align* the wheels of my car.
(c) join sb as an ally; come into agreement with sb :
The Socialist Party has *align*ed itself with the Communists.

alien : (a) foreign; strange; unfamiliar:
They were in an *alien* environment.
(b) contrary to sth; hateful to sb:
Such principles are *alien* to their religion.
Cruelty is quite *alien* to my nature.

34. ALIMENTARY/ELEMENTARY

alimentary : of food and digestion :
What is an *alimentary* canal?

elementary : simple; not developed; in the beginning stage :
You should fully comply with the *elementary* rules of social conduct.

35. ALLAY/ALLEY

allay : make sth less; relieve :
My efforts to *allay* her fears met with success.

alley : narrow passage between or behind houses:
It is a blind *alley*.

36. ALLEVIATE/MITIGATE

alleviate : ease; make sth less severe :
The doctor gave her an injection to *alleviate* the pain.
They *alleviated* the boredom of waiting by singing songs.

mitigate : make sth less violent, severe or painful; moderate :
I did my best to *mitigate* his sufferings.
They should endeavour to *mitigate* distress.
It is an attempt to *mitigate* the unfavourable reaction.

37. ALLUDE/ELUDE

allude : mention sb/sth briefly or indirectly :
He *alluded* to her love affairs in the past.

elude : avoid; escape capture, especially by means of a tric
He eluded his enemies.
A criminal cannot *elude* justice for ever.

38. ALLURE/LURE

allure : tempt or attract sb by raising the expectation of gaining sth :
Many settlers were *allured* by promises of easy wealth.
A man is often *allured* by the charm of important position.

lure : attract or tempt a person or an animal :
She *lured* him into a trap.

39. ALLUSION/ILLUSION

allusion : indirect reference to :
I made an *allusion* to the teachings of Mahatma Gandhi.

illusion : (a) false idea, belief or impression; delusion :
I have no *illusions* about my ability.
(b) imaginary thing that a person wrongly believes to exist; false perception :
That was an optical *illusion*.
In the hot sun, the surface of the road seems wet, but that is only an *illusion*.

40. ALTAR/ALTER

altar : raised, flat-topped platform on which offerings are made to a God in a place of worship :
I placed my offerings on the *altar*.

alter : make or become different; change in position, size, shape, etc:
The plane *altered* the course.
She had to *alter* her clothes after losing weight.

41. ALTERNATE/ALTERNATIVE

alternate : (a) happening or following one after the other :
This is a pattern of *alternate* circles and squares.
He passed through *alternate* triumph and despair.
(b) every second :
I meet her on *alternate* days.

alternative : available in place of sth else; other:
He found *alternative* means of transport.
The *alternative* book to study for the examination is New Approach Leaner's Grammar.

42. AMIABLE/AMICABLE

amiable : pleasant and good-tempered; showing and in- spiring friendliness:
He has an *amiable* character.
I have always found her a very *amiable* lady.

amicable : showing friendliness; without hostility; done in a friendly way; peaceable :
They settled the dispute in an *amicable* way.

43. ANALYST/ANNALIST

analyst : person skilled in making, especially chemical *analyses* :
He is a food *analyst*.

analyst : person who writes annals :
He is a noted *annalist*.

44. ANCIENT/OLD

ancient : belonging to times long past :
These are *ancient* monuments.
Tell me something about *ancient* India.

ol : (a) advanced in age; having lived for a long time, no longer young :
Old people cannot be so active as young people.
What will you do when you grow *old*?
He is too *old* for you to marry.

(b) having been in existence or use for a long time:
Old customs die hard.
Discard your *old* clothes.

(c) not recent or modem:
Can you discard *old* religious practices?
Things were different in the *old* days.

(d) familiar; known for a long time :
She is an *old* friend of mine.

(e) former; previous :
What was your *old* job?
We had a larger garden at our *old* house.

(f) having much experience or practice:
He is very *old* in diplomacy.

45. ANNEAL/ANNUAL

anneal : make metals, etc. tough by cooling slowly after heating :
Do you know how to *anneal* metals?

annual : (a) happening every year :
This is my *annual* visit to this city.

(b) calculated for the year :
Can you tell me something about the *annual* course of the Sun?

46. ANSWER/REPLY

answer : (a) say, write or do sth in response to :
Think carefully before you *answer*.
Did you *answer* to his question?

(b) satisfy; be suitable for sth :
Your qualifications and experience do not *answer* to our needs.

(c) correspond to or match the description of sb/sth :
The photograph *answers* to the description of the wanted man.

(d) be responsible or blamed for sth :
You will have to *answer* for your crimes one day.

(e) speak on behalf of sb or in support of sth :
I agree but I cannot *answer* for him.
As I know her well, I can certainly *answer* for her honesty.

(f) be responsible to sb :
Whom do you *answer* to in your new job?
You will answer to me for any damage to the car.

reply : respond to a letter, etc :
She did not *reply* to my letter.

47. ANTIC/ANTIQUE

antic : absurd or exaggerated movement or behaviour intended to amuse people :
People were laughing at the clown's silly *antics*.

antique : belonging to the distant past :
She is fond of collecting *antique* coins, etc.

Note : *Antique,* as a noun, means an old object, for example, a piece of China or furniture, which is valuable because of its beauty or rarity.
His house was filled with *antiques*.

48. ANXIOUS/EAGER

anxious : (a) worried; uneasy; feeling anxiety :
I am very *anxious* about her health.
(b) causing anxiety :
We had a few *anxious* moments before landing safely.
(c) strongly wishing sth :
I am *anxious* for your safety.

eager : full of interest or desire; keen :
I am *eager* to please her at any cost.
Are you *eager* for brilliant success in life?

49. APOLOGY/PARDON

apology : statement of regret for doing wrong, being impolite, or hurting sb's feelings :
She accepted my *apology* for my being impolite to her.

pardon : (a) forgiveness :
I sought her *pardon* for my rudeness.
(b) cancellation of a punishment incurred for a crime :
He was granted a *pardon* after new evidence proved his innocence.

50. APPOSITE/OPPOSITE; *ALSO REFER TO P. 155*

apposite : very appropriate for a purpose or an occasion :
I found his speech wholly *apposite* to the current debate.
Her comments were entirely *apposite* to the subject under discussion.

opposite : (a) having a position on the other side of sb/sth; facing:
His house is on the *opposite* side of the road.
She entered the room through the *opposite* door.
(b) facing a specified person or thing :
I asked the man *opposite* if he would open the door.
(c) entirely different; contrary :
They were travelling in *opposite* directions.

51. APPRAISE/APPRISE

appraise : assess the value or quality of sb/sth :
He *appraised* the ability of his pupils.
Let us *appraise* her work.
It would be unwise to buy the house before having it *appraised*.

apprise : inform sb of sth :
I was *apprised* of the committee's decision.

52. ARTIST/ARTISTE

artist : (a) person who practises any of the fine arts, especially painting :
He is a great *artist.*
(b) person who does sth with great skill :
The carpenter has made this cupboard beautifully-he is a real *artist.*

artiste : professional entertainer, such as a singer, a dancer, an actor, etc :
She is a famous *artiste.*

53. ASCENT/ASSENT

ascent : (a) act of ascending :
He was the first man to make an *ascent* in a balloon.
(b) upward path or slope :
The last part of the *ascent* is very steep.

assent : to agree to a suggestion, idea, etc :
The Director *assented* to the Board's proposals.

Note : *Assent*, as a noun, means agreement to a suggestion or idea :
The committee is waiting for the Chairman to give his *assent.*

54. ASSAY/ESSAY

assay : test of the fineness, purity or quality of metals, ores, etc :
He made an *assay* of an ore.

essay : piece of writing, usually short and in prose, on anyone subject :
We had to write four *essays* in the history examination.

55. ASSUME/PRESUME

assume : (a) accept sth as true before there is proof :
I cannot *assume* anything in this case.
We are *assuming* that the present situation is going to continue.
(b) put on or display sth falsely; pretend :
He *assumed* ignorance of the accident.
She *assumed* an air of great concern for my safety.
The look of innocence she *assumed* had us all fooled.
(c) take on; undertake; begin to act in or exercise sth :
He will *assume* his new responsibilities next week.
The problem is beginning to *assume* massive proportion.

presume : (a) suppose sth to be true; take sth for granted :
I *presume* that an agreement will eventually be reached.
Ten passengers are missing, *presumed* dead.
(b) venture to do sth; be so bold as to do sth :
May I *presume* to advise you?
I shall not *presume* to disturb her.

56. ASTONISHMENT/SURPRISE/WONDER

astonishment : great surprise:
He looked at her in *astonishment.*

surprise : (a) feeling caused by sth happening suddenly or unexpectedly :
To my *surprise,* the plan succeeded.
She looked up in surprise when I shouted.

(b) event or thing that causes this feeling :
This gift came as a complete *surprise* to me.

wonder : feeling of surprise mixed with admiration, bewilderment or disbelief :
The children watched the conjurer in silent *wonder*.
They were filled with *wonder* at the sight.

57. AUDIENCE/SPECTATORS

audience : (a) group of people gathered to hear or watch sb/sth :
I have addressed *audiences* all over the country.
(b) number of people who watch, read or listen to the same thing :
An *audience* of millions watched the royal wedding on T.V.
(c) formal interview with a ruler or a very important person:
We had an *audience* with the President this forenoon.

spectators : persons who watch, especially a show or game :
There were noisy *spectators* at the football match.

58. AUGER/AUGUR

auger : tool for boring holes in wood :
The carpenter used the *auger* with skill.

augur : foretell; be a sign of sth :
This does not *augur* well for our team.
The quality of your work *augurs* well for the examinations next month.

59. AUGUST/AUGUST

august : the eighth month of the year, next after july :

august : majestic and imposing; inspiring feelings of respect and awe :
He was probably the most *august* figure in the Lok Sabha.
I attended the meeting of an *august* body of elder statesmen.

60. AUTHENTIC/GENUINE

authentic : (a) known to be true :
Is it an *authentic* document?
(b) reliable; trustworthy :
What he has said is an *authentic* statement.

genuine : (a) real; truly what it is said to be; not fake or artificial :
She looked at me in *genuine* astonishment.
It is a *genuine* pearl.
(b) honest; sincere:
She seems *genuine*, but can I trust?
They seemed nice, *genuine* persons.

61. AVENGE/REVENGE

avenge : (a) take or get revenge for a wrong done to sb/oneself :
She *avenged* her father's murder.
(b) take or get revenge on sb/sth for such a wrong :
She avenged herself on her father's killers.

revenge : do sth to get satisfaction for an offence, etc; avenge sb :
He will *revenge* himself on those who helped the thief to escape.

62. AVERT/OVERT

avert : (a) turn sth away :
He *averted* his glance from the terrible sight.
(b) prevent sth; avoid :
I *averted* a crisis by prompt action.
She managed to *avert* suspicion.

Overt : not secret or hidden; done or shown openly or publicly:
I am aware of their *overt* hostility.

63. AVOCATION/VOCATION

avocation : something done for pleasure; hobby :
Gardening is his *avocation*.

vocation : (a) person's trade or profession :
By *vocation*, he is a lawyer.
You should find your true *vocation* in life.
(b) feeling that one is called to, and qualified for, a certain kind of work :
He has a *vocation* to become a priest.
Nursing is a *vocation* as well as a profession.

64. AVOID/OVOID

avoid : (a) keep oneself away from sb/sth :
I think she is *avoiding* me.
Avoid driving in the middle of the road.
(b) prevent; stop sth happening :
Try to *avoid* accidents.
I just *avoided* running over a little child.

ovoid : egg-shaped :
There is an *ovoid* table in our office.

Note : *Ovoid*, as a noun, means an egg-shaped object.

2

First Word of Each Group Beginning With-B

1. BABBLE/BABE/BAUBLE/BUBBLE

babble : (a) talk quickly or in a way that is difficult or impossible to understand:
Stop *babbling* and speak more slowly.
(b) chatter in a thoughtless or confused way :
What are you *babbling* about?

Note : Babble, as a noun, means :
(a) foolish talk:
I dislike your *babble*.
(b) talk that is difficult or impossible to understand :
I heard the *babble* of many voices.

babel : scene of noisy talking and confusion:
There is a *babel* of voices in the busy market.

bauble : showy ornament of little value:
She is fond of wearing bauble.

bubble : (a) floating ball formed of liquid and containing air or gas :
These are soap *bubbles*.
Children love blowing *bubbles*.
(b) ball or air or gas in a liquid or in a solidified liquid such as glass:
Champagne is full of *bubbles*.
This glass vase has a *bubble* in its base.

2. BABY/BOOBY/BOBBY/BEVY

baby : (a) very young child or animal :
Both mother and *baby* are doing well.
He is a *baby* boy.
(b) youngest member of a family or group :
He is the baby of our team.
(c) childish or timid person:
Stop crying, and don't be such a *baby*.
(d) very small of its kind:
He has bought a *baby* car.

Note: Baby, as a verb, means *treat sb like a baby; pamper* :
Don't *baby* her.

booby : foolish person :
They say you are a booby.

bobby : policeman :
The hawker sitting under the tree is a *bobby* in disguise.
A *bobby* was run over by a speeding car.

bevy : (a) large group :
A *bevy* of beautiful girls called on me last evening.
(b) block of birds, especially quails :
A *bevy* of quails was there in the field.

3. BAG/BEG/VAGUE

bag : (a) container made of flexible material with an opening at the top :
He bought a *bag* yesterday.
(b) such a container with its contents; the amount it contains:
He needs four *bags* of coal.
(c) thing resembling a bag :
There are *bags* under his eyes.
(d) all the birds, animals, etc. shot or caught :
We got a good bag today.
(e) fussy, unattractive or bad-tempered, usually older women :
She is an awful old *bag*.

Note: *Bag*, as a verb, means :
1. put into a *bag* or *bags* :
2. kill or catch sth.
They *bagged* nothing except a couple of birds.
3. take sth without permission but without intending to steal :
Who has *bagged* my matches?
She *bagged* (occupied) the most comfortable chair.
Try to *bag* an empty table.

beg : (a) ask for money, food, clothes, etc. as a gift or as charity; make a living in this way :
There are thousands *begging* in the streets.
He was so poor that he had to *beg* for money from the passers-by.
He made a living by *begging* from the rich.
(b) ask earnestly or humbly for sth :
I *beg* of you not to take any risks.
She *begged* me for forgiveness.
He *begged* mercy of the President.

vague : (a) not clearly expressed or perceived :
She gave a *vague* answer to my question.
(b) not exact or specific; imprecise :
It is a *vague* estimate of the cost.
(c) undecided or uncertain about sth :
He is *vague* about his plans.
(d) suggesting unclear thinking or absent- mindedness :
She made a *vague* gesture.
(e) indistinct; not clear :
It is the *vague* outline of a ship.

4. BAIL/BALE

bail : (a) money paid, by or for a person accused of a crime, as security that he will return for his trial if he is allowed to go free until then :
He was released on a bail of five thousand rupees.
(b) permission for a person to be released on such security :
The magistrate granted him *bail*.

bale : large bundle of paper, goods, straw, etc. pressed together and tied with rope or wire ready to be moved, sold, and so on :
The cloth was packed in *bales.*

5. BAIT/BAT/BET/VAT

bait : food or imitation food put on a hook to catch fish or placed in nets, traps, etc. to attract prey :
The fish nibbled at the *bait.*

baton : (a) usually wooden implement of a specified size and shape, and with a handle, used for hitting the ball in games such as cricket, etc :
He needs a *bat.*

(b) small mouse-like animal that flies at night and feeds on fruit and insects :
Do you like to see a *bat?*
He dashed around like a *bat* out of hell.

bet-n : (a) arrangement to risk money, etc. on an event of which the result is doubtful :
He made a *bet* on the horse race.
He lost a *bet* in the recent past.

(b) opinion; prediction:
My *bet* is that she had got held up in the traffic.

Note: *Bet,* as a verb, means risk money on a race or on some other event of which the result is doubtful :
He spends all his money *betting* on horses.

vat-n : tank or large container for holding liquids, etc. in distilling, brewing, dyeing and tanning :
Vats are being manufactured in that industry.

6. BALANCE/VALANCE/VALENCE

balance : (a) difference between two columns of an account-money received and money spent:
I must check my bank *balances.*

(b) amount of money still owed after some payment has been made :
The *balance* of two thousand rupees will be paid within ten days.

(c) remainder of sth after part has already been used, taken, etc:
When will you take the *balance* of your annual leave?

(d) sanity; steadiness of mind :
His wife's sad and sudden demise upset the *balance* of his mind.

(e) even distribution of weight; steadiness:
Riders need a good sense of *balance.*

(f) condition that exists when two opposites are equal or in correct proportions :
Try to achieve a better *balance* between work and play.
This newspaper maintains a good *balance* in its presentation of different opinions.

(g) Pleasing proportion of parts in a whole :
This painting has a pleasing *balance* of shapes and colours.
All the parts of the building are in perfect *balance.*

(h) Instrument used for weighing :
He bought a *balance* yesterday.

valance : short curtain or frill hung around the frame of a bed:
The valance on your bed is very charming.

valence : capacity of an atom to combine with, or be replaced by, another or others as compared with that of the hydrogen atom :
Elements whose atoms lose electrons, such as hydrogen and the metals, have a positive *valance*.

7. BALD/BOLD

bald : (a) having little or no hair on the scalp :
You are going *bald*.
He has a large *bald* patch.

(b) without elaboration; plain or dull :
He has adopted a *bald* style of writing.
The *bald* fact is that the first five years were wasted.
Let me know the *bald* facts of the case.

bold : (a) confident and brave; daring; enterprising :
She is a *bold* young lady.
I have taken a *bold* action in the matter.

(b) distinct; vivid; clearly visible :
It is a *bold*, legible handwriting.

(c) printed in thick type :
The head words should be in *bold* type.

8.BALL/BAWL

ball : (a) solid or hollow sphere used in games:
Children are playing with a *ball*.

(b) round mass of material that has been pressed together, rolled or wound into shape :
I am a rich man.
I have a gold *ball*.

bawl : shout or cry loudly :
Your baby has been *bawling* for hours.
She *bawled* at me across the road.

9. BALLET/VALET

ballet : (a) style of dancing used to tell a story in a dramatic performance with music but without speech or singing :
Was that a classical *ballet*?

(b) story performed in this way:
Have you seen this *ballet* before?

(c) group of dancers who regularly perform *ballet* together:
They are the members of the National *Ballet*.

valet : (a) man's personal servant who looks after his clothes, serves his meals, and so on :
Our *valet* is both regular and punctual in his attendance.

(b) hotel employee with similar duties :
The *valet* of this room performs his duty faithfully.

10. BAN/BANE

ban : prohibition; order that bans :
The government has put a *ban* on import of cloth.

Note: *Ban*, as a verb, means :
(a) officially forbid sth :
The film was *banned* by the censor.
The use of chemical weapons should be *banned*.
(b) officially forbid sb to do sth :
She has been *banned* from driving for six months.
He was *banned* from attending the meeting.

bane : cause of sb's ruin or trouble :
She has been the *bane* of my life.
Drink was the *bane* of his life.

11. BANAL/VENAL

banal : uninteresting; common place :
Nobody likes your *banal* comments.

venal : (c) ready to accept money for doing sth dishonest :
Venal officials and officers should be severely punished.
Give the *venal* politicians a wide berth.
(b) influenced by or done for bribery :
Appropriate steps should be taken to wipe out *venal* practices.

12. BAND/BEND/END

band : (a) thin flat strip, hoop orloop used for fastening things together, or for placing round an object to strengthen it :
Papers have been kept together with a rubber *band*.
(b) organised group of people doing sth together with a common purpose.
The police have arrested a *band* of robbers.
(c) group of people playing wind instruments :
Do you like to see a military *band*?

bend : (a) force sth into an angle; make curved or crooked :
It is hard to bend an iron bar.
Touch your toes without bending your knees.
(b) become curved or angular:
The road *bends* to the left after a few metres.
(c) bow or stoop :
He *bent* forward to listen to the child.
(d) cause sb/sth to bow or stoop :
They refused to *bend* to the hijacker's demand.
(e) turn sth in a new direction :
We should bend the age-old customs for the progress of society.

vend : offer small articles for sale :
Tell me what you *vend*.

13. BANISH/VANISH

banish : (a) send sb away, especially out of the country, as a punishment:
He was *banished* from his country for life.
(b) drive thoughts, etc. out of the mind :
He *banished* all thoughts of a restful holiday from his mind.

vanish : (a) disappear completely and suddenly :
The thief vanished into the crowd.
(b) fade away or cease to exist :
My hopes of success have *vanished*.

14. BANK/BUNK

bank : (a) land sloping up along each side of a river or canal; ground near a river :
Can you jump over to the opposite *bank*?
My house is on the North *bank* of the river.
(b) flat-topped mass of cloud, snow, etc. especially one formed by the wind :
The sun went behind a bank of clouds.
(c) establishment for keeping money, valuables, etc. safely:
I have money in the *bank*.
(d) store of valuable things, information, etc :
I have built up a bank of useful references.

bunk: (a) narrow bed built into a wall like a shelf :
This *bunk* is for keeping my night dress.
(b) one of a pair of single beds, fixed one above the other, especially for children :
It is a *bunk* with nice stairs.

15. BAR/BARE/BEAR

bar : (a) obstruct sth so as to prevent progress :
Poverty *bars* the way to progress.
Soldiers *barred* the road, so we had to turn back.
(b) prevent sb from using or doing sth :
she was *barred* from entering the competition because of her age.

bare : reveal; uncover sth :
She *bared* her chest.

Note : Bare, as an adjective, means without covering or protection:
He goes out generally with his head *bare*.

bear : (a) show sth; display; carry visibly :
The document does not *bear* my signature.
She *bears* much resemblance to her mother.
The title of the essay *bears* little relation to the contents.
(b) be known by sth; have :
A married woman usually *bears* her husband's surname.
(c) carry sb/sth, especially while moving :
He was *bearing* a heavy load.
(d) sustain; support sb/sth :
The ice is too thin to *bear* your weight.
(e) shoulder; take responsibility, etc. on oneself :
Who will *bear* the cost of your wedding?
You have to *bear* the blame.
She *bears* her responsibilities lightly.
(f) endure sth; tolerate; stand:
I cannot *bear* to be laughed at.
She *bore* her sorrow without complaint.
The pain was almost more than he could *bear*.
(g) be fit for sth; allow :
The plan will not *bear* close inspection.
His sufferings do not *bear* thinking about.
Her joke does not *bear* repeating.

(h) keep feelings, etc. in the mind :
She *bears* a grudge against me.
He *bore* her no ill will.

(i) move, behave or conduct oneself in a specified way :
He *bears* himself like a soldier.
He *bore* himself with dignity at a difficult time.

(j) give birth to sb :
She has *borne* seven daughters.

(k) produce sth; yield :
The trees are *bearing* pink blossom.
His efforts *bore* no result.

(l) go or turn in the specified direction :
This road *bears* to the west.
When you get to the park, *bear* to the right.

16. BARB/VERVE/VERB

barb : hurtful remark :
Your *barbs* of ridicule have angered her.

verve-n : enthusiasm, spirit or vigour, especially in artistic or literary work :
She always sings with *verve*.
The performance lacked *verve*.

verb-n : word or phrase indicating an action, an event or a state :
Advise is a *verb* but advice is a noun.

17. BARBARISM/BARBARITY

barbarism : (c) state of being uncivilised, ignored or rude :
Everyone detests *barbarism*.

(b) use of a word or expression that is unacceptable :
We are teaching students to rid their writings of *barbarism*.

barbarity : savage cruelty :
The *barbarities* of modern warfare baffle expression.

18. BARGE/VERGE : *ALSO REFER TO P. 232*

barge : (a) rush or lump heavily and clumsily :
Stop *barging* into people.
She *barged* past me in the crowd.

(b) enter or interrupt sth rudely or clumsily :
I tried to stop him coming through the door but he just *barged* in.
He always *barges* into others' conversation.

verge : be very close or similar to sth; be approaching sth :
This is a situation *verging* on the ridiculous.
As she is *verging* on 85 now, she needs constant attention.

19. BARK/BURKE

bark : (a) make sharp, loud sound :
Our dog always *barks* at strangers.

(b) say sth in a sharp harsh voice:
When she is angry, she often *barks* at the children.

Note: *Bark*, as a noun, means :

1. tough outer covering of tree trunks and branches.
2. sharp harsh sound made by dogs and foxes.

burke : (a) avoid :
I always *burke* publicity.
(b) suppress :
He tried to *burke* the inquiry.

20. BARLEY/BURLY

barley : grass-like plant producing grain used for food, and for making beer and whisky :
Do you know how to grow *barley* plants?

burly : with a strong heavy body; sturdy :
There is a *burly* policeman waiting for you.

21. BARN/BURN

barn : (a) simple building for storing hay, grain, etc. in a farm:
A farmer stores his erops in a *barn*.
(b) any unattractive large building:
They live in that *barn* of a house.

burn : (c) destroy, damage, injure sb/sth by fire, heat or acid :
The house was *burnt* to the ground.
All his belongings were *burnt* in the fire.
(b) make a hole or mark by burning :
The cigarette *burnt* a hole in the carpet.
(c) use sth as fuel :
Do you *burn* coal as well as wood on this fire?
(d) be killed by fire :
Ten persons were *burnt* to death in the hotel fire.
(e) be able to catch fire easily :
Paper *burns* easily.
(f) be full of strong emotion :
He was *burning* with rage.
(g) want to do sth very much :
He was *burning* to avenge the death of his father.

Note: *Burn*, as a noun, means :
1. injury or mark caused by fire, heat or acid :
He died of the *burns* he received in the fire.
2. small stream.

22. BASAL/VASSAL/VESSEL : *ALSO REFER TO P. 223-224*

basal : fundamental; pertaining to base :
Let me know the basal rights guaranteed to the citizens under the Constitution.

vassal : person or nation dependent on another:
India is not a vassal state.

vessel : (a) a ship or a large boat :
I had seen many ocean-going vessels.
(b) any hollow container for holding liquids :
(c) tube-like structure in the body of an animal or a plant, conveying or holding blood or other fluid :
Tell me something about blood vessels.

23. BASE/BASIS

base : (a) lowest part of sth :
Where was the *base* of the pillar?
(b) starting point; underlying principle :
Padma used her family's history as a *base* for her novel.
His arguments had a sound economic *base*.

Note: 1. Base, as an adjective, means :
(i) dishonourable; despicable :
He was acting from *base* motives.
(ii) not pure :
It is a base coin.
(c) low in value :
We do not use *base* metal.
2. Base as a verb, means :
(i) use sth as grounds, evidence, etc. for sth else :
My novel is *based* on historical facts.
Direct taxation is usually *based* on income.
(ii) provide sb with a *base* or centre to work :
Where are you *based* now?
Most of our staff are *based* in Kolkata.

basis : (a) foundation; main principle that underlies sth :
Her arguments have a firm *basis*.
Rates of work are calculated on a weekly *basis*.
(b) starting point for a discussion :
No *basis* for negotitation has been agreed upon.
This agenda will form the *basis* of our next meeting.

24. BASK/BUSK

bask : sit or lie enjoying warmth :
Let us *bask* in the sunshine.
She is *basking* in his favour.

busk : entertain people in a public place for money :
He earns his living by *busking*.

25. BASS/BUS

bass : (a) a man with lowest male voice :
Is he a *bass* or a baritone?
(b) singer with such a voice.
He is a very fine *bass*.

Note: *Bass* also means any of several fresh water or sea fish.
They caught ten *basses*.

bus : large vehicle carrying passengers between stopping places along a fixed route:
Shall we walk or go by *bus*?

26. BAST/BASTE

bast : fibre from the inner bark of certain trees, used for tying and weaving baskets, mats, and so on :
Do you know how to use the *bast*?

baste : (a) sew pieces of material together with long temporary stitches :
(b) pour oil, butter, etc. over sth to keep it moist during cooking :

27. BASTARD/BUSTARD

bastard : (a) illegitimate child :
He is a *bastard* child.
(b) ruthless or cruel person :
He is a real *bastard*, leaving his young wife in that way.
(c) thing that causes pain, difficulty, and so on :
Your headache is a real *bastard*.
(d) not genuine or authentic; showing an odd mixture :
He writes in a bastard style.

bustard : large land bird that can run very fast :
I have never seen a *bustard*.

28. BATH/BATHE

bath : (a) washing of the whole body, especially while sitting or lying in water :
I take a hot *bath* every morning.
(b) large, oblong container for water in which a person sits to have a bath.
Plese run a *bath* for me.
(c) water placed in this container ready for use :
Plese run a *bath* for me.
(d) an indoor public swimming-pool :
Let us go to the heated swimming-*baths*.

Note : *Bath*, as a verb, means :
1. give a *bath* to sb/sth :
Have you *bathed* the baby?
2. take a *bath* :
I bath every night.

bathe : (c) apply water to sth; soak in water :
The doctor told her to *bathe* her eyes twice a day.
The nurse *bathed* the wound.
(b) go swimming in the river, a lake, etc. for enjoyment :
On hot days, we often bathe in the river.

Note : *Bathe*, as a noun, means action of swimming in the river, etc.
It is a sunny day. Let us go for a *bathe*.

29. BATHOS/PATHOS

bathos : sudden change in writing or speech from what is deeply moving or important to what is foolish or trivial; anticlimax :
His writings are almost always full of bathos.

pathos : quality, especially in speech, writing, acting, etc. that causes a feeling of pity or sadness :
They have eyes full of *pathos*.
That was a scene of real *pathos*.

30. BATIK/BOUTIQUE

batik : (a) method of printing coloured designs on cloth by waxing the parts that are not to be dyed :
This artist is good at making *batik*.
(b) material dyed in this way :
He bought a *batik* dress.

boutique : small shop selling clothes and other articles of the latest fashion :
My *boutique* runs well.

31. BATON/BUTTON

baton : (a) short thin stick used by the conductor of a band or orchestra :
The music director's *baton* is a rythmic tool.
(b) short stick that indicates a certain rank.
It is a Field-Marshal's *baton*.
(c) short stick carried and handed on in a relay race :
Queen's *baton* went round the common wealth countries before the games commenced.

button : (c) knob or disc made of wood, metal, etc. sewn onto a garment as a fastener or as an ornament :
He bought twenty trouser *buttons*.
(b) small knob that is pressed to operate a doorbell, a switch on a machine, and so on :
Which *button* do I press to turn the radio on?

Note: *Button*, as a verb, denotes:
1. fasten sth with *buttons* :
Please *button* your shirt.
2. be fastened with buttons :
This dress *buttons* at the back.
3. complete sth successfully :
This contract should be *buttoned* up by tomorrow.

32. BATTER/BETTER

batter : hit sb/sth hard and often :
He kept *battering* at the door.

Note : *Batter*, as a noun, means beaten mixture of flour, eggs, milk, etc. for cooking.
She is fond of fish fried in *batter*.

better : (a) of a more excellent or desirable kind:
She resolved to lead a better life in future.
He is a *better* man than you.
Life was difficult then, but things have got *better* and *better* over the years.
(b) of a more precise or suitable kind:
Having talked to the witnesses, I now have a *better* idea of what happened.
Can't you think of a *better* word than nice to describe your holiday?
(c) partly or fully recovered from an illness :
The patient is much *better* today.
Her ankle is getting *better*.

Note: 1. *Better*, as a noun denotes that which is better :
I had hoped for *better*.
I expected *better* of you.
2. *Better*, as an adverb, means :
(i) in a more pleasant, efficient, desirable, etc. way :
She sings *better* than you.
You would write *better* if you had a good pen.

(ii) to a greater degree; more :
1like him *better* than (I like) her.
You will like it *better* when you understand it more.
The *better* I know her, the more I admire her.

(iii) more usefully :
His advice is *better* ignored.
If the roads are icy, you would be *better* advised to delay your departure.

3. *Better*, as a verb, means :

(i) do *better* than sth; surpass :
This achievement cannot be *bettered*.

(ii) improve sth :
The government hopes to *better* the conditions of the workers.

(iii) get a better social position or status :
You should always try your best to *better* yourself.

33. BATTLE/WAR

battle : (a) a combat between organised armed forces:
Who fought the *battle* of Panipat?

(b) any contest or struggle:
There was a *battle* of words between them.
His whole life was a constant battle against abject poverty.

war : (a) state of fighting between nations or groups within a nation using military force :
The border incident led to *war* between the two countries.
The government wanted to avoid the civil *war* at all costs.

(b) instance or period of such fighting :
I had fought in two *wars*.
I had been a student in London during the Second World *War*.

(c) competition, conflict or hostility between people, group, etc:
There was a state of *war* between the rivals.

(d) efforts made to eliminate disease, crime, and so on :
It is a major step in the *war* against cancer.

(e) campaign of verbal abuse :
As the election approaches, the *war* of words between the main political parties becomes increasingly intense.

34. BATTY/BOOTEE/BOOTY

batty : crazy; slightly mad:
I totally dislike your batty ideas.
He must be going *batty*.

bootee : (c) woman's short lined boot :
Sita's *bootee* is elegant.

(b) baby's woollen boot :
The *bootee* of this child is comfortable.

booty : things taken by thieves or captured from an enemy in war; loot; plunder :
The pirates buried the *booty* which they had captured on Treasure Island.

35. BAWDY/BODY

bawdy : amusing in a coarse or indecent way :
I detest your *bawdy* jokes.

body : (a) whole physical structure of a human being or an animal :
Children's *bodies* grow steadily.
(b) main part of a human body, apart from the head and limbs; trunk; torso :
He has a strong *body*, but rather thin legs.
(c) main part of sth, especially a vehicle or building :
The body of the bus was damaged.
The main *body* of the book deals with the author's political career.

36. BEACH/BEECH

beach : stretch of sand or pebbles along the edge of the sea or a lake; shore between high and low water mark:
Hundreds of holiday-makers were sunbathing on the *beach*.
We had a walk along the *beach*.

beech : type of tree with smooth bark, shiny leaves and small triangular nuts :
Cricket bats are made of *beech* wood.

37. BEAD/BID

bead : (a) small piece of material with a hole through it for threading with others on a string, or for sewing onto material :
It is a string of glass beads.
(b) drop of liquid :
There are *beads* of sweat on her forehead.

bid : (c) price offered in order to buy sth, especially at an auction :
He made a bid of five thousand rupees for a painting.
(b) effort to do, obtain, achieve, etc. sth; attempt :
He failed in his *bid* to reach the summit.
They made a *bid* for popular support.

38. BEAM/VIM

beam : (a) long thick bar of metal, wood or concrete etc, supported at both ends, that carries the weight of part of a building or some other structure :
He bought ten *beams* for the building.
(b) ray or stream of light from a lamp, the sun, or the moon, etc :
The *beam* of light from the car's headlamp could be seen for miles.
(c) bright and happy look or smile :
His face wore a *beam* of pleasure.

Note : *Beam* is also used as a verb to mean :
(i) (of the sun) send out light and warmth :
The sun beams majestically.
(ii) smile happily and cheerfully :
The winner *beamed* with satisfaction.

vim : energy or vigour :
He is full of *vim*.
You shuold put more *vim* into your acting.

39. BEAT/BEET/BIT

beat : (a) hit sb/sth repeatedly :
Some body was *beating* at the door.
Who is *beating* the drum?
(b) reduce sb to a specified state by hitting repeatedly :
The police beat the prisoner unconscious.
(c) expand and contract rhythmically, especially the heart :
He is alive - his heart is still *beating*.
(d) defeat sb; win against sb; do better than sb :
Your team was easily *beaten*.
(e) be better than sth; defeat :
Nothing *beats* home cooking.
The government's main aim is to *beat* inflation.

Note : *Beat*, as a noun, means :
1. stroke or regular sequence of strokes :
We heard the *beat* of a drun.
2. emphasis repeated regularly, marking rhythm in music or poetry :
The song has a good *beat*.
3. route along which sb goes regularly, allocated to a policeman watchman, etc :
The Policeman is out on his beat.

beet: type of plant with a fleshy root which is used as a vegetable or for making sugar :
Do you use *beet* as a vegetable?
Can you make sugar from *beet*?

bit: (a) small piece or amount of sth :
I gave her a *bit* of sound advice.
(b) slightly; rather :
These trousers are a *bit* tight.
(c) short time or distance.
Wait a *bit*.
[Move up a *bit*.]
(d) metal part of a bridle put in a horse's mouth as a way of controlling it :
Bit of the bridle helps keep nurse under control.

40. BEAU/BOO

beau: (a) man who pays great attention to women :
In a party a *beau* is a centre of a ttraction of women in a party.
(b) girl's admirer or lover :
She says you are her *beau*.

boo : *boo*: sound made to show disapproval or contempt :
The Prime Minister's speech was greeted with *boos* and jeers.

Note : *Boo*, as a verb,means show disapproval or contempt to sb/sth by shouting *boo* :
You can hear the crowd *booing*.

41. BEER/VEER

beer : alcoholic drink made from malt and flavoured with hops, etc :
Would you like to have a glass of *beer*?

(a) change direction or course :
The car suddenly *veered* of the road.
The wind has *veered* round.

(b) of a conversation, sb's behaviour or opinion, change suddenly or very noticeably :
The discussion *veered* away from religion and came round to politics.

42. BELLOW/BELOW

bellow : (a) make a deep loud noise like a bull; roar, especially with pain :
The bull *bellowed*. angrily.

(b) say sth loudly or angrily; shout:
The music was so loud that we had to *bellow* at each other to be heard.
The officer *bellowed* orders at the platoon.

below : at or to a lower position, level, rank, etc. than sb/sth:
Don't write *below* this line.
We looked down from the mountain to the valley *below*.
An inspector in Delhi Police force is *below* an assistant commissioner of police.
The standard of his work is well *below* the average of his class.

43. BELLY/VALLY

belly : (a) part of the body below the chest, containing the stomach, bowels and digestive organs; abdomen :
Don't go out with an empty *belly*.

(b) bulging or rounded part of sth.
Many things are kept in the *belly* of a ship.

valley : stretch of lands between hills or mountains, often with a river flowing through it :
He likes to see a *valley*.

44. BENCH/BUNCH

bench : (a) long seat made of wood or stone :
(b) judge's seat in court :
(c) judges or magistrates as a group :
(d) judges or magistrates hearing a case :

bunch : (c) number of things growing, fastened or grouped together :
Give me a *bunch* of grapes.
Where is the *bunch* of keys?

(b) group of people; gang; mob :
They are a *bunch* of thugs.

45. BENEFICENT/BENEFICIAL

beneficient : showing active kindness; generous; charitable :
A *beneficent* ruler wins the loyalty of his people.
He is our *beneficent* patron.

beneficial : having a helpful or useful effect; advantageous :
Fresh air is *beneficial* to one's health.
Such a system will be *beneficial* to society.

46. BERTH/BIRTH

berth : (a) sleeping-place on a ship, train, etc. :

(b) place for a ship to be tied up in a harbour, or to be at anchor :
To *berth* a ship is to moor it in a suitable place.
(c) job or position, especially an enjoyable one :
He is running after a cosy *berth*.

birth : (c) being born or bearing young one; emergence of young one from the mother's body :
The baby weighed six pounds at *birth*.
There were five births at the hospital yesterday.
He has been blind from *birth*.
(b) beginning; coming into existence :
Tell me something about the *birth* of capitalism in India.
(c) family origin; descent :
Padmini is of noble *birth*.
She is Indian by *birth* but French by marriage.

47. BESIDE/BESIDES

beside : (a) at the side of sb/sth; next to :
She sat *beside* me.
I keep a dictionary *beside* me when I am writing.
(b) compared with sb/sth :
Beside your earlier work, this piece seems rather disappointing.
You are quite tall *beside* your brother.
(c) having lost one's self-control because of the intensity of the emotion one is feeling :
He was *beside* himself with joy.

besides : (c) in addition to sb/sth :
There will be four of us for dinner, *besides* Champa Devi.
The play was badly acted, *besides* being far too long.
(b) apart from; except :
No one writes to me *besides* you.
She has no relations *besides* an aged aunt.

Note : *Besides*, as an adverb, means 'in addition'; also :
He is my youngest child, and I have three others *besides*.
I don't like that new dictionary; *besides*, it is too expensive.

48. BEST/VEST

best-adj : of the most excellent, desirable, suitable, etc. kind :
Who is your *best* friend?
That was the *best* dinner I have ever had.
What is the best way to get there?

Note : 1. *Best*, as an adverb, denotes :
(i) in the most excellent manner :
This is the *best* kept garden in the town.
She is the person *best* able to cope with the task.
Do as you think *best*.
(ii) to the greatest degree, most :
Who is the *best*-loved politician in the country?
2. *Best*, as a noun, means :
(i) that which is best; the outstanding thing or person among several :
She wants the best of everything.

He was acting from the *best* of motives.
We are the *best* of friends.
He is among the *best* of our workers.

(ii) most important advantage or aspect of sth :
That is the *best* of having a car.
The best we can hope for is that nobody gets killed.

3. *Best*, as a verb, means defeat sb; outwit :
He was *bested* in the debate.

vest-n : (a) garment worn under a shirt,etc. next to the skin : He wears cotton *vests*.

(b) special, usually sleeveless garment covering the upper part of the body :
The Prime Minister wears a bullet-proof *vest*.

Note : *Vest*, as a verb, means give sth as a firm or legal right to sb/ sth; confer sth on sb/sth:
Authority is *vested* in the people.
Parliament is vested with the power of making laws.

49. BETWEEN/AMONG

between : (a) in or into the space separating two or more points, objects, persons, etc :
I lost my keys somewhere *between* the car and the house.
His job is somewhere *between* a typist and a personal assistant.

(b) in the period of time separating two days, years, events, etc.:
It is cheaper *between* 6 p.m. and 8 a.m.
I am usually free *between* Friday and Sunday.

(c) from one place to another:
He flies *between* Delhi and Kolkata twice a week.

(d) indicating a connection or relation:
There is an obvious link *between* unemployment and crime rate.

(e) shared by two persons or things :
They drank a bottle of milk *between* them.
This is just *between* you and me.

(f) by the actions or contributions of :
They wrote the book *between* them.
We can afford to buy a house *between* us.

Note : Between, as an adverb, means :

1. in or into the space separa ting two or more points, objects, people, etc. :
One village ends where the next begins, and there is a road that runs *between*.
You would have a good view of the river from here except for the block of flats in between.

2. in the period of time separating two dates, events, etc. :
We have two meetings this morning, but there is some free time in *between*.

among : (c) Surrounded by sb/sth:
He works among the poor.
She found it among a pile of old books.

(b) in the number of sth; included in :
I was *among* the last to leave the meeting.
Among those present were the President and his wife.
He is only one *among* many who need financial assistance.

(c) to each member of a group :
He distributed the books *among* the class.

(d) between :
Politicians are always arguing *among* themselves.
There is honour *among* thieves.

Note : 1. *Between* is used of people or things, either two in number or more than two considered individually :
She divided her possessions equally *between* her four children.
There is a lot of disagreement *between* the main political parties on this issue.

2. *Among* is used of people or things considered as a group :
Share out the books *among* the class.
They talked *among* themselves while they waited for the bus.
Many children were standing *among* the crowd at the football match. '

3. The form *amongst* is also used to mean the same as *among* :

4. The following is the general difference between the said two words :
Between is used of two persons or things, whereas *among* is used of three of more persons or things.

50. BLANCH/BLENCH

blanch : (c) prepare food, especially vegetables, by putting briefly in boiling water; scald :
People *blanch* almonds to remove their skins.

(b) become pale with fear, cold, etc. :
The little child *blanched* with fear at the sight of the hare.

blench : make a sudden movement because of fear; flinch:

51. BLAND/BLEND

bland : (c) gentle or casual in manner; suave; showing no strong emotions :
Do you like his *bland* nature?

(b) tasteless, very mild in flavour :
He eats only *bland* food because of his ulcer.

(c) uninteresting; without striking features :
He has a *bland* appearance.

blend : (c) mix; form a mixture :
Oil does not *blend* with water.

(b) look or sound good together; combine with sth in a harmonious way :
Their voices *blend* well.
Those cottages *blend* perfectly with the landscape.

(c) shade gradually into each other :
The sea and the sky seemed to *blend* into each other.

(d) mix different types of sth in order to get a certain quality :
I dislike *blended* tea.

52. BLOC/BLOCK

bloc : group of countries or parties united by a common interest :
India is not in favour of joining any power bloc.

(a) large solid piece of wood, stone, metal, etc., usually with flat surfaces :
It is a *block* of concrete.

(b) large building divided into separate flats or offices :
There are many *blocks* of flats in the city.

(c) group of buildings bounded by streets on four sides :
Let us go for a walk round the *block.*

(d) length of one side of such a *block* :
She lives four *blocks* away from here.

(e) large quantity of things regarded as a single unit:
They occupied a block of six seats in the theatre.

(f) piece of wood or metal with designs engraved on it for printing:
Block making was invented in China.

(g) obstacle, obstruction :
The government's stubborn attitude was a *block* to further talks.

Note : *Block,* as a verb, means :

1. make movement or flow difficult or impossible on or in sth; obstruct sth :
A large crowd *blocked* the corridors and exits.
My nose is *blocked* up.
2. prevent sb/sth from moving or progressing; hinder; obstruct :
The accident *blocked* traffic in the town centre.

53. BLUNDER/ERROR/MISTAKE

blunder : stupid or careless mistake:
I made a terrible *blunder* in introducing that beautiful girl to my husband.

Note : *Blunder,* as a verb, means make a blunder :
The police *blundered* badly by arresting the wrong man.

error : (a) thing done wrongly :
There are many spelling *errors* in your essay.

(b) state of being wrong in belief or behaviour :
The letter was sent to you in *error.*
The accident was the result of human *error.*

mistake : (c) wrong idea or opinion; misconception :
You cannot arrest me. There must be some *mistake.*
It was *mistake* to go there on holiday.
I made the *mistake* of leaving our bedroom window open.

(b) thing done incorrectly through ignorance orwrong judgement; error :
The waiter made a *mistake* over the bill.
It was a big *mistake* to leave my umbrella at home.
Your article is full of *mistakes.*

Note : *Mistake, error* and *blunder* refer to something done incorrectly or improperly :
Mistake is the most general, used of everyday situations.
Error is more formal.
Blunder is a careless *mistake,* often unnecessary or resulting from misjudgement.

54. BOAR/BORE/BOOR

boar : male wild pig :

bore : persons or thing that is tiresome; nuisance :
She has become an awful *bore* since she got married.
Don't be such a *bore*.
We have run out of petrol. What a *bore*?

Note : 1. *Bore,* as a verb, means make sb feel tired and uninterested by being dull or tedious :
I have heard all his stories before; they *bore* me.
I hope you are not getting *bored* by my conversation.

2. There is another *bore* used both as a verb and a noun :
(i) *Bore,* as a verb, means :
(a) make a hole, well, tunnel, etc. with a revolving tool or by digging :
This drill can *bore* through rock.
Let him *bore* a hole in the wood.
(b) move by burrowing:
The mole *bored* its way underground.
(ii) *Bore,* as a noun, means:
(a) deep hole made in the ground to find water or oil :
(b) hollow part inside a gun barrel :
He has bought a twelve-*bore* shotgun.

3. There is still another *bore*. It means high tidal wave that moves along a narrow estuary from the sea :

boor : rough, rude or insensitive person :
She says you are a *boor*.

55. BOARDER/BORDER

boarder : (c) person who boards at sb's house :
(b) pupil who lives at a boarding-school during the term :
The school has 400 *boarders* and 200 day pupils.

border : (a) frontier; line dividing two countries or areas :
The dacoits escaped across the *border*.
There were some *border* incidents in the recent past :
(b) band or strip, usually ornamental, around or along the edge of sth :
Let me see the *border* of the photograph.
I bought a tablecloth with an embroidered *border*.
(c) Strip of ground along the edge of a lawn or path for planting flowers or shrubs.

Note : *Border*, as a verb, means :
1. be a border to sth; be on the border of sth :
Our garden is bordered on one side by a canal.
Tell me the number of countries that *border* India.
2. put a border on sth :
His handkerchief is *bordered* with lace.
3. be next to sth; adjoin sth :
The new shopping centre *borders* on the national highwa y.
4. be almost the same as sth; verge on sth :
Your reply to her question was *bordering* on rudeness.
Our task *borders* on the impossible.

56. BOAST/BOOST

boast : talk about one's own achievements, abilities, etc. with too much pride and satisfaction:
He is always *boasting* about his brilliant success at college.
He *boasted* of being the best player in the team.

boost : increase the strength or value of sth; help or encourage sb/ sth :
We should boost production.
The unexpected win *boosted* the team's morale.

Note : *Boost*, as a noun, means encouragement; help; increase :
There was a *boost* in sales of clothes.
I gave her confidence a *boost*.

57. BOB/BOOB

bob : style of hair-cut (woman's) :
She wears her hair in a *bob*.

Note : 1. *Bob*, as a verb, means cut a woman hair-short, so that it hangs loosely above shoulders:
She wears her hair *bobbed*.
2. There is another *bob*.
(i) As a verb, it means:
(a) move quickly up and down :
A toy boat is *bobbing* up and down on the waves.
(b) come to the surface quickly :
She dived below the surface, then *bobbed* up like a cork again a few seconds later.
(ii) Asa noun, it means quick movements, down and up; jerk:
Why did you make a bob of your head?

boob : make a silly mistake :
He has *boobed* again.

58. BOD/BODE

bod : person, especially a man :
He is an odd *bod*.

bode : (a) be a sign of sth coming; foretell :
This *bodes* us no good.
(b) be a good or bad sign for sb/sth. :
The bad trading figures do not *bode* well for the company's future.
Your idle habits *bode* bad for your future.
Her expression *boded* bad for somebody.

59. BOG/BUG

bog : area of wet spongy ground formed of decaying vegetation :
Let us keep to the path-parts of the moor are *bog*.

Note : *Bog*, as a verb, denotes :
1. cause sth to sink into mud or wet ground :
The tank got *bagged* down in the mud.
2. cause sth to become stuck and unable to make progress :
Our discussions got *bogged* down in irrelevant detail.

bug : (a) small flat foul-smelling insect infesting dirty houses and beds :

(b) illness caused by a germ or infectious virus :
He thinks he has caught a *bug*.
(c) Obsessive interest :
He was never interested in cooking before, but now he has been bitten by the *bug*.
(d) defect in a machine :
There is a *bug* in the system.
(e) small hidden microphone placed, so that conversations can be heard at a distance :
He searched the room for *bugs*.
We planted a *bug* in house of my rival.
Our intelligence services planted a *bug* in that foreign embassy.

Note : *Bug*, as a verb, means :

1. fit a room, telephone, etc. with a hidden microphone for listening to conversations :
This office is *bugged*.
2. Listen to a conversation, etc. with a hidden microphone :
Be careful what you say; may be our conversation is being *bugged*.
3. annoy sb; irritate :
Tell me what is *bugging* you?
That girl really *bugs* me.

60. BOGGY/BOGIE/BOGY

boggy : soft and wet :
You cannot run on *boggy* ground.

bogie : undercarriage with wheels fitted below the end of a railway vehicle and pivoted for going round curves :

bogy : (c) thing that causes fear often without reason; bug-bear :
Inflation is the *bogy* of many a government.
(b) Imaginary evil spirit used to frighten children :
If you don't sleep, *bogy* will come.

61. BOLT/VOLT/VAULT

bolt : (a) metal bar that slides into a socket to lock a door, window, etc :
(b) metal pin withaheadatoneend, and a thread used with a nut for fastening things together :
The *bolts* are all tight enough.
(c) flash of lightning :
(d) quantity of cloth, etc. wound in a roll :
(e) sudden dash :
When the police arrived, he made a *bolt* for the door.

volt : Unit of electrical force :

vault : (a) arched roof; series of arches forming a roof :
(b) cellar or underground room used for storing things at a cool temperature :
(c) underground room, especially in a bank and protected by locks, alarms, thick walls, etc. used for keeping money and other valuable safe :

62. BONE/BOON

bone : any of the hard parts that form the skeleton of an animal's body :
He has broken a *bone* in his arm.

boon : (a) advantage; benefit; thing that one is thankful for :
Parks are a great *boon* to people in big cities.
A warm coat is a real *boon* in cold weather.
(b) request or favour :
She asked a *boon* of my helping her with five thousand rupees.

63. BONNY/BONY

bonny : attractive or beautiful; healthy-looking :
She has given birth to a *boony* baby.

bony : (a) of or like bone :
(b) full of bones :
This fish is very *bony*.
(c) thin and having prominent bones :
He has *bony* figures.
He is a tall *bony* man.

64. BOROUGH/BORROW

borough : (a) (In England) town or district with a corporation and certain rights of self-government :
(b) any of the administrative areas of Greater London :

borrow : (a) receive or obtainsth temporarily from sb/sth with the promise or intention of returning it :
I *borrowed* ten thousand rupees from the bank.
(b) take and use sth as one's own; copy sth :
Can I *borrow* freely from other writers?
He *borrowed* music from other composers.
She *borrowed* my ideas and wrote an essay.
(c) adopt a word or phrase from another language.
The expression shigram is *borrowed* from Sanskrit.

65. BOUGH/BOW

bough : any of the main branches of a tree :
He climbed a *bough* of the banyan tree.

bow : piece of wood bent into a curve by a tight string joining its ends, used as a weapon for shooting arrows :
They were hunting with *bows* and arrows.

Note : There is another *bow* used both as a noun and a verb :
1. *Bow*, as a noun, means bending of the head or body as a greeting, etc.
She acknowledged my greetings with a *bow*.
He made a *bow* and left the room.
2. *Bow*, as a verb, means :
(i) bend the head or body as a sign of respect or as a greeting:
We all *bowed* to the President.
The actor *bowed* as the audience applauded.
The congregation *bowed* their heads in prayer.
(ii) bend sb/sth under or as if under a weight:
His back was *bowed* with age

66. BOWEL/BOWL

bowel : (a) part of the alimentary canal below the stomach; intestine :
Do you have a *bowel* complaint?
He suffers from cancer of the *bowel*.
(b) deepest or innermost part of a place :
There are many a thing in the *bowels* of the earth.

bowl : (c) deep round dish, used for holding food or liquid :
Where is the sugar *bowl*?
(b) amount contained in a *bowl* :
She ate three *bowls* of rice.
Let me have a *bowl* of soup.
(c) hollow rounded part of certain objects :
I need a spoon with a big *bowl*.
He filled the *bowl* of his pipe with tobacco.

67. BOY/BUOY

boy : (a) male child; son :
His eldest *boy* is in university.
(b) young man; lad; youth :
I lived in New York as a *boy*.
How many *boys* are there in your class at college?

buoy : floating object anchored to the bottom of the sea, river, etc. to mark places that are dangerous for boat or to show where boats may go :
Be guided by *buoy* while sailing in a rough sea.

68. BRAKE/BREAK

brake : device for reducing the speed of or stopping a car, train, bicycle, etc. :
He applied the *brakes* to avoid an accident.
His *brakes* failed on a steep hill.
Ignorance acts as a *brake* to progress.
The government is deternrnined to put a *brake* on public spending.

Note: *Brake*, as a verb, means slow down using a *brake* :
The driver *braked* hard as the child ran onto the road in front of him.

break : (a) separate into two or more parts as a result of force or strain (but not by cutting) :
She dropped the plate and it *broke* into pieces.
(b) cause a whole object to do this :
He *broke* a cup.
She fell of a ladder and *broke* her arm.
(c) fail to observe a law, promise, etc.; not obey or follow sth :
You should not *break* the law.
He was *breaking* the speed limit.
(d) stop doing sth for a while; pause:
Let us *break* for tea.
(e) interrupt; destroy the continuity of sth :
Don't *break* my concentration.
We *broke* our journey to Kolkata at Patna.

(f) cause sth to end :
She *broke* the silence by coughing.

(g) bring sth to an end by force :
We had to *break* the blockade.

(h) change suddenly after a settled period :
The fine weather *broke* at last.

(i) disperse; show an opening :
The clouds *broke* and the sun came out.

(j) come into existence :
Dawn was *breaking*.

(k) begin suddenly and violently :
The storm *broke*.

(l) become known; be revealed :
There was a public outcry when the scandal *broke*.

(m) weaken or destroy sth :
We *broke* their morale.
Break the power of the trade unions.
The scandal *broke* him.

(n) become weak or be destroyed :
The thief *broke* under questioning and confessed everything.

(o) overwhelm sb with a strong emotion :
The death of his wife broke him completely.

(p) change tone because of emotion :
Her voice *broke* as she told the dreadful news.

(q) do better than or surpass a record :
Rajni Devi *broke* the Olympic 100 metres record.

(r) curl and fall in waves :
The sound of waves was *breaking* on the beach.
The sea was *breaking* over the wrecked ship.

(s) solve; decipher:
Can you *break* this code?

Note: *Break*, as a noun, means :

1. broken place; opening made by *breaking* :
   There was a *break* in the wall.
2. gap; space :
   There is a *break* in the clouds.
   Wait for a *break* in the traffic before crossing the road.
3. interval between periods of work; pause :
   I work for four hours without a *break*.
   She took an hour's *break* for lunch.
4. change or interruption in sth continuous :
   There was a *break* in her education.
5. discontinuation or end of a relationship:
   She has been depressed since the *break* with her boyfriend.
   There was a *break* in diplomatic relations between the two countries.

69. BRASH/BRUSH

brash : (a) confident in a rude or aggressive way; impudently self-assertive :
Her *brash* answer annoyed the interviewers.

(b) garish; showy :
Children are fond of wearing *brash* clothes.

brush : (a) implement with bristles of hair, wire, nylon, etc. set in a block of wood, etc., and used for scrubing, sweeping, cleaning, painting, tidying the hair, etc. :
I need a hair *brush*.

(b) act of brushing:
He gave his clothes a good *brush*.

(c) light touch made in passing :
He knocked a glass off the table with a *brush* of his coat.

(d) short unfriendly encounter with sb; quarrel :
He had a *brush* with the police in the recent past.
She has a nasty *brush* with her boss this forenoon.

Note : *Brush*, as a verb, means :

1. use a *brush* on sb / sth; clean, polish, make tidy or smooth with a *brush* :
You should *brush* your teeth every morning.
2. put sth into a particular state with a *brush* :
Brush your teeth clean.
3. touch sb lightly in passing :
Did you *brush* her cheek?
His hand *brushed* hers.

70. BRASSERIE/BRASSIERE

brasserie : type of restaurant serving beer with food :

brassiere : Woman's undergarment worn to support the breasts :

71. BREACH/BREECH

breach : (a) breaking or neglect of a law, an agreement, a duty, etc :
There was a *breach* of contract.
There was a *breach* of the law in the town.
I sued her for *breach* of contract.

(b) break in friendly relations between people or groups :
There was a *breach* of diplomatic relations between the two countries.

(c) opening:
The huge waves made a *breach* in the sea wall.
The sheep got out of the field after one of them had made a *breach* in the hedge.

Note : *Breach*, as a verb, means make a gap in a defensive wall, etc :
Our tanks have *breached* the enemy defences.

breech : back part of a gun barrel where the bullet or shell is placed :
It is a *breech*-loading gun.

72. BREATH/BREATHE

breath-n (a) air taken into and sent out of the lungs :
His *breath* smelt of garlic.

(b) single act of taking air into the lung :
He took a deep *breath*.

(c) slight movement of air :
There was not a *breath* of air.

(d) slight suggestion or rumour of sth; hint of sth :
There was a *breath* of scandal involving her.
This is the first *breath* of spring.

(e) person or thing that is a welcome and refreshing change :
Her smile is a *breath* of fresh air in this gloomy office.

breathe-v : (a) take air into the lungs and send in out again :
People *breathe* more slowly when they are asleep.
He was *breathing* hard after racing for the train.

(b) say sth softly; whisper :
He *breathed* loving words in her ear.

(c) exude :
The team *breathed* confidence before the match.

73. BREEZE/BRIDGE

breeze : (a) light wind :
A gentle *breeze* was blowing.
There is not much *breeze* today.

(b) thing that is easy to do or enjoy :
Some people think that learning to drive is a *breeze*.

(c) noisy quarrel :
There was a *breeze* among the people.

Note : *Breeze*, as a verb, means move in cheeful and carefree way :
Look who has just *breezed* in.
He *breezes* through life, never worrying about anything.

bridge : (a) structure of wood, iron, concrete, etc., providing a way across a river, road, railway, etc. :
There is a *bridge* across the river.

(b) thing that provides a connection or contact between two or more things:
Cultural exchanges are a way of building *bridges* between nations.

(c) bony upper part of the nose :

(d) part of a pair of glasses that rests on the nose :

(e) device for keeping false teeth in place, fastened to natural teeth on each side :

Note : *Bridge*, as a verb, means :

1. build or form a bridge over sth :
   People *bridged* the canal.
2. fill an awkward or empty space :
   A snack in the afternoon *bridges* the gap between lunch and supper.
   She *bridged* a gap in the conversation.
3. reduce the distance between widely contrasting groups :
   How can we *bridge* the gap between the rich and the poor?

74. BRETHREN/BROTHERS

brethren : plural form of brother when brother refers to a member of certain evangelical Christian sects, a religious order, especially a monk :
Brother Luke will address the audience.
The *Brethren* hold a prayer meeting every Friday.

Note : 1. *Brethren* is in the plural number. It is old use for brothers :
2. *Brethren* is, in general, used to mean members of the same society :
It is in the larger interest of the nation that Muslims live peacefully with their Hindu *brethren*.

brothers : plural form of brother when *brother* refers to :
(a) man or boy having the same parents as another person :
She has three *brothers*.
Lohit and Rohit are real *brothers*.
We are like *brothers*.
(b) person united with others by belonging to the same group, society, profession, and so on :
We are all *brothers* in the same fight against corruption.
She was greatly respected by her *brother* doctors.

Note : It should be remembered that in expressions like brother doctors, only doctor would be in the plural form. Brothers doctors or brothers doctor would be wrong.

75. BRIDAL/BRIDLE

Bridal : of a bride or wedding:
The *bridal* party has already arrived.
She was still wearing her *bridal* costume.

Bridle : part of a horse's harness that goes on its head, including the metal bit for the mouth, the straps and the reins :
Without a *bridle* it is not possible to control a horse.

Note : *Bridle*, as a verb, means :
1. put a *bridle* on :
2. keep feelings, etc. under control; restrain :
You should *bridle* your temper.
3. show anger, resentment, etc. because of sth :
She *bridled* with anger at your offensive remarks.

76. BRING/FETCH

Bring : (a) come carrying sth or accompanying sb :
She *brought* her boyfriend to the party.
The new manager *brings* ten years' experience to the job.
Bring me a cup of tea.
(b) result in sth; cause; produce :
These pills bring relief from pain.
The sad news *brought* tears to her eyes.
The revolution *brought* many a change.
(c) produce sth as profit or income :
His writing *brings* him ten thousand rupees a month.
(d) cause sb/sth to be in a certain state or position :
His incompetence has *brought* the company to the brink of bankruptcy.
(e) cause sb to move in the way specified :
Her cries *brought* the neighbours running.
(f) put forward charges, etc. in a law court :
She *brought* a charge against him.

(g) force or make oneself do sth :
He could not *bring* himself to tell her the tragic news.

fetch : (a) go for and bring sb/sth :
Fetch a doctor at once.
Please *fetch* the children from school.
(b) be sold for a price :
Those old books *fetched* him four thousands rupees at auction.
The old car will not *fetch* you much.
(c) give a blow to sb :
She *fetched* him a terrific slap in the face.

Note : The meaning off *fetch* at
(a) above is of utmost importance. In such a sense, you must not use the verb go with *fetch*. Let us observe the first usage :
Fetch a doctor at once.
This is the correct sentence. You must not say, go and *fetch* a doctor at once, because the sense of go is implied in the verb *fetch*.

77. BROACH/BROOCH

broach : (a) open a bottle, etc. to use the contents :
Let us broach another bottle of milk.
(b) make a hole in a barrel to draw off the liquid inside:
(c) begin a discussion of a topic:
He broached the subject of a loan with the bank manager.

brooch : ornament with a hinged pin and clasp, worn on women's clothes:
This woman has a lovely gold brooch pinned to her blouse.

78. BROAD/BROOD

broad : (a) wide; large in size from one side to the other :
He is tall, *broad* and muscular.
There is a broad street ahead.
He has *broad* shoulders.
(b) from side to side; in breadth :
Have you seen a river two hundred metres *broad*?
(c) covering a wide area; extensive :
There is *a broad* expanse of water behind the airport.
There is broad support for the government policies.
(d) clear; obvious; unmistakable :
She gave me a *broad* cheeful smile.
He always speaks with a *broad* smile on his face.
The minister gave a *broad* hint that he intends to raise taxes.
(e) general; not detailed :
What is the *broad* outline of your plan?
The negotiators reached *broad* agreement on the main issues.
She is feminist in the *broadest* sense of term.
(f) tolerant; liberal :
He is a man of broad views.
(g) Indecent; coarse :
She detests your *broad* humour.

brood : all the young birds (or other animals) produced atone hatching or birth :
It is lovely to see a hen with her *brood* of chicks.

Note: *Brood,* as a verb, means :
1. sit on eggs to hatch them :
   The hen is *brooding* the eggs.
2. think about sth for a long time in a troubled or resentful way :
   Don't *brood* over the past.

79. BROKE/BROOK

broke : having no money; penniless; bankrupt :
He had taken the job because he was *broke.*
Could you lend me two hundred rupees? I am completely *broke.*

brook : small stream :

Note : There is another brook used as a verb in the sense of tolerate sth; allow :
I shall not *brook* anyone interfering with my affairs.
The matter is urgent; it *brooks* no delay.

80. BRUIT/BRUTE

bruit : spread a rumour or report :
It has been *bruited* that he is going abroad for higher studies.
The news of the impending marriage was *bruited* abroad.

brute : (a) animal (except man), especially a large or fierce one :
That dog looks a real *brute.*
(b) brutal and insensitive person :
His father was a drunken *brute.*
(c) unpleasant or difficult thing:
It is a *brute* of a problem.
This lock is a *brute*—it just will not open.

Note : *Brute,* as an adjective, means not involving thought or reason; unthinking:
You should not resort to *brute* force in order to solve a problem.

81. BUREAU/BURROW

bureau : (a) writing desk with drawers :
(b) agency; office :
He runs a travel *bureau.*
Let us visit the information *bureau.*

burrow : hole made in the ground and used as a home or shelter by foxes, rabbits, and so on :

Note : *Burrow,* as a verb, means :
1. make sth by digging :
   Rabbits had *burrowed* holes in the grassy bank.
2. dig a hole :
3. move in a direction by or as if by digging :
   The fox *burrowed* its way under the fence to reach the chickens.
   The prisoners escaped by *burrowing* under the wall.
   We had to *burrow* through a mass of files to find the documents we wanted.

82. BUST/VAST

bust : (a) sculpture of a person's head, shoulders and chest :
(b) woman's breasts; bosom :
A woman's *bust* is her bosom.
(c) measurement round a woman's chest and back :
May I know your *bust* size, Madam?

Note : *Bust*, as a verb, denotes :
1. break sth; smash :
I dropped my camera on the pavement and *bust* it.
2. raid a house or arrest sb :
He has been *busted* for drugs.
3. reduce sb to a lower military rank; demote :
He was *busted* for being absent without leave.

vast : (a) very large in area, size, quantity or degree; immense :
His business empire was truly *vast*.
I incurred a *vast* expense in constructing this house.
There was a *vast* crowd at the Ramlila Ground.
(b) very great :
He has inherited a *vast* fortune.
I had to spend a *vast* sum of money to decorate the office rooms and the conference hall.

83. BUT/BUTT

but : (a) on the contrary :
He does not like music *but* his wife does.
She tried to do it *but* could not.
(b) however; yet; in spite of this :
He cut his knee badly *but* did not cry.
This restaurant serves cheap *but* excellent food.
He is hard-working, *but* not very clever.
(c) yet also; at the same time :
He was tired *but* happy after the long walk.

Note : (a) *But*, as an adverb, means only :
He is *but* a boy.
She left *but* an hour ago.
We can *but* try.
If I had *but* known that she was ill, I would have visited her.
(b) *But*, as a preposition, means except, apart from, other than :
The problem is anything *but* easy.
Everyone was there *but* him.
Nothing *but* trouble will come of this plan.
(c) *But*, as a relative pronoun, means who/that do/does not :
There is no man *but* feels pity for the poor.
There is not one of us *but* wishes to help her.

butt : (a) thicker end of a tool or weapon :
It is a rifle butt.
(b) Short piece at the end of a cigar or cigarette that is left when it has been smoked; stub :
The ashtray is full of *butts*.

(c) person or thing that is often mocked or teased :
He is the *butt* of everyone's jokes.
You are the *butt* of the whole college.
(d) mound of earth behind the targets on a shooting-range :
(e) large cask or barrel for storing wine or beer :
(f) large barrel for collecting rain water :
(g) buttocks; bottom :
Get off your *butts* and do some work.

Note : 1. The expression, the *butts*, means shooting-range :
2. *Butt*, as a verb, means :
(i) hit or push sb/sth with the head (like a goat) :
Don't *butt* her in the stomach.
(ii) hit one's head on sth :
He *butted* his head against the shelf as he was getting up.
(iii) interrupt sb/sth or interfere in sth :
May I *butt* in on your conversation?
Don't *butt* in like that when Iam speaking.

84. BUY/VIE

buy : (a) purchase:
Where did you *buy* that coat?
Did you *buy* your car new or second-hand?
She has *bought* a present for her boyfriend.
(b) be the means of obtaining sth :
Money cannot *buy* happiness.
A sum of hundred rupees today *buys* much less that it did a year ago.
(c) obtain sth by a sacrifice :
His fame was *bought* at the expense of health and happiness.
(d) accept sth as valid; believe :
No one will *buy* that excuse.
(e) bribe sb :
You cannot *buy* me.
He cannot be *bought*.

Note: *Buy*, as a noun, means act of buying sth; thing bought:
Best *buys* of the week are carrots and cabbages, which are plentiful and cheap.

vie : compete keenly with sb for sth; rival sb for sth :
The two girls *vied* with each other for the first place:
Businesses *vied* with each other to attract customers.

3

First Word of Each Group Beginning With-C

1. CAB/CAVE

cab-n : taxi :
Shall we walk or go by *cab*?

cave-n : hollow place in the side of a cliff or hill, or underground:
The hills are riddled with *caves*.

Note : *Cave*, as a verb, means :
1. explore *caves* as a sport :
He likes *caving*.
2. collapse; fall inwards :
The roof of the tunnel *caved* in on the workmen.

2. CABAL/CABLE

cabal : group of people involved in a secret political plot; secret intrigue:
Don't join their *cabal*.

cable : (a) thick strong rope made of fibre or wire :
(b) rope or chain of an anchor :
(c) one-tenth of a nautical mile :
(d) set of insulated wires for carrying messages by telegraph :
(e) set of insulated wires for carrying electricity overhead :

3. CACHE/CATCH

cache: (a) place for hiding weapons, treasure or food :
Police discovered a *cache* of weapons in the terrorists' hideout.
(b) hidden store of weapons, drugs, treasure, etc :
The police arrested two dacoits with an arms *cache*.

catch : (a) act of catching :
(b) amount of sth *caught* :
The angler had a huge *catch* of fish.
(c) device for fastening sth :
The *catch* on my handbag is broken.
(d) hidden difficulty or disadvantage :
The house is very cheap. There must be a *catch* somewhere.

4. CAD/CADE

cad : man who behaves dishonourably :
As he is a *cad*, I always avoid him.

Cade : tame, domesticated :

5. CADGE/CAGE

cadge : get or try to get sth from sb by asking, often unreasonably :
Could I *cadge* a lift with you?
He is always *cadging* meals from his friends.

cage : structure made of bars or wires in which birds or animals are kept or carried :
There are two parrots in that *cage*.

6. CAFE/CAP/CAPE

cafe : small inexpensive restaurant serving light meals :
Do you often visit that *cafe*?

cap : (a) soft head-covering worn by men and boys :
He was wearing a flat *cap*.
(b) protective cover or top for a pen, bottle, etc. :

cape : (a) loose sleeveless garment like a cloak, but shorter :
He has gone to put on a *cape*.
Waving a red *cape*, he provoked the bull to charge.
(b) large piece of high land sticking out into the sea from the coast:
Where is the *Cape* of good hope?

7. CALENDAR/CALENDER/COLANDER

calendar : (a) chart showing the days, weeks and months of a particular year :
Do you have next year's *calendar*?
(b) device that can be adjusted to show the date each day :
He needs a desk *calendar*.

calender : machine for pressing and smoothing cloth or paper :

colander : metal or plastic bowl with many small holes to drain water from vegetables, etc. after cooking :

8. CALF/COUGH/CUFF/CUP

calf : (a) young of cattle :
(b) fleshy back part of the leg below the knee :
The muscle on back of a person's leg is called the *calf*.

cough : (a) act or sound of coughing :
She gave a quiet *cough* to attract my attention.
(b) illness, infection, etc. that causes a person to cough often:
He has a bad *cough*.

Note : Cough, as a verb, means :

1. send out air horn the lungs violently and noisily to clear one's throat, or when one has a cold, etc. :
   She was *coughing* all night.
2. get sth out of the throat or lungs by coughing:
   He had been *coughing* up blood.
3. say or produce sth reluctantly :
   She owes me money, but she won't *cough* it up.

cuff : end of a coat of shirt sleeve at the wrist :
Your shirt has hayed *cuffs*.

cup : small bowl-shaped container with a handle; its contents :
Give me a *cup* of coffee.
She drank a whole *cup* of milk.

Note : *Cup*, as a verb, means form into the shape of a *cup*:
She *cupped* her hands round her mouth and shouted.

9. CALL/CULL

call : (a) say loudly to attract sb's attention; shout; cry :
I thought I heard somebody *calling*.
She *called* her father for help.

(b) order or ask sb/sth to come to a specified place by Shouting, telephoning, writing, etc; summon :
Call the fire brigade.
Call the children; it is time for tea.
The doctor has been *called* to an urgent case.

(c) make a short visit :
She *called* at our house last night.

(d) stop at a place :
The train on platform 4 is for Kolkata, *calling* at Allahabad and Patna.

(e) telephone sb :
I shall *call* you again later.

(f) announce; order sth to take place :
We shall *call* a meeting to be held on Tuesday, the 4th of August, 20 at 4.30 p.m.

(g) wake sb :
Please *call* me at clock tomorrow morning.

(h) describe or address sb / sth as :
How dare you *call* me fat?
Her name is Mamta but we *call* her Madhu.
He has not got anything published and he *calls* himself a writer.

(i) regard as; consider sb/sth to be :
I *call* your behaviour mean and selfish.

Note: Call, as a noun, means :

1. shout; cry :
   She came at my *call*.
2. short visit :
   I paid a *call* on her last evening.
   He has five *calls* to make this afternoon.
3. act of telephoning; conversation on the telephone :
   Were there any *calls* for me while I was out?
4. Invitation, order, signal, etc. to come or meet :
   I am waiting for a *call* to the Prmie Minister's office.
5. request or demand for sth :
   The President made a *call* for national unity.
6. need or occasion for sth :
   There was no *call* for such rudeness.
7. demand on sb/sth :
   He is a busy man with many *calls* on his time.

cull : (a) select or obtain sth from various different sources :
This information has been *culled* from various reference books.

(b) kill a certain number of weaker animals in a herd, in order to reduce its size :
Deer are *culled* by hunters.

(c) reduce the herd in this way :
The herd must be *culled*.

10. CALM/COME

calm: (a) untroubled; quiet; not excited, nervous or agitated:
You should keep *calm* in an emergency.
The city is *calm* again after yesterday's riots.

(b) not windy :
It is a *calm,* cloudless day.

(c) still; without large waves :
The sea is *calm* at the moment.

come: (a) move to, towards, into, etc. a place :
She *came* into the room and shut the door.
He has *come* all the way from Srinagar to look for a job.

(b) arrive at a place :
What time will you be *coming*?
Have any letters *come* for me?

(c) move in order to be with sb or be present at an event:
Would you like to *come* to dinner next Friday?
Are you *coming* to my party?

(d) travel a specified distance:
We have *come* forty miles since lunch.
Our company has *come* a long way in the last five years.

(e) move in the way specified:
She *came* hurrying to see me as soon as she heard I was ill.
The children *came* running to meet us.

(f) occuopy a particular position in space or time; occur:
Triveni *came* first in the examination.
Diwali *comes* early this year.
Her death *came* as a terrible shock to us.
His resignation *came* as a surprise.

(g) be available :
This dress *comes* in four sizes.
Do these shoes *come* in black?
New cars don't *come* cheap.

(h) behave like or play the part of sth :
She tried to *come* the innocent with me.

11. CAN/CANE

can: (a) metal or plastic container for holding or carrying liquids:
It is a petrol *can.*

(b) sealed tin in which food or drink is preserved and sold:

(c) contents of or amount contained in a can:
He bought a *can* of peaches.
He drank two *cans* of milk.

cane: (a) hollow jointed stem of certain plants, such as bamboo, *sugarcane,* etc :

(b) such stems used as a material for making furniture, etc. :
It is a *cane* chair.

(c) length of *cane* used as a walkingstick or for beating people as a punishment:

Note : *Cane,* as a verb, means:

1. punish sb by beating with a *cane.*
   The headmaster *caned* ten boys for disobedience.
2. defeat sb totally :
   We really *caned* them in the last match.

12. CANNON/CANON

cannon: (a) large heavy gun firing solid metal balls :
(b) automatic gun firing shells from an aircraft, a tank, etc. :

canon: (a) general rule, standard or principle by which sth is judged :
This film offends against all the *canons* of good taste.
(b) list of sacred books accepted as genuine :
(c) set of writings, etc. accepted as being truly the work of a particular author :
Can you tell me something about the Shakes- pearian *canon*?
(d) priest with special duties in a cathedral :

13. CANVAS/CANVASS

canvas: (a) Strong coarse cloth used for making tents, sails, etc :
This is a *canvas* bag.
(b) a piece of above used for oil painting, etc :
The artist showed me his *canvas*.

canvass: go round an area asking people for political support:
Our party candidate will *canvass* the constituency next month.
He is *canvassing* for the Communist candidate.

14. CAR/CUR

car: motor vehicle with wheels for carrying passengers:
What kind of *car* do you have?
We are going to Madras by *car*.

cur: (a) vicious or bad-tempered dog :
(b) cowardly or worthless man :
Are you a *cur*?

15. CARD/CURD

card: (a) thick stiff paper or thin pasteboard :
(b) piece of this for writing or printing on, used to identify a person or to record information, or as proof of membership :
Where is your identity *card*?
(c) piece of this with a picture on it, for sending greetings, messages, etc :
I sent you a birthday *card* and a Diwali *card*.
(d) wire brush or toothed instrument for cleaning or combing wool:

curd: thick soft substance formed when milk turns sour, used to make cheese :
I am fond of *curd* and whey.

16. CAREER/CARRIER

career: (a) profession or occupation with opportunities for advancement or promotion :
She chose an academic *career*.
(b) progress through life :
Do you look back on your successful *career*?
(c) quick or violent forward movement :
He ran in full *career*.

Note : *Career*, as a verb, means move about quickly and often dangerously:
He was *careering* down the road on a bicycle.
The car *careered* off the road into a ditch.

carrier: (a) person or thing that carries sth :
(b) person or company that *carries* goods or people for payment :
Your *carrier* for this flight is Air India.
(c) framework fixed to a bicycle, etc. for carrying luggage or a person or child :
This bicycle has a strong *carrier*.
(d) person or animal that can transmit a disease to others without suffering from it :
Mosquitoes are *carriers* of malaria.

17. CARRY/CURRY

carry : (a) support weight of sb / sth and take him/ it from place to place:
The train *carries* hundreds of commuters to and from work.
She *carried* her baby in her arms.
(b) contain and direct flow of; take; conduct :
The veins *carry* blood to the heart.
(c) have sth with :
Ten policeman *carried* gums.
I never *carry* much money with me.
(d) support the weight of sth :
These pillars *carry* the weight of the roof.
A road bridge has to *carry* a lot of traffic.
(e) possess :
His voice *carries* the ring of authority.
(f) have sth as a result; involve; entail :
Power *carries* great responsibility.
Crimes of violence *carry* heavy penalties.
(g) take sth to specified point or direction :
The war was *carried* into enemy territory.
His ability *carried* hjm to the top of his profession.
She *carries* modesty to extremes.
(h) approve sth by majority of votes :
The resolution was *carried* by 304 votes to 201.
(i) win the support or sympathy of sb :
His moving speech was enough to *carry* the audience.
(j) hold or move one's head or body in a specified way :
She *carries* herself well.
(k) of a newspaper or broadcast, include sth in its content; contain :
Today's newspapers *carry* full reports of the President's visit.

curry : dish of vegetables, etc. cooked with certain hot-tasting spices :
Don't eat too much *curry*.

18. CART/CURT

cart : vehicle with two or four wheels used for carrying loads:

curt : rudely brief; adrupt :
She gave a *curt* answer to my question.
He is rather *curt* when he is angry.

19. CARTON/CARTOON

carton : light cardboard or plastic box for holding goods :
Give me a *carton* of cream.

cartoon : amusing drawing in newspaper or magazine, especially one that comments satirically on current events :
He can draw very informative and didactic *cartoons*.

20. CARVE/CURB/CURVE/KERB

carve: (a) form sth by cutting away material from wood or stone:
The statue was *carved* out of stone.
(b) inscribe sth by cutting on a surface :
He *carved* his initials on a tree trunk.

crub : (a) thing that restrains or controls :
You sould put a *curb* on your anger.
The government has put *curbs* on spending.
(b) strap or chain passing under a horse's jaw, used to restrain the horse :

curve : line of which no part is straight, and which changes direction withou angles :
He drew a *curve* on a graph.

Note : *Curve*, as a verb, means *form* a *curve*.
The road *curved* suddenly to the left.

kerb-n : stone or concrete edge of a pavement at the side of a road:
Stop at the *kerb* and look both ways before crossing the road.

21. CAST/CASTE

cast-n : (a) act of throwing sth :
Make a *cast* with a net.
(b) object made by pouring or pressing soft material into a mould:
This ice cream *cast* is very small.
(c) all the actors in a play :
This is a film with a distinguished *cast*.
(d) type of sth :
She has an unusual *cast* of mind.
(e) slight squint :
He has a *cast* in one eye.

Note : *Cast*, as a verb, means :

1. throw sth with force :
   He *cast* a stone into the water.
2. turn or send sth in a particular direction; direct :
   He *cast* a furtive glance at her.
   The tree *cast* a long shadow on the grass.
   The tradgedy *cast* a shadow on their lives.
3. make an object :
   The novel is *cast* in the form of a diary.
4. choose actors to play parts in a play, etc :
   We are *casting* next week.
5. give sb a part in a play, etc :
   Alok was *cast* as the husband in the play.
6. make damaging or derogatory remarks about sb/sth :
   Don't *cast* aspersions on her character.
7. give a vote :
   Please *cast* your vote in my favour.

8. abandon or reject sb/sth :
She has *cast* off four boyfriends in a month.

caste-n : (a) any of the hereditary social classes:
He is a Brahmin by *caste*.
Are you in favour of the *caste* system?
(b) any exclusive social class :
The highest *caste* is Brahmins.
(c) social system based on rigid distinctions of birth, rank, wealth, and so on :
Don't judge a man by his *caste*.

22. CASUAL/CAUSAL

casual-adj : (a) happening by chance :
I had a *casual* friendship with her.
He had a *casual* meeting with me.
(b) made or done without much care or thought; off hand :
Your *casual* remark offended her.
(c) irresponsible; nonchalant; showing little concern :
Her attitude to her job is rather *casual*.
(d) not serious; not methodical or thorough :
I had a *casual* glance at the newspaper.
(e) not formal; for informal occasions :
These clothes are for *casual* wear.
She wears *casual* clothes in bright colours.
(f) not permanent; irregular; part-time :
He earns his living by *casual* labour.
Are you a *casual* journalist?
(g) slight; superficial :
I have a *casual* acquaintance with that young lady.

causal-adj: (a) relating to cause and effect.
There is a *causal* connection between hard work and success.
Is there any *causal* connection between food and health?
(b) in grammar, expressing or indicating a cause:
Because is a *causal* conjunction.

23. CATTLE/KETTLE

cattle-n : animals with horns and cloven hoofs, such as cows, bulls and bullocks :
He has ten heads of *cattle*.
I saw a herd of *cattle* grazing in the field.

kettle-n : container with a spout, lid and handle, used for boiling water:
Let her boil water in the *kettle* and make some tea.

24. CAUSE/REASON

cause-n: (a) that which produces an effect; thing, event, person, etc. that makes sth happen :
What was the *cause* of the fire?
Smoking is one of the *causes* of heart disease.
(b) aim, principle or movement that is strongly defended or supported :
His life was devoted to the *cause* of justice.

Note : *Cause*, as a verb, denotes make happen; be the *cause* of sth :
Smoking can *cause* lung cancer.
She is always *causing* trouble for people.
The cold weather *caused* the plants to die.

reason-n: (a) motive or justification for sth :
Give me the *reason* for your going.
He has adequate *reason* for doing so.
(b) power of the mind to think, understand, form opinions, etc :
Only man has *reason*.
(c) what is right or practical or possible; common sense or judgement :
There is a good deal of *reason* in what you say.

Note : A *cause* of something is what makes something happen:
The police are investigating the *cause* of the explosion.
Reason for something has a wider use. It can be the explanation that people give for why something is done.
What was the *reason* for his resignation?
She did not give any *reasons* for leaving.

25. CEASE/SEIZE/SIEGE *: ALSO REFER TO P. 199-200*

cease-v : stop; come or bring sth to an end :
The officer ordered his men *cease-fire*.
That office has *ceased* to exist.

seize-v : (a) take hold of sth suddenly and violently; grab :
She *seized* me by the wrist.
(b) take stolen goods, illegal drugs, etc. away from sb :
10 kilos of heroin were *seized* yesterday at the airport.
(c) capture sth; take :
The enemy troops *seized* the airport in a surprise attack.
(d) see an opportunity, etc. and make use of it eagerly and at once:
Seize any opening you can.
(e) affect sb. suddenly and overwhelmingly:
Panic *seized* us.
We were *seized* by a sudden impulse to run.

siege-n : surrounding of a town, etc. by armed forced in order to capture it or force it to surrender :
The town was under *siege* for ten days.

26. CEDE/SEED

cede-v : give up one's rights to or possession of sth :
We shall never *cede* even an inch of our territory to any neighbouring state.
(a) part of a plant from which a new plant of the same kind can grow :
Give me a handful of grass *seed*.
Pea *seed* can be sown in April.
(b) begin to look shabby or become less able, efficient, etc :
He started to drink too much and gradually ran to *seed*.

27. CEILING/ROOF

Ceiling: (a) top inner surface of a room :
Don't bump your head on the low *ceiling*.

(b) maximum altitude at which a particular aircraft can normally fly :
It is an aircraft with a *ceiling* 18,000 ft.
(c) upper limit :
There is a *ceiling* on business rate increases.

roof : structure covering or forming the top of a building, vehicle, etc.
This is a house with a slate *roof*.
How can you live under the same *roof* as that woman?

28. CELL/SELL

cell-n: (a) very small room :
The prisoner was locked in a *cell*.
(b) compartment in a honeycomb :
(c) device for producing an electric current by chemical action:
My torch battery is made up of three *cells*.
(d) microscopic unit of living matter, containing a nucleus:
Human tissue is made of *cells*.
Do you know anything about cancer *cells*?
(e) small group of people forming a centre of political activities:
There is a Leftist *cell* within the Congress organisation.

sell-v : (a) give goods, etc. to sb who becomes their owner-after paying money :
Will you *sell* your car?
(b) have a stock of sth for sale :
That shop *sells* fruit, vegetables, etc.
Do you *sell* stamps?
(c) be sold, find buyers :
Will such a long novel *sell*?
The badges *sell* at 50 paisa each.
This shop *sells* a wide variety of goods.
(d) deceive; disappoint :
I have been *sold*.

Note : *Sell* is also used as a noun to mean disappointment, deception.
It is a real *sell*: the food seems cheap but you pay extra for vegetables.

29. CELLAR/SELLER

cellar-n : underground room for storing things:
That firm has a coal *cellar*.

seller-n : (a) person who sells :
He is a book *seller*.
(b) item that is sold :
This book is a best *seller*.
That model is a poor *seller*.

30. CEMETERY/SYMMETRY : ALSO REFER TO P. 218

cemetery-n : area of land used for burying the dead:
Mary goes to the *cemetery* each week to put flowers on her father's grave.

symmetry-n: exact match in size and shape between the two halves of sth:
The *symmetry* of the Taj Mahal is immensely pleasing to the eyes.

31. CENSER/CENSOR/CENSURE

censer-n : container in which incense is burnt in temples, churches, etc :

censor-n : person authorised to examine books, films, plays, letters, etc. and remove parts which are considered indecent, offensive, politically unacceptable or threat to security :
The film, "Private Life of a Woman", was banned by the *censor*.
The *censor* gave A certificate to our film.

Note : Censor, as a verb, means examine or remove parts from sth, as a censor :
This is the *censored* version of the film.

censure-n : strong criticism or condemnation; reprimand :
The Parliament passed a vote of *censure* against the Prime Minister.

Note : Censure, as a verb, means criticize sb severely; rebuke sb formally :
Five members of Parliament were censured by the Speaker of the Lok Sabha.

32. CENT/SCENT

cent-n: (a) one 100th part of a US dollar:
(b) coin of this value :
I have seventy *cents* with me at the moment.

scent-n : (a) characteristic smell of sth, especially a pleasant one:
Do you like the *scent* of new-mown hay?
Modem roses have no *scent*.
(b) feeling of the presence of sth :
She felt a *scent* of fear.

33. CEREAL/SERIAL

cereal-n : (a) any of various types of grass producing edible grains, such as wheat, oats, barely, etc :
(b) grain produced by such a grass:
(c) food made from the grain of *cereals*:
These are breakfast *cereals*.

serial-adj: (a) of, in or forming a series :
Files are numbered in *serial* order.
(b) (of a story, etc.) appearing in parts in a periodical, etc. or on T.V. or radio :
Our new *serial* thriller begins at 8.30 this evening.

34. CEREMONIAL/CEREMONIOUS

ceremonial : of, used for or involving a ceremony; formal:
He bought a *ceremonial* dress.
The *ceremonial* part of a marriage is very important.
She invites me on *ceremonial* occasions.

Note : *Ceremonial*, as a noun, means system of rules and procedures for *ceremonies* or formal occasions :
You should observe the *ceremonials* of religion.
Everything was performed with due *ceremonial*.

ceremonious :
(a) full of ceremony; very formal :
Don't be *ceremonious* with your fast friends.
I bid her an unusually *ceremonious* farewell.
(b) elaborately perfomed :
He unveiled the picture with a *ceremonious* gesture.

35. CESSION/SESSION

cession-n : (a) action of ceding sth, especially land or rights:
We shall never agree to the *cession* of Kashmir to Pakistan.
(b) thing that is ceded, especially land :

session-n: (a) meeting or series of meetings of a Parliament, law court, etc. for discussing or deciding sth :
Parliament is in *session*.
(b) school or university year :
(c) Single continuous period spent in one activity :
She was present at the recording *session*.

36. CHAFE/CHAFF

chafe-v: (a) become irritated or impatient because of sth :
The passengers sat *chafing* at the long delay.
She *chafed* under an illness.
(b) cause sth to become sore by rubbing :
His shirt collar *chafed* his neck.
(c) become sore by rubbing :
Her skin *chafes* easily.
(d) warm sb by rubbing, especially with the hands :
He *chafed* the baby's feet.

chaff-n : (a) outer covering of com, etc., separated from the grain by threshing or winnowing :
(b) hay or straw cut up as food for cattle:

Note: There is another chaff used, both as a verb and a noun :
1. *Chaff,* as a verb, means tease'sb in a good-natured Way:
They *chaffed* him about his love life.
2. *Chaff,* as a noun, means good-na tured teasing or joking:
Your *chaff* offended him.

37. CHALK/CHOCK/CHOKE/CHUCK

chalk-n : (a) type of white rock used for burning to make lime:
(b) this or similar substance made into white or coloured sticks for writing or drawing on black-boards:
Give me a stick of *chalk*.
This is a picture drawn in *chalk*.

Note: Chalk, as a verb, means :
1. write, draw or mark sth with chalk:
2. draw with chalk.
The boys *chalked* out goal-posts on the play ground wall.
3. achieve or register a success :
The team has *chalked* up its fourth win in a row.

chock-n : block or wedge used to prevent a wheel, barrel door, etc. from moving :

choke-v : (a) be unable to breathe because one's windpipe is blocked by sth :
He *choked* to death on a fish bone.
(b) cause sb to stop breathing by blocking the wind-pipe; make sb unable to breathe easily :
The fumes almost *choked* me.
(c) become speechless :
She was *choking* with emotion.
(d) cause sb to become speechless :
Anger *choked* his words.
(e) block; clog or smother sth :
The drains are *choked* up with dead leaves.

chuck-v : (a) throw sth carelessly or casually :
Chuck it in the dustbin.
Chuck me the newspaper if you have finished reading it.
(b) abandon; give up sb/sth :
That girl has just *chucked* her boyfriend.

Note: *Chuck*, as a noun, means playful touch or stroke under the chin.
I gave the baby a *chuck*.

38. CHASTE/CHEST

Chaste-adj :
(a) not having had sexual intercourse; virgin :
(b) not having sexual intercourse except with the person to whom one is married :
(c) pure; virtuous :
(d) simple in style; not ornate :
Try to write in *chaste* English.

chest-n : (a) large strong box for storing or shipping things in :
He needs a tea *chest*.
(b) upper front part of the body from the neck to the stomach:
He has a hairy *chest*.
What size are you round the *chest*?

39. CHEAP/CHIEF/CHIP/CHEEP

cheap-adj: (a) low in price; costing little money :
Cabbages are very *cheap* at the moment.
(b) charging low prices :
He visits a *cheap* restaurant.
(c) of poor quality :
I do not buy *cheap* furniture.
(d) Insincere :
She dislikes your *cheap* flattery.
(e) despicable; contemptible; not worthy of respect :
His brother is a *cheap* crook.
His treatment of her made her feel *cheap*.
That was a *cheap* trick to play on her.

chief-adj : (a) main; most important; principal :
Smoking is one of the *chief* cause of lung cancer.
Name the *chief* rivers of India.
(b) having the highest authority or rank :
He is the *chief* priest of the Birla Temple.

chip-n : (a) thin piece cut or broken off from wood, stone, glass, etc :
It is a *chip* of wood.
(b) thin strip of potato fried in deep fat :
Bring me a plate of *chips*.

cheep-n : weak shrill cry of a young bird :

40. CHEAT/CHIT

cheat-v: (a) act dishonestly or unfairly in order to win an advantage or profit :
She accused me of *cheating* at cards.
(b) trick or deceive sb/sth :
Do you *cheat* the income tax department?

chit-n : (a) a spirited and usually disrespectful young woman:
She is a mere *chit* of a girl :
(b) short written note or letter :
(c) note showing an amount of money owed :
Can I sign a *chit* for the drinks I have ordered?

41. CHECK/CHEQUE

check-v: (a) make sure of sth by examining or investigating it :
Go and *check* if the baby is asleep.
(b) cause sb/sth to stop or go more slowly; slow down; control :
Check the flow of blood from the wound.
The government is determined to *check* the growth of public spending.

Note: Check, as a noun, means :
1. examination to make sure that sth is correct, safe, satisfactory or in good condition :
You should conduct regular *checks* on the quality of your products.
2. investigation : The police made a *check* on all the victim's friends.

cheque-n : special printed form on which one writes an order to a bank to pay a sum of money from one's account to oneself or to another person:
I paid her by *cheque*.

42. CHEEK/CHICK

cheek-n : (a) either side of the face below the eye :
She has healthy pink *cheeks*.
They were dancing *cheek* to *cheek*.
(b) impertinent talk or behaviour; impudence :
He had the *cheek* to ask me to do his work for him.
(c) either of the buttocks :

chick-n : (a) young bird, especially a young chicken, just before or after hatching :
He bought a hen with her *chicks*.
(b) young woman :
She is a real *chick*.

43. CHILDISH/CHILDLIKE

childish-adj : (of an adult) immature; silly :
Don't be so *childish*.

childlike-adj : like or characteristic of a child; innocent; not devious :
I highly laud her *childlike* honesty.

44. CHOIR/COIR

choir-n : (a) organised group of singers, especially one that performs in church services :
She sings in the church *choir*.
(b) part of a church where these singers sit:

coir-n : fibre from the outer husk of coconuts, used for making ropes, matting, and so forth :

45. CHOLER/COLLAR/COLOUR

choler-n : anger :
He spoke in *choler* about the plight of the poor.

collar-n : (a) band, upright or folder cover, round the neck of a shirt, coat, dress, and so on :
She grabbed him by the *collar*.
(b) band of leather, metal, etc. put round an animal's, especially a dog's neck :
Our dog has its name on its *collar*.
(c) metal band or ring joining two pipes, rods, etc. in a machine:

Note: Collar, as a verb, means :
1. seize sb by the collar; capture :
The policeman *collelred* the thief.
2. take sth without permission :
Who has *collared* my pen?

colour-n : (a) visible quality that objects have, produced by rays of light:
The garden was a mass of *colour*.
(b) redness of the face or complexion, usually regarded as a sign of good health :
She has a high *colour*.
The fresh air brought colour to her cheeks.
(c) interesting detail or qualities; vividness :
His description of the area is full of *colour*.

46. CHORD/CORD

chord-n : (a) in music, combination of notes, usually sounded together in harmony :
(b) (mathematics) straight line that joins two points on the circumference of a circle or the ends of an arc :
(c) string of a harp, etc :

chord-n : (a) piece of long, thin, flexible material made of twisted strands, thicker than string and thinner than rope :
He tied the parcels with *cord*.
(b) part of the body like a *cord* in being long, thin and flexible:
What is a spinal *cord*?

47. CITE/SIGHT/SITE

cite-v : (a) quote; speak or write words taken from a passage, a book, an author, etc :
She *cited* a verse from a poem by Tagore.

(b) mention sth as an example or to support an argument; refer to:
He *cited* many examples in support of his argument.
I *cited* the high unemployment figures as evidence of the failure of government policy.
(c) officially commend, especially a soldier, for bravery; mention:
He was *cited* in dispatches.
(d) summon sb to appear in a court of law :
She is the woman who was *cited* in his divorce action.

sight-n : (a) ability to see; vision:
He has very good *sight*.
Some drugs can affect your *sight*.
(b) action of seeing sb/sth:
When can I have a *sight* of your new house?
(c) range within which sb can see or sth can be seen:
The train is still in *sight*.
The car was out of *sight* behind the house.
(d) thing to be seen, or worth seeing, especially sth remarkable:
The flowers are a lovely *sight* in spring.
A suffering animal is a distressing *sight*.
(e) person or thing that looks ridiculous, untidy, etc :
What a *sight* you look in those old clothes?

Note: Sight, when used in the sense at (e) above, must be preceded by the indefinite article, "a" :

site-n : (a) place where a building, town, etc. was, is, or will be situated:
This is a *site* for a new college for girls.
Deliever the material to the building *site*.
(b) place where sth has happened or will happen or for a particular activity:
Rescue workers rushed to the *site* of the plane crash.

48. CLACK/CLUCK

clack-n : short sharp sound of hard objects being struck together :
I heard the *clack* of high heels on the stone floor.
Is it the *clack* of the typewriter?

cluck-n : noise that a hen makes :

49. CLENCH/CLINCH

clench-v : (a) close sth tightly or press two things firmly together :
Clench your fist.
He *clenched* his teeth.
(b) grasp or hold sb/sth firmly :
He *clenched* the railings with both hands.

clinch-v : (a) fix a nail firmly in place by hammering sideways the end that sticks out:
(b) confirm or settle sth finally :
Let us *clinch* the bargain.
(c) (of boxers) hold each other tightly with the arms :
The boxers *clinched* and the referee had to separate them.
The scene ended as the lovers *clinched*.

50. CLEW/CLUE

clew-n : (a) metal loop attached to the lower corner of a sail:
(b) loop holding the strings of a hammock:

clue-n : (a) fact or piece of evidence that helps to solve a problem or reveal the truth in an investigation :
We have no *clue* as to where she went after she left home.
There was no *clue* to the identity of the murderer.
(b) word or words indicating the answer to be inserted in crossword puzzle:
The *clues* to this cross word puzzle are interesting.

51. CLICK/CLIQUE

click-n : short sharp sound like that of a key turning in a lock:
He saluted with a *click* of his heels.

Note : *Click*, as a verb, means :

1. make a slight sharp sound :
The door *clicked* shut.
The new part *clicked* into place.
2. cause sth to make a slight sharp sound:
He *clicked* his fingers.
3. become friendly at once:
We met on holiday and just *clicked* immediately.
4. become popular with sb :
The film has really clicked with young audiences.
5. suddenly become clear or understood :
I puzzled over it for hours before it finally *clicked*.

clique-n : small group of people, often with shared interests, who associate closely and exclude others from their group :
This club is dominated by a small *clique* of intel-lectuals.

52. CLIENT/CLIENTELE

client-n : (a) person who receives help or advice from a professional person, such as a lawyer, an architect, etc :
(b) customer in a shop:

clientele-n : (a) customers or clients as a group :
He has an international *clientele*.
(b) patrons of a theatre, restaurant, etc :

53. CLIMATE/WEATHER

climate-n : (a) regular pattern of weather conditions-temperature, rainfall, winds, etc-of a particular region :
Kashmir has a cold *climate*.
(b) area or region with certain weather conditions:
She moved to a warmer climate.
(c) general attitude or feeling; atmosphere :
Tell me something about the present political *climate* of India.
I dislike the changing *climate* of public opinion.
There is a *climate* of suspicion about his statement.

weather-n : condition of the atmosphere at a certain place and time, with reference to temperature and the presence of rain, sunshine, wind, and so on :
I like sunny *weather*.
The success of the crop wholly depends on the *weather*.

54. CLOAK/CLOCK

cloak-n : (a) sleeveless outer garment hanging loosely from the shoulders, usually worn out of doors :

(b) thing that hides or covers :

The dacoits escaped under the *cloak* of darkness.

The spy's activities are concealed by the *cloak* of diplomacy.

Note : *Cloak*, as a verb, means cover or hide as if with a *cloak* :

The negotiations were *cloaked* in secrecy.

clock-n : (a) Instrument for measuring and showing time :

I was late for school as the home *clock* was ten minutes slow.

(b) instrument, such as a taximeter or a milimeter, for measuring and recording things other than time :

This is a second-hand car with 20,000 miles on the *clock*.

55. CLOTH/CLOTHE/CLOTHES

cloth-n : material made by weaving cotton, wool, silk, etc :

He has enough woollen *cloth* to make a suit.

clothe-v: (a) put clothes on sb/oneself; dress :

She was *clothed* from head to foot in white.

(b) provide clothes for sb. :

He can barely feed and *clothe* his family.

(c) cover sth as if with *clothes*:

The landscape was *clothed* in mist.

clothes-n : garments; covering for a person's body :

Put on your warm *clothes*.

Note : *Clothes* is always used in the plural number.

He was wearing expensive *clothes*.

56. COACH/COUCH

coach-a : (a) bus for carrying passengers over long distance:

They travelled by a *coach* to Allahabad.

(b) large four-wheeled carriage pulled by horses and used for carrying passengers:

Children are fond of travelling by a *coach*.

Note : There is another *coach*, used both as a noun and a verb:

1. Coach, as a noun, means :
   (i) teacher who gives private lessons to prepare students for examinations :

   I need a *coach* for my youngest son.

   (ii) person who trains sportsmen :

   Who is your tennis *coach*?
2. *Coach*, as a verb, means :
   (i) teach or train sb for an examination or a sporting contest:

   He *coached* a swimmer for the Olympics.

   She *coaches* me in English.

   You have talent but you still need *coaching*.

   (ii) work or act as a coach :

   He will be *coaching* all summer.

couch-n : long bedlike seat for sitting or lying on; sofa:

There is a lovely *couch* in her drawing-room.

Note : *Couch*, as a verb, means :

1. express a thought, an idea, etc. in words:
   His letter was *couched* in insolent terms.
   I sent her a carefully *couched* reply.
2. (of animals) lie flat, either in hiding or ready to jump forward :
   A deer *couched* on a grassy bank.

57. COARSE/COURSE

coarse-adj : (a) not fine; consisting of large particles :
Do you need *coarse* sand?
(b) rough or loose in texture :
These are bags made from *coarse* linen.
(c) (of food, etc.) of low quality; inferior:
Poor people eat *coarse* grain.
(d) vulgar; not refined :
Nobody likes your *coarse* manners.

course-n : (a) forward movement in time :
In the *course* of my long life, I have known many changes.
I did not sleep once during the entire *course* of the journey.
(b) direction or route followed by a ship, river or an aircraft:
The plane was on *course*.
The *course* of the ship was due north.
The *course* of the argument suddenly changed.
(c) way of acting or proceeding :
The wisest *course* would be to ignore it.
The government's present *course* will only lead to disaster.
(d) (education) series of lessons, lectures, etc :
He took an elementary *course* in mathematics.
(e) (medical) series of treatments, pills, etc :
The doctor prescribed a course of injections.
(f) any of the separate parts of a meal :
The dinner consisted of six *courses*.
The main *course* was a vegetable stew.

Note : *Course*, as a verb, means move or flow freely :
The blood *coursed* through his veins.
Tears *coursed* down her rosy cheeks.

58. COAT/QUOTE

coat-n : (a) long outer garment with sleeves, fastened at the front with buttons :
It is a waterproof *coat*.
(b) woman's jacket worn with a skirt :
She was wearing a tweed *coat* and skirt.
(c) layer of paint of some other substance put on a surface at one time :
Give the table a second *coat* of paint.

quote-v : (a) repeat in speech or writing words previously said or written by another person :
He is always *quoting* verses from Gitanjali.
I think he is going to resign, but please don't *quote* me.
(b) mention sb/sth in support of a statement :
Can you *quote* an example of what you mean?

(c) name an amount as the price of sth :
The shares are currently being *quoted* at fifty rupees a share.
This is the best price I can *quote* you.

59. COAX/COX

coax-v : (a) persuade sb gently or gradually :
I *coaxed* her to take her medicine.
She *coaxed* him out of his bad temper.
(b) obtain sth from sb by gentle persuasion :
I had to *coax* the information out of him.
She *coaxed* a smile from her child.

cox-n : person who steers a rowing boat, especially in races :

60. COD/CODE

cod-n : large sea fish :

code-n : (a) system of words, letters, symbols, etc. that represent others, used for secret messages or for presenting or recording information briefly :
She sent me a letter in *code*.
(b) set of laws or rules arranged in a system:
What is a penal *code*?
(c) set of moral principles accepted by society or a group of people:
You should observe the *code* of behaviour.

61. COLD/COOL

cold-adj : (a) of low temperature, when compared to the temperature of the human body :
Do you feel *cold*?
The weather is getting *colder*.
(b) without friendliness, kindness or enthusiasm; without emotion:
She gave me a *cold* welcome.

Note : Cold, as a noun, means :
1. lack of heat or warmth; low temperature:
He was shivering with *cold*.
Don't stand outside in the *cold*.
She does not seem to feel the *cold*.
2. infectious illness of the nose or throat or both, with sneezing, coughing, etc :
As he had a *cold*, he could not attend the meeting.

cool-adj : (a) fairly cold; not hot or warm; between warm and cold :
Let us sit in the shade and keep *cool*.
The tea is not *cool* enough to drink.
(b) calm; unexcited :
Champa always remains calm, *cool* and collected in a crisis.
He was always *cool* in the face of danger.
Do you have a *cool* head?
(c) not showing interest, enthusiasm or friendliness:
She was totally *cool* about my proposal.
They gave the Prime Minister a *cool* reception.
(d) calmly bold or impudent:
You should have seen the *cool* way she took my radio without even-asking.

(e) of sums of money, distances, etc :
My new car cost me a *cool* seventy thousand rupees.
She suggested that we should walk a *cool* four miles farther.

62. COLLAGE/COLLEGE

collage-n : an art picture made by a combination of pieces of paper, string, matchsticks, cloth, photographs, metal, etc. and glued to a surface :
He is expert in making *collage*.

college-n : institution for higher education or professional training:

63. COLLISION/COLLUSION

collision-n: (a) instance of one object or person striking against another; instance of colliding; crash :
There was a head-on *collision* between two cars.
The two ships came into *collision*.

(b) strong disagreement; conflict or clash of opposing aims, ideas, opinions, etc :
His political activities brought him into *collision* with the law.

collusion-n : secret agreement or co-operation between two or more persons with the aim of deceiving or cheating others :
She acted in *collusion* with the other witness.
There was *collusion* between the two witnesses.
The dacoit was in *collusion* with the servant of the house.

64. COMA/COMMA

coma-n : state of deep unconsciousness, usually lasting a long time and caused by severe injury or illness:
He was in a *coma* of twenty days.

comma-n : punctuation mark (,) to indicate a slight pause or break between parts of a sentence:

65. COMFORT/COMPORT

comfort-n : (a) state of physical or mental well-being; state of being free from suffering, pain or anxiety :
Do you live in *comfort*?
She did everything for my absolute *comfort*.

(b) consolation; help or kindness to sb who is suffering:
He sent me a few words of *comfort*.
The news brought *comfort* to all of us.

(c) person or thing that brings relief or consolation:
My children are a great *comfort* to me.
It is a great *comfort* to know that she is safe and sound.

(d) thing that creates physical ease or well-being:
The hotel has all modem *comforts*.
He likes his *comforts*.

Note : *Comfort*, as a verb, means give comfort to sb :
They *comforted* the dying man.
The boy ran to his mother to be *comforted*.

comport-v : behave; conduct oneself in the specified way :
You should *comport* yourself with dignity.
She always *comports* in a dignified manner.

66. COMIC/COMICAL

comic-adj: (a) funny; causing people to laugh; intended to amuse :
She sang a *comic* song.
(b) containing or using comedy :
Are you a *comic* actor?

comical-adj : amusing; odd :
There is something *comical* about you.
Do you like his *comical* activities?

67. COMMAND/COMMEND

command: (a) order; tell sb that he must do sth :
Do as I *command* you.
The officer *commanded* the soldiers to fire.
(b) have at one's disposal; be able to use sth :
He *commands* great wealth.
A government minister *commands* the services of many officials.
Our house *commands* a very fine view.
(c) deserve and get sth :
Great men *command* our respect.
The plight of the famine victims *commands* everyone's sympathy.

Note : *Command*, as a noun, means :

1. order :
   Her *commands* were quickly observed.
   Give your *commands* in a loud, confident voice.
2. control; authority :
   He took *command* of a regiment.
   He has fifty soldiers under his *command.*
   Who is in *command* of this department?
3. ability to use or control sth; mastery :
   He has a good *command* of the English language.
   She has enormous funds at her *commands.*
   Do you have *command* over yourself?

commend: (a) speak favourably to or of sb/sth; praise sb/sth:
I highly *commend* her teaching.
They *commended* the chef on the excellent meal.
(b) recommend sb/sth :
That is excellent advice; I *commend* it to you .

68. COMPARE/CONTRAST

compare-v : (a) examine people or things to see how they are alike and how they are different:
Compare the style of the two poems.
If you *compare* her work with his, you will find hers is much better.
(b) show the likeness between two dissimilar things, ideas or persons :
Poets have *compared* sleep to death.

contrast-v : (a) compare (two persons or things), so that differences are clear :
Contrast my work with hers.
(b) show a difference when compared :

Her actions *contrasted* sharply with her promises.
His actions and promises *contrasted* sharply.

69. COMPEER/COMPERE

compeer-n : person of equal status or ability :
He is much respected by his *compeers.*

compere-n : person who introduces the performers in a variety programme or game show :
He acted as a *compere* on many an occasion.

70. COMPLACENT/COMPLAISANT

complacent : self-satisfied; calmly satisfied with oneself, one's work, and so forth:
Don't be *complacent* about your achievements; there is still a lot to be done.
She talked to me with a *complacent* smile.

complaisant : obliging; ready to please :
He is a *complaisant* husband.
As she is *complaisant,* I like her much.

71. COMPLEMENT/COMPLIMENT

complement : (a) thing that goes well or suitably with sth else, or makes it complete :
Rice makes an excellent *complement* to a curry dish.
(b) the complete number or quantity needed or allowed: .
We have taken on our full *complement* of new trainees for this year.

compliment : (a) expression of praise, admiration, etc :
She likes to hear *compliment* on her appearance.
He paid me very charming *compliment* on my paintings.
(b) greeting, usually as part of a message:
My *compliments* are to your father.
The flowers are with the *compliments* of the management.

Note : Compliments, the plural form of *compliment,* must be use in the sense at (b) above.

72. COMPRISE/CONSIST

comprise-v : (a) be made up of; have as parts or members :
The committee *comprises* people of widely differing view.
(b) be the parts or members of sth :
Ten small boys and a dog *comprised* the street entertainer's audience.

consist-v : be composed of sth :
The *committee* consists of seven members.

Note : 1. *Comprise* and *consist* mean one and the same thing.
Consist, when used in the said sense, is always followed by the preposition of. On the other hand, of is not used with *comprise.* Left us observe the following two usages:
(i) The Indian Parliament *comprises* the President, the Rajya Sabha and Lok Sabha.
(ii) The Indian Parliament *consists* of the President, the Rajya Sabha and the Lok Sabha.

2. The expression *consist* in means have sth as its chief or only element or feature :
The beauty of the plan *consists* in its simplicity.
The happiness of a country *consists* in the freedom of its citizens.

73. CON/CONE

con-n : instance of cheating sb; confidence trick:
The whole thing was a big *con.*
This so-called bargain is just a *con.*

Note : Con, as a verb, means swindle or persuade sb after gaining his trust :
You cannot con me- you are not really ill.
I was *conned* into buying a useless car.

(a) solid body that narrows to a point from a circular flat base:
A church stuple is *cone* shaped.
(b) sth of this shape, whether solid or hollow, as a warning sign for road-workers, etc :
(c) fruit of certain evergreen trees :
A pine *cone* is the fruit of a pine tree.

Note : Cone, as a verb, denotes mark or separate sth with *cones* :
They *coned* off a section of motorway during repairs.
Cone off parking spaces that must not be used.

74. CONCERT/CONSORT

concert-n : musical entertainment given in public by one or more performers:
Let us give a *concert* for charity.
Did you like the orchestral *concert?*

consort-n : husband or wife, especially of a ruler :
I had an audience with queen *consort.*

75. CONCUR/CONKER/CONQUER

concurt-n : (a) agree; express agreement :
I *concur* with her in condemning what has been done.
The judge *concurred* with earlier findings.
(b) happen together; coincide :
Everything *concurred* to produce a successful result.

conker-n : horse-chestnut :

conquer-v : (a) take possession of sth by force :
We do not want to *conquer* any neighbouring country.
(b) gain the admiration love, etc. of sb/sth :
She has *conquered* the hearts of many healthy and wealthy men.
He set out to *conquer* the literary world of Delhi.
(c) defeat a rival in competition :
India *conquered* their main rivals in the first round of the competition.
(d) overcome :
The Himalayas were *conquered* many years ago.
Smallpox has finally been *conquered.*
You must *conquer* your fear of driving.

76. CONFIDANT/CONFIDENT

confidant-n : trusted person to whom one speaks about one's private affairs or secrets:
Who is your *confidant?*

confident-adj : feeling or showing trust in one's ability :
Are you *confident* of success?
I feel *confident* of victory.
She gave me a *confident* smile.

77. CONFIRM/CONFORM

confirm-v : (a) establish the truth of sth; provide evidence for the truth or correctness of sth :
Please *confirm* your telephone message by letter.
The announcement *confirmed* my suspicions.
(b) ratify; make definite or establish more firmly:
After a six-month probationary period, she was *confirmed* in her post.

conform-v : (a) keep to or comply with (rules, standards, etc.) :
The building does not *conform* to safety regulations.
She refused to *conform* to the normal social conventions.
(b) agree or be consistent with sth :
His ideas do not *conform* with mine.

78. CONSCIENTIOUS/CONSCIOUS

conscientious: (a) careful to do what one ought to do, and do it as well as one can :
He is a *conscientious* worker.
(b) done with great care and attention:
This essay is a most *conscientious* piece of work.

conscious : knowing what is going on around one because one is able to use bodily senses and mental powers; awake:
She spoke to us in her *conscious* moments.
He was in a coma for seven days, but now he is *conscious* again.

79. CONTAGIOUS/INFECTIOUS

constagious : (a) (of a disease) spreading by contact:
Scarlet fever is highly *contagious.*
It was as *contagious* as smallpox.
(b) spreading easily from one person to another:
Yawning is *contagious.*
Her confidence was *contagious.*

infectious : (a) (of a disease) caused by bacteria; etc :
Influenza is highly *infectious.*
(b) In danger of infecting others :
While you have this rash, you are still *infectious.*
(c) quickly influencing others; likely to spread to others:
I find her enthusiasm *infectious.*
What an *infectious* laugh he has?

80. CONTEND/CONTENT

contend-v : (a) struggle in order to overcome a rival, difficulty or competitor:
Several teams are *contending* for the prize.
I have a lot of problems to *contend* with.
(b) assert; argue :

I would *contend* that unemployment is our most serious social evil.

content-adj : happy; not wanting more; satisfied with what one has :
Are you *content* with your present salary?
He is *content* to remain where he is now.
She is *content* to stay in her present job.

Note : There is another content, a noun, not related to the *content* dealt with above. This content means :

1. that which is contained in sth :
   The drawer had been emptied of its *contents*.
   At the front of the book is a table of *contents*, giving details of what is in the book.
2. that which is written or spoken about in a book, an article, a speech, etc :
   The *content* of your essay is excellent, but it is not very well-expressed.
3. amount of sth contained in sth else:
   Take food with a high fat *content*.

81. CONTINUAL/CONTINUOUS

continual : always happening; very frequent and without cessation; going on all the time without stopping, or repeatedly:
I am tired of their *continual* talking.
How do we prevent these *continual* breakdowns?
Are you not tired of this *continual* rain?

continuous : going on without stopping or being interrupted :
Our political institutions are in *continuous* evolution.
There is *continuous* increase in our military capacity.

Note : *Continual* describes an action which is repeated again and again:
Please stop your *continual* questions.
She was chided for *continual* interruptions.
Continuous indicates that the action carries on without stopping or interruption:
There was a *continuous* flow of traffic.
They chattered *continuously* for an hour.

82. COOP/COUP/COUPE

coop-n : cage for poultry:

coup-n : surprising and successful action:
She made a great *coup* in getting the Prime Minister to agree to an interview.

coupe-n : (a) two-door car with a sloping back :
(b) closed horse-drawn carriage with an inside seat for two persons and an outside seat for the driver :

83. COP/COPE

cop-n : policeman :

cope-v : manage successfully; be able to deal with sth difficult :
Can you *cope* with the problem?

84. CORPS/CORPSE

corps-n : (a) military force made up of two or more divisions :
(b) group of people involved in a particular activity :
Are you a member of the diplomatic *corps*?

corpse-n : dead body, especially of a human being:

85. COT/COTE

cot-n : (a) bed for a young child, usually with sides to prevent the child from falling down:
The baby sleeps in a *cot*.
(b) small, narrow, easily movable bed:
(c) small building for sheltering animals:

cote-n : shed or shelter for domestic animals or birds:

86. COUNCIL/COUNSEL

council-n : advisory or deliberative assembly /body :
He is a member of the U.P. Legislative *Council*.

counsel-n : (a) advice; suggestions :
You should listen to the *counsel* of your elders.
(b) barrister/lawyer conducting a law case:
He is the *counsel* for the prosecution.

Note : *Counsel*, as a verb, means :

1. give professional advice to sb :
   He is a psychiatrist who *counsels* alcoholics.
2. advise :
   I *counselled* them to give up the plan.
   He *counselled* caution in such a case.

87. COURTESY/CURTSY

courtesy-n : (a) good manners; courteous behaviour :
She did not even have the *courtesy* to apologize.
(b) courteous remark or act :
Do me the *courtesy* of listening (i.e. Please listen) to what I have to say.

curtsy-n : a woman's act of respect to a person of higher rank, done by bending the knees and lowering the head and shoulders :
She made a *curtsy* to the officer.

88. CREAK/CREEK/CRICK

creak-v : make a harsh sound like that of an unoiled door hinge, or badly fitting floor-boards when trodden on :
The wooden cart *creaked* as it moved along.

creek-n : (a) narrow stretch of water flowing inland from a coast :
(b) small river; stream :

crick-n : painful stiffness, especially in the neck :
He had a *crick* in his neck.

89. CRITIC/CRITIQUE

critic-n : (a) person who expresses a low opinion of sb/sth; points out faults in sb/sth, etc :
I am my own severest *critic*.
She confounded her *critics* by breaking the record.

(b) person who evaluates and describes the quality of sth :
He is an excellent literary *critic.*
This is a play highly praised by the *critics.*

critique-n : critical analysis :
The book presents a *critique* of the government's policies.

90. CROAK/CROCK/CROOK

croak-n : deep hoarse sound, like that made by a frog:
The *croak* of a frog is not a musical sound.

crock-n : (a) old or worn-out person or animal:
What does a young girl like you want with an old *crock* like him?
(b) old useless vehicle:

crook-n : person who is habitually dishonest:
That used car salesman is a real *crook.*

Note : *Crook,* as an adjective, means ill :
I am feeling a bit *crook.*

91. CRUD/CRUDE

crud-n : (a) unpleasant person:
She says that you are a *crud.*
(b) slimy or sticky substance; sth dirty or unwanted:
There is *crud* at the bottom of the sauce pan.

crude-adj : (a) unrefined; in the natural state:
Do you need *crude* oil?
(b) not well finished; rough:
He adopted a *crude* method to cheat him.
Your paintings are rather *crude.*
This is a *crude* sketch of the plan.
(c) coarse; not showing taste or refinement:
Don't make *crude* jokes in the presence of girls.
I detest his *crude* manners.

92. CUE/QUEUE

cue-n : (a) thing said or done to signal sb's turn to say or do sth, especially in theatrical or other performance:
Actors have to learn their *cues* as well as their own lines.
When I nod my head, that is your *cue* to interrupt the meeting.
(b) example of how to behave, what to do, etc :
Follow her *cue,* and one day you will be a great scholar.

queue-n : line of people, vehicle, etc. waiting for sth or to do sth :
This is the *queue* for the bus.

93. CURRANT/CURRENT

currant-n : small sweet, dried, seedless grape used in cookery:
He is fond of *currant* cakes.

current-adj : (a) happening now; of the present time:
He spoke on *current* political issues.
Where is the *current* issue of the magazine?
Who is her *current* boyfriend?
(b) in common or general use; generally accepted:
There are many words that are no longer *current.*

Note : There is another *current,* a noun, used to mean :

1. movement of water, air, etc. flowing in a certain direction :
   The swimmer was swept away by the *current*.
   She had to swim against the *current*.
2. flow of electricity through sth or along a wire or cable:
   Please turn on the *current*.

(c) trend; course or movement (of events, opinions, etc.) :
Nothing disturbs the peaceful *current* of life in the village.

94. CUT/CUTE

cut-n : (a) wound made with a knife, etc :
There are *cuts* on his face.
(b) reduction in amount, length, size, etc:
He had to take a *cut* in his salary.
(c) act of removing part of a play, film, book, etc :
There are several *cuts* in the film.
(d) style in which a garment is made by *cutting* :
I don't like the *cut* of your new suit.
(e) remark, etc. that hurts sb's feelings :
What she said was a *cut* at me.

cute-adj : (a) attractive; pretty and charming:
She is a *cute* baby.
(b) clever; sharp-witted:
It was *cute* of you to spot that.
I have had enough of your *cute* remarks.

95. CYMBAL/SYMBOL

cymbal-n : one of a pair of round brass plates struck together or hit with a stick to produce a changing sound:
A clash of *cymbal* is a part of our orchestra.

symbol-n : (a) image, object, etc. that suggests or refers to sth else; emblem :
The cross is the *symbol* of Christianity.
The lion is the *symbol* of courage.
(b) mark or sign with a particular meaning, such as punctuation marks, plus and minus signs in mathematics, musical notation, etc :
Red cross is a popular *symbol*.

4

First Word of Each Group Beginning With-D

1. DAB/DUB

dab-v : (a) press lightly and gently :
He *dabbed* his eyes with a tissue.
(b) lightly touch sth by pressing but not rubbing :
I *dabbed* at the cut with cotton wool.

dub-v : (a) give sb a nickname :
They *dubbed* him 'shorty' because he was very tall.
(b) create, add or replace the soundtrack of a film in a different language :
This is a Bengali film *dubbed* into Hindi.

2. DAFT/DEFT

daft-adj : foolish; silly :
He has gone a bit *daft* in the head.
Don't be so *daft*.

deft-adj : skilful and quick :
Are you *deft* at dealing with young women?
With *deft* fingers, he untangled the wire.

3. DAILY/DALL Y

daily-adj; adv : done, produced or happening everyday :
What is your *daily* routine.
Most newspapers appear *daily*.
The machines are inspected *daily*.

Note : *Daily*, as a noun, means newspaper published every weekday:
Do you subscribe a *daily*?

dally-v: (a) waste time :
Don't *dally*.
She *dallies* over her work and rarely finishes it.
(b) treat sb/sth frivolously :
She merely *dallied* with his affections.

4. DAIRY/DIARY

dairy-n : (a) place where milk is kept and milk products are made :
Don't buy milk from Mother *Dairy*.
(b) shop where milk, butter, etc. are sold :

diary-n : book used for a daily record of events, thoughts, appointments, etc :
Do you keep a *diary*?

DAM/DAMN

dam-n : barrier built across a river to hold back water and form a reservoir, to prevent flooding, etc :
Bhakra *dam* is famous in India.

damn-v : criticise sth severely :
The play was *damned* by the reviewers.

DAMP/DUMP

damp-v : slightly wet; not completely dry :
Don't wear *damp* clothes.

dump-v : (a) put unwanted things in a place and leave as rubbish :
Dump your rubbish in the canal.
(b) leave or abandon sb :
She *dumped* the kids at her mother's and went to the theatre.
He has *dumped* his wife and gone off with one of his girl students.

Note : Dump, as a noun, denotes place where rubbish may be unloaded and left; rubbish-heap; dirty or unattractive place :
How can you live in this *dump*?

DANCE/DUNCE

dance-v : (a) move rhythmically in a series of steps, alone, with a partner, or in a group in tune to music :
They *danced* to the disco music.
I *danced* with her all night.
(b) cause sb to *dance* :
He *danced* the baby on his knee.
She *danced* the little child round the room.

dunce-n : person who is stupid or slow to learn :
He is the *dunce* of the class.

DANK/DUNK

dank-adj : unpleasantly damp and cold :
Don't enter the *dank* cellar.

dunk-v : (a) dip in liquid before eating :
Dunk a biscuit in your tea.
(b) submerge sb/sth briefly in water :
We *dunked* her in the swimming pool as a joke.

DARK/DIRK

dark-adj : (a) with no or very little light :
The child is afraid of entering the *dark* room.
(b) hidden; mysterious :
What is the *dark* secret about it?
(c) difficult to understand; obscure :
Your meaning is too *dark* for me.
(d) gloomy; sad :
Don't look on the *dark* side of thing.

dirk-n : type of dagger :

10. DART/DIRT

dart-v : (a) move suddenly and quickly :
swallows are *darting* through the air.
The child *darted* into the doorway to hide.
(b) to throw suddenly and quickly :
She *darted* an angry look at him.

Note : *Dart* is also used as a noun in the sense of sudden fast movement :
She made a *dart* for the exit.

dirt-n : (a) filth :
Your clothes are covered with *dirt*.
(b) obscene thought or talk :
I don't want to hear your *dirt*.
(c) malicious gossip :
He likes to hear all the *dirt* about his colleagues.

11. DEAF/DEEP/DIP

deaf-adj : (a) unable to hear at all or to hear well :
He is *deaf* in one ear.
She is getting *deafer* in her old age.
(b) unwilling to listen to sth :
He is *deaf* to my advice.

Note : The term *deaf* means deaf people.

deep-adj : (a) extending a long way from top to bottom:
It is a *deep* well.
(b) extending down, back or in :
The canal has water ten feet *deep*.
People stood twenty *deep* to see her go past.
(c) taking in or giving out a lot of air :
He took a *deep* breath.
(d) far down in sth :
He stood with his hands *deep* in his pockets.
(e) absorbed in sth :
Don't disturb her : She is *deep* in thought.
(f) very involved in sth :
He was *deep* in difficulties.
(g) learned; profound :
He is a *deep* scholar.

dip-v : put or lower sth into a liquid :
Dip your pen into the ink.

Note : *Dip* is also used as a noun to mean :
1. quickly swim or bathe :
He has gone for a *dip*.
2. downward slope :
There is a *dip* in the road.

12. DEAL/DILL

deal-v : (a) distribute cards in a game :
Whose turn is it to *deal* the cards?
She *dealt* me four cards.

(b) hit sb/sth :
She *dealt* me a tremendous blow with the poker.

(c) cause a shock, setback, etc :
Her death *dealt* them a terrible blow.

(d) trade in sth :
They *deal* in wheat.

(e) behave towards sb :
You should *deal* politely with angry customers.

(f) manage sth; attend to :
You *dealt* with an awkward situation very tactfully.
Have you not *dealt* with that letter yet?

(g) take or have sth as a subject; discuss sth :
The next chapter *deals* with adjectives.
herb with scented leaves and seeds used for flavouring pickles :

13. DEAN/DIN

dean-n : head of a university department of studies :
He is the *dean* of the faculty of law.

din-n : continuing loud confused noise :
They made so much *din* that I could not hear you.

14. DEAR/DEER

dear-adj : (a) greatly valued; loved by sb :
Is she your *dear* friend?
She is very *dear* to me.

(b) expensive :
He was wearing *dear* clothes.

Note : *Dear* is also used both as an adverb and a noun :

1. *Dear*, as an adverb, means at a high cost :
If you want to make money, buy cheap and sell *dear*.
2. *Dear*, as a noun, denotes lovable person :
Isn't that little child a *dear*?
Be a *dear* and (i.e. Please) give me that pen.

deer-n : any of several types of graceful, quick-running, ruminant animals, the male of which has antlers :
The *deer* in the park have large, branching antlers.

15. DECEASE/DISEASE

decease-n : a person's death :
The *deceased* had died of old age.

disease-n : illness of the body, of the mind, or of plants :
He suffers from a *disease* of the nervous system.

16. DECENT/DISSENT/DESCENT

decent-adj: (a) proper; acceptable :
We must provide *decent* housing for the poor.

(b) modest; not likely to embarrass others :
She was wearing *decent* clothes.
Never tell stories that are not *decent*.

(c) Satisfactory; quite good :
Are you earning a *decent* living?
That was quite a *decent* lunch.
He is a thoroughly *decent* man.

dissent-v : have or express opinions which are opposed to official views, religious teaching, etc :
I strongly *dissent* from what the last speaker has said.

descent-n : (a) coming or going down :
The plane began its *descent* into Patna.
(b) slope :
(c) ancestry; origins :
He traces his *descent* from the Mughal kings.
(d) inconvenient or unexpected visit :
There was a sudden *descent* by tax officials.

17. DEEM/DIM

deem-v : consider; regard :
I *deem* it a great honour to be invited to address you.

dim-adj : (a) not bright :
That is a *dim* corridor with no windows.
Don't read by *dim* candle-light.
(d) faint; not clearly remembered :
I have a *dim* recollection of the accident.

18. DEFER/DIFFER

defer-v : delay sth until a later time; postpone sth :
He *deferred* his departure to a later date.

Note : There is another *defer* not related to *defer* dealt with above. This *defer* means give way to sb or sb's wishes, judgement, etc. out of respect:
On technical matters, I *defer* to the experts.
I *defer* to her greater experience in such things.

differ-v : (a) be unlike; not be the same as sb/sth :
The brothers *differ* widely in their tastes.
In this respect Hindi *differs* from Urdu.
(b) disagree :
I *differ* with you on that.
We *differ* on many a things.

19. DEFERENCE/DIFFERENCE

deference : giving way to the views, wishes, etc. of others out or respect; respect :
You should treat your elders with due *deference*.
In *deference* to our host, I decided not to challenge his controversial remarks.

difference: (a) way in which two persons or things are not the same, or in which sb/sth has changed :
What are the *differences* between the two children?
Do you notice a *difference* in her?
(b) amount or degree in which two things are not the same or sth has changed :
There is an age *difference* of four years between him and his wife.

(c) disagreement :
Settle your *differences* and be friends again.
We had a *difference* of opinion over who had won.

20. DEFY/DEIFY

defy-v : (a) disobey or refuse to respect :
They *defied* their parents and got married.
(b) refuse to give in to sb/sth; resist boldly :
The army *defied* the enemy's forces.
(c) be so difficult as to make sth impossible :
The problem *defied* solution.

deify-v: make a god of sb/sth; worship as a God :
Primitive people *deified* the Sun.

21. DEMUR/DEMURE

demur-v : express a doubt about sth or an objection to sth :
I suggested putting the matter to a vote, but the chairman *demurred*.

Note : *Demur*, as a noun, means without objecting or hesitating:
He finished the work without *demur*.

demure-ad : (a) pretending to be quiet, serious and modest :
She is very *demure* young lady.
(b) suggesting that one is demure :
She talked to me with a *demure* smile.

22. DEN/DEIGN

den-v : (a) animal's hidden home :
That is a lion's *den*.
(b) secret meeting place :
Two policemen went to a *den* of thieves.
(c) room in a home where a person can study or work without being disturbed :
He has retired to his *den*.

deign-v : be kind or gracious enough to do sth; condescend :
She walked past me without even *deigning* to look at me.

23. DEPART/DEPORT

depart-v: (a) leave; go away :
They *departed* for Madras at 10 a.m.
(b) behave in a way that differs from what is usual or expected :
Don't *depart* from the truth.

deport-v : legally force an unwanted person to leave a country :
He was convicted of drug offences and *deported*.
The spy was imprisoned for two years and then *deported*.

24. DEPARTMENT/DEPORTMENT

department: (a) each of several divisions of a government, business, shop, university, etc :
He is the head of the sales *department*.
(b) area of activity or knowledge :
Don't ask me about our finances: that is my wife's *department*.

deportment : (a) way of standing and walking; bearing:
It is in your interest to have lessons in *deportment*.
(b) behaviour :

25. DEPENDANT/DEPENDENT

dependant-n : person who depends on others for a home, food, and so forth :
He has four *dependants* to support.
I can feed only one *dependant*.

dependent-adj : needing support from sb :
She is a woman with four *dependent* children.
Are you *dependent* on your parents?

26. DESERT/DESSERT

desert-v : (a) go away from a place without intending ever to return :
Many persons *deserted* the village.
(b) leave sb without help or support; abandon:
He *deserted* his wife and went abroad.
(c) fail sb when needed :
His courage *deserted* him.

Note:
1. *Desert* is also used as a noun in the sense of large area of barren land, with very little water and vegetation, often sand-covered :
Vast areas of land have become *desert*.
2. The word deserts mean what one deserves :
He was punished according to his *deserts*.
He met with his just *deserts*.

dessert-n : (a) any sweet dish eaten at the end of a meal :
Do you like pineapple *dessert*?
(b) course in which this dish is served :
Shall we move on to *dessert*?

27. DEVICE/DEVISE

device-n : (a) thing made or adapted for a special purpose :
This is an explosive *device*.
(b) scheme; trick :
Her illness is merely a *device* to avoid seeing him.

devise-v : think out; invent :
He *devised* a new type of transistor.

28. DEVOTE/DEVOUT

devote-v : dedicate; give to sb/sth :
You should *devote* all your efforts to your task.
He *devoted* himself to a noble cause.

devout-adj : (a) pious; sincerely religious :
She is a *devout* old lady.
(b) Sincere; deeply felt :
She is one of my *devout* supporters.

29. DEW/DUE

dew-n : tiny drops of moisture condensed on cool surfaces from water vapour in the air :
The grass was wet with *dew*.

due-adj (a) owed as an obligation or a debt :
Have you paid the money *due* to her?
He has still *due* ten days leave.
(b) deserving sth; owed sth :
I am *due* for promotion soon.
(c) requiring immediate payment :
My house rent will fall *due* on the 10th instant.
(d) expected; scheduled; arranged :
My book is *due* to be published in March.
The train is *due* in five minutes.
(e) suitable, right, proper :
I decided the matter after *due* consideration of all the relevant facts.
(f) caused by sb/sth; because of sb/sth :
The team's success was largely *due* to your efforts.

Note : 1. *Due* is also used both as an adverb and a noun :
(i) *Due*, as an adverb, means exactly :
Walk four kilometres *due* West.
(ii) *Due*, as a noun, denotes thing that should be given to sb by right :
He received a large reward, which was no more than his *due*..
2. The word dues means charges or fees :
I have not paid my *dues* yet.

30. DINGHY/DINGY

dinghy-n : (a) any of various types of small open boat :
(b) inflatable rubber boat used for rescuing passengers from ships and aircraft :

dingy-adj : drab; dirty looking; not cheerful or bright :
He stays in a *dingy* room in a cheap hotel.

31. DISCARD/DISCORD

discard-n : (a) throw sth out or away :
Those are old *discarded* clothes.
(b) stop using, wearing, etc :
You should *discard* your winter clothes in spring.
Discard outdated beliefs.

discord-n : disagreement; quarrelling :
A note of *discord* crept into their relationship.

32. DISCREET/DISCRETE

discreet-adj : careful or showing good judgement in what one says or does not too devious :
It was not very *discreet* of you to ring me up at the office.

discrete-adj : separate; distinct :
It is a series of *discrete* events.

33. DISCUS/DISCUSS

discus-n : heavy disc thrown in athletic contests :

discuss-v : talk or write about sth :
I shall *discuss* the problem with her.
My latest book *discusses* the problems of the blind.

34. DISINTERESTED/UNINTERESTED

disinterested : not influenced by personal feelings or interests; unbaised :
A judge should always be *disinterested*.
My advice is absolutely *disinterested*.

uninterested: having or show no interest or concern; indifferent :
She is *uninterested* in your harangue.
I am *uninterested* in what you want to do.

35. DIVERS/DIVERSE

divers-adj : various; several :
He adopted *divers* tricks to cheat her.

diverse-adj : of different kinds; varied :
Her interests are very *diverse*.
People from *diverse* cultures attended the meeting.
He is a man of *diverse* talents.

36. DODDLE/DOODLE

doddle-n : task or activity that is easily performed :
That hill is an absolute *doddle* to climb.

doodle-v : make meaningless drawings, scribbles, etc., while one is or should be thinking about sth else :
Stop *doodling* on my notebook.
She *doodled* on my papers.

37. DOILY/DOLLY

doily-n : small ornamental mat of lace, paper, etc. placed under a dish or under a cake, etc. or plate :

dolly-n : (a) doll :
The little girl played at putting her *dolly* to bed.
(b) movable support for a cine or televison camera :

38. DOLE/DOLL

dole-v : distribute food money, etc. in small amounts :
Allowances are grudgingly *doled* out to the elderly.

doll-n : (a) model of a bay or an adult :
The child is playing with a *doll*.
(b) attractive young woman :
Their daughter is a little doll.

Note : Doll, as a verb, means dress sb/oneself in a smart or showy way :
She was all *dolled* up for the party.
That young lady was all *dolled* up in the latest fashion.

39. DOLLAR/DOLOUR

dollar-n : (a) unit of money in the U.S.A. and a few other countries:
Oil from these fields is priced in *dollars*.
They spent half a million *dollars* on the campaign.
(b) banknote or coin worth one dollar :
Have you got any *dollars*?

dolour-n : grief or sorrow :
Can I do anything to lesson your *dolour*?

40. DOOR/DOUR

door-n : movable barrier that closes the entrance to a building, room, car, etc :
Open the *door*.
Shut the front *door*.

dour-adj : stern; severe; gloomy looking; joyless :
His *dour* looks frightened the child.
She faced me with her usual *dour* expression.

41. DOSE/DOZE

dose-n : (a) amount of medicine to be taken at one time :
Let her take a *dose* of this medicine.
(b) any experience of sth unpleasant :
He had a *dose* of malaria in the recent past.
(c) any experience of sth enjoyable :
What you need is a *dose* of laughter.
What he needed was a large *dose* of courage.
(d) venereal infection:
Have you caught a *dose*?

doze : (a) sleep lightly :
He *dozed* in the armchair.
(b) fall into a light sleep :
She *dozed* off during the film.

Note : *Doze* is also used as a noun in the sense of short, light sleep:
I had a quick *doze* on the train.

42. DOT/DOTE

dot-n : (a) small round mark :
Let him join the *dots* up to complete the drawing.
(b) anything resembling a *dot;* a small quantity :
I like just a *dot* of milk in my tea.

dote-v : show too much fondness for sb/sth :
He *dotes* on his grandchildren.

43. DRAFT/DRAUGHT/DROUGHT

draft-n : (a) rough preliminary version of sth :
This is the *draft* of my speech.
Make a *draft* of the reply to be sent.
(b) written order to a bank to pay money to sb :
It is a *draft* on the State Bank of India.
(c) group of people chosen from a larger group for a special purpose :
We are sending a fresh *draft* of doctors and nurses to the worst hit area.

draught-n: (a) current of air in a room or some other enclosed space :
As the train began to move, a pleasant *draught* cooled us all douwn
(b) one continuous process of swallowing liquid; the amount swallowed :
He took a long *draught* of milk.

He emptied his glass of water at one *draught*.
Take a deep *draught* of air into your lungs.

drought-n : period of continuous dry weather, when there is not enough water for people's needs :
Last year the state was hit by a severe *drought*.

44. DRAWL/DROLL/DROOL

drawl-v : speaker say sth in a slow lazy manner:
He *drawled* out a few words.

droll-adj : amusing or odd in a quaint way :
I am not interested in your *droll* story.

drol-v : (a) let saliva flow the mouth; dribble:
Why are you *drooling*?
(b) show in a ridiculous way how much one enjoys or admires sb/sth :
They are *drooling* over a photograph of a beautiful girl.

45. DROOP/DROP

droop-v : bend or hang downwards through tiredness or weakness :
Flowers were *drooping* for lack of water.
Her head *drooped* sadly.
His spirits *drooped* at the news.

drop-n : (a) small rounded mass of liquid :
Pour the oil in *drops* into the mixture.
These are *drops* of rain.
(b) decrease :
There was a *drop* in prices of vegetables.

Note : Drop, as a verb, means :

1. fall or allow sth to fall :
The bottle *dropped* and broke.
The climber slipped and *dropped* to his death.
2. become weaker, less or lower :
Her voice *dropped* to a whisper.
3. allow sb to get out of a car, etc :
She *dropped* me near our house.
4. Send a letter, etc. to sb :
I *dropped* him a letter yesterday.
5. Stop seeing sb :
She has *dropped* most of her old friends.
6. Stop doing or discussing sth :
Let us *drop* the formalities; call me "Sweety."
Look, can we just *drop* the subject?

46. DUAL/DUEL/DWELL

dual-adj : double; having two parts or aspects :
He has *dual* role as producer and director.
She has *dual* nationality.

duel-n : contest or struggle between two person, groups, etc :
They were engaged in a *duel* of words.

dwell-v : (a) live as an inhabitant of or reside at a place :
I don not know where she *dwells*.
Do you still *dwell* in your old abode?
(b) think, write or speak at length about sth :
Let us not *dwell* on her past mistakes.
He began to *dwell* on memories of his mother.

47. DUD/DUDE

dud-n : thing or person that fails to work properly :
Two of the fireworks in the box were *duds*.
The new manager is a complete *dud*.

Note : *Dud*, as an adjective, means worthless; defective
It is a *dud* cheque.
His father is a *dud* person.

(a) a man, guy :
Who is that *dude* over there?
(b) American English for a city man, especially an Easterner in the West :

Note : *Dude* ranch means a holiday place that offers activities, such as horse riding, etc.

5

First Word of Each Group Beginning With-E

1. EARLY/YEARLY

early : (a) near to the beginning of a period of time :
I shall visit you in *early* spring.
She is in her *early* twenties.
(b) before the usual or expected time :
Are you an *early* riser?
We had an *early* breakfast today.
The bus arrived five minutes *early*.

yearly : occurring every year or once a year :
Our *yearly* conference will be held on Monday, the 10th instant, at 4.30 p.m.

2. EARN/YARN/YEARN

earn-v : (a) get money by working:
He *earns* four thousand rupees a month.
(b) get money as a return on a loan or investment:
Money *earns* more in a high interest account.
(c) gain sth deserved in return for achievements, behaviour, etc :
His honesty earned him great respect.
His bad manners *earned* him a sharp rebuke.

yarn-n: (a) fibres that have been spun for knitting, weaving, etc :
(b) story; traveller's tale, especially one that is exaggerated or invented :
She narrated a humorous *yarn*.

Note : *Yarn* is also used as a verb to mean *tell stories* :
We stayed up yarning until midnight.
The beggar spun a long *yarn* about his misfortunes. .

yearn-v : desire strongly or with tenderness or affection; be filled with longing :
He *yearned* for his home and family.
She *yearned* to return to her native country.

3. EAST/YEAST

east-n : point of the horizon where the Sun rises; one of the four main points of the compass :
The wind is blowing from the *east*.
He lives to the east of the Red Fort.

Note : *East* is also used as an adjective as well as an adverb:
1. *East*, as an adjective, means in or towards the east:
He lives on the east coast.
2. *East*, as an adverb, means towards the east:
My window faces *east*.
We are going to a place *east* of the Yamuna.

yeast-n : fungous substance used in brewing beer, and in making of bread :

4. ECONOMIC/ECONOMICAL

economic : (a) of economics :
We are passing through an *economic* crisis.
I don't support the government's *economic* policy.
(b) designed to give a profit:
It is not always *economic* for buses to run on Sunday.

economical : not wasteful; careful in spending of money, time, etc. and in the use of resources:
She is *economical* in her use of salt when cooking.
I have an *economical* sytle of writing.

5. EDICT/ADDICT

edict-n : order or proclamation issued by an authority :
We must obey the *edicts* of the governments.

addict-n : (a) person who is unable to stop taking drugs, alcohol, etc :
Are you a heroin *addict*?
(b) person who is strongly interested in sth :
He is football *addict*.
She is a T.V. *addict*.

6. EDIT/ADIT

edit-v : (a) prepare a piece of writing, often another person's, for publication :
I edited one of Tagore's plays for use in schools.
(b) prepare book, newspaper, film, etc. for publication or broadcast :
Do you edit any monthly magazine?
(c) remove unwanted words, phrases, etc. from a book, script, etc. in the process of editing:
Do you know how to edit a book?

adit-n : almost horizontal entrance to a mine :

7. EERIE/EYRIE

eerie-adj : causing a feeling of mystery and fear:
I heard an *eerie* scream coming from that direction.
I had the *eerie* feeling that someone was watching me.
There was *eerie* silence in the deserted village.

eyrie-n : eagle's nest; nest of other birds of prey built high up among rocks:
Do you want to see an *eyrie*?

8. EFFLUENT/AFFLUENT

effluent-n : discharge of liquid waste matter, sewage, etc :
The *effluent* from the factory makes the river unsafe for swimming.

affluent-adj : rich; prosperous:
He lives an *affluent* lifestyle.
His parents were very *affluent*.

9. EGO/AGO

ego-n : opinion of one's own worth; part of the mind that can think, feel and act; self-esteem :
Losing the match made quite a dent in his ego.

ago-adv : gone by; in the past :
He came here ten years *ago*.
How long *ago* is it that you last saw her?

10. ELICIT/ILLICIT

elicit-v : draw out; cause to come out:
I *elicited* the truth of the case.
Threats to reimpose the tax *elicited* jeers from the opposition,
In ten minutes I had *elicited* all their family history.

illicit-adj : (a) illegal; not allowed by law:
They were prosecuted for *illicit* sale of drugs.
(b) not approved by the normal rules of society :
Do you have an *illicit* relationship with that beautiful and charming girl?

11. ELIGIBLE/ILLEGIBLE

eligible-adj : having the right qualifications; fit, suitable, to be chosen :
He is *eligible* for the post.
You are *eligible* for membership in our club.

illegible-adj : not legible; difficult or impossible to read:
The document bears an *illegible* signature.
Her handwriting is *illegible*.

12. ELITE/ALIGHT

elite-n : social group considered to be the best or most important because of their power, talent, wealth, etc :
I belong to a small intellectual *elite*.
Do you belong to the ruling *elite*?

alight-v : (a) get down from a horse or vehicle :
You should never *alight* from a moving bus.
(b) come down from the air and settle :
The sparrow *alighted* on the roof of the house.
(c) find sth by chance:
My eyes *alighted* on a dusty old book at the back of the shelf.

Note: There is another alight, an adjective, used to mean on *fire; lit* :
A burning cigarette set the dry grass *alight*.
Her dress caught *alight* in the gas fire.

13. ELUSIVE/ILLUSIVE

elusive-adj : tending to escape :
He is an *elusive* criminal.
Happiness is an *elusive* quality.

illusive-adj : deceptive; based on illusion :
What he says is *illusive*.

14. EMIGRANT/IMMIGRANT

emigrant-n : person who emigrates :
They are *emigrants* to France.

immigrant-n : person who has come to live permanently in a foreign country :
They are illegal *immigrants*.

15. EMIGRATE/IMMIGRATE

emigrate-v : leave one's own country to go and live in another :
He *emigrated* from India to England five years ago.

immigrate-v : enter a foreign country in order to live there permanently,
Do you want to *immigrate* to Japan?

16. EMINENT/IMMINENT

eminent: (a) (of a person) famous and distinguished :
He is an *eminent* architect.
She is *eminent* for her virtues.
(b) (of qualities) remarkable; outstanding :
He is a man of *eminent* goodness.

imminent : likely to happen very soon; about to happen :
There is no warning of *imminent* danger.

17. ENVELOP/ENVELOPE

envelop-v : cover or surround; wrap sth/sb up :
The baby was *enveloped* in a blanket.
The mountains are *enveloped* in cloud.

envelope-n : wrapper or covering, especially made of paper for a letter:
Give me an airmail *envelope*.
I don't have writing paper or *envelopes*.

18. ERRAND/ERRANT

errand-n : (a) short journey to take a message, get or deliver goods, etc :
I am tired of running *errands* for her.
(b) object or purpose of such a journey :
I have come on a special *errand*.

errand-adj : misbehaving; doing wrong :
She has an *errant* husband.

19. ERUPTION/IRRUPTION

eruption-n : (a) outbreak of a volcano :
The *eruption* of a volcano destroyed a few villages.
(b) outbreak of war, disease, etc.
The eruption of hostilities between the two countries is imminent.
(c) sudden appearance of spot, etc. on the skin.
There was an *eruption* of black spots on her right cheek.

irruption-n : sudden and violent entry:
The *irruption* of the noisy group of revellers disturbed us.

20. EXALT/EXULT

exalt-v : (a) make sb higher in rank or greater in power :
She was *exalted* in the estimation of the general public on account of her selfless services for the uplift of the poor.
(b) praise highly:
People *exalt* him for his honesty, and tenacity of purpose.

exult-v : rejoice greatly; get great pleasure from sth :
She *exulted* at her sister's tremendous success.

21. EXCITE/INCITE

excite-v : (a) cause strong feeling of eagerness, happiness, nervousness, etc:
Everybody was *excited* by the news of the victory.
It is nothing to get *excited* about.
(b) cause or bring about sth by arousing strong feelings in sb :
Criminals *excited* a riot in the town.
Agitators were *exciting* the people to rebel against the government.
(c) arouse emotion in sb :
The recent discoveries have *excited* great interest among doctors.

(d) arouse sexual desire :
Some people are sexually *excited* by pornographic magazines.

incite-v : (a) urge or persuade sb to do sth by making him very angry or excited:
The union leaders *incited* the workers to violence.
The colonel was accused of inciting other officers to mutiny.
(b) create or cause sth :
They incited a breach of peace.

22. EXERCISE/EXORCISE

exercise-n: (a) use or practice through effort or action:
The doctor admired me to take more *exercise.*
Jogging is a healthy form of *exercise.*
(b) use or application :
The *exercise* of patience is essential in diplomatic negotiations.

exorcise-v : drive out or expel an evil spirit by prayers or magic :
A priest *exorcised* the ghost from the house.

23. EXPAND/EXPEND

expand-v : (a) make or become greater in size, number or importance:
Metals *expand* when they are heated.
I shall *expand* my story into a novel.
(b) unfold; spread out :
His face *expanded* in a smile of welcome.

expend-v : (a) spend, use (money, etc.) in doing sth :
You have to *expend* a lot of time, effort and money on the project.
(b) exhaust; use up :
He has already *expended* all his ammunition.

24. EXPANSE/EXPENSE

expanse-n : wise and open area :
Look at the blue *expanse* of the sky.
Where is the wide *expanse* of the grassy fields?

expense-n : (a) spending of money, etc., cost :
They are constructing a building at a great *expense* of time, energy and money.
He hired a plane regardless of the *expense.*
(b) cause of spending :
Running a car is big *expense.*
(c) money spent in doing a specific job, or for a specific purpose :
Let me know the details about your travelling *expenses.*
Who is meeting the *expenses* of your trip?

25. EXTANT/EXTEND/EXTENT

extant-adj : still in existence:
This is an ancient but *extant* law.
Where is the earliest *extant* manuscript of this poem?

extend-v : make longer or larger :
Can you *extend* your visit a few days longer?
The fence should be *extended.*

extent-n : length, area, range :
I was amazed at the *extent* of her knowledge.
Let me see the full *extent* of the park.
The race track is nearly five kilometres in *extent.*

6

First Word of Each Group Beginning With-F

1. FAD/FADE

fad-n: fashion, interest, enthusiasm, preference, etc. that is not likely to last :
She is full of *fads* and fancies.
His interest in collecting foreign stamps is just a fad.

Fade-v: (a) lose colour, freshness or vigour :
Flowers soon *fade* when cut.
She is *fading* fast.

(b) cause sth to lose colour, freshness, etc :
The strong sunlight has *faded* the curtains.

(c) become indistinct; disappear gradually :
His hopes *faded*.
All memory of her childhood had *faded* from her mind.
The sound of the cheering *faded* in the distance.

(d) disperse; die :
The crowd just *faded* away.
He is *fading* away.

2. FAINT/FEINT

faint-adj: (a) indistinct; that cannot be clearly perceived by senses; not intense in colour or sound or smell :
The sounds of music grew *fainter* in the distance.
She called for help in a faint voice.

(b) vague :
There is a *faint* hope that she may be cured.

(c) lacking strength :
His breathing became faint.

(d) giddy :
He feels *faint*.

(e) weak :
He made a faint attempt to do the work.
That was a *faint* show of resistance.

Note : There is another faint that is used both as a verb and as a noun :

1. Faint, as a verb, means lose consciousness :
   She *fainted* from hunger.
2. *Faint*, as a noun, means act to state of fading :
   He fell to the ground in a dead *faint*.

feint-n : (a) pretended attack to distract an opponent's attention from the main attack :
Feint technique is popular in boxing.
(b) pretence :
He made a *feint* of doing the work.

3.FAIR/FARE

fair-adj : (a) impartial :
He deseres a *fair* trial.
(b) average; moderately good :
He has a *fair* chance of success.
You have a *fair* amount of sense.
(c) dry and fine :
Let us hope for *fair* weather.
(d) pale; light in colour; blond :
Does your child have a *fair* complexion?

Note : There is another *fair*, a noun, used to mean :
1. market held regularly in a particular place, often with entertainments.
I enjoy food *fair* held in my locality.
2. Large-scale exhibition of commercial and industrial goods.
Did you visit the trade *fair*?

fare-n : money charged for a journey by bus, train, ship, taxi, etc :
What is the bus *fare* to Lucknow?

4. FALLOW / FELLOW

fallow-adj : ploughed but left unplanted to restore its fertility :
Allow land to lie *fallow* for a short period.

fellow-n : (a) companion; comrade :
Who are your *fellow*?
(b) of the same class, kind, etc :
I shall always support my *fellow* countrymen.
(c) man or boy :
You are a nice *fellow*.

5. FAN/FEIGN/FEN

Fan-n : (a) device with rotating blades, operated mechanically to create a current of cool air :
It is so hot-please turn the *fan* on.
(b) object held in the hand and waved to create a current of cool air :
When there is no electricity in summer, people use *fan*.

Note : There is another fan, a noun. It means enthusiastic or supporter of sth/sb.
Are you a football *fan*?

feign-v : pretend :
I *feigned* illness to avoid meeting her.
She *feigned* ignorance of the accident.

fen-n : area of low marshy land :
Can you run on a *fen*?

6. FAR/FUR

far-adj : (a) distant :
Don't journey into *far* regions.
(b) more remote :
His house is at the *far* end of the road.

Note : Far is also used as an adverb to mean :

1. at or to a great distance :
How *far* is it to Meerut from here?
How *far* have we walked?
2. by a great distance :
I shall go *far* beyond the bridge.
3. a long way :
We dancedfar into the night.
4. to a great extent :
He lives *far* beyond his means.
5. considerably; very much :
He runs *far* faster than his brother.
6. to the place mentioned, but no further :
I have read as *far* as the fourth chapter.
I shall walk with you as *far* as the airport.

fur-n: (a) soft thick hair covering the bodies of certain animals:
This is a coat made of *fur*.
(b) garment made of *fur* :
I have her an expensive *fur* for her birthday.

7. FARM/FIRM

farm-n : (a) area of land, and the buildings on it, used for growing crops or raising animals :
He has lived on this *farm* for ten years.
(b) *farm* house and the buildings near it :
He has gone to get some eggs at the *farm*.

firm-adj : (a) fairly hard :
This wet ground is not firm enough to walk on.
(b) strongly fixed in place; secure or solid:
Our house has a firm concrete fencing.
(c) steady and strong :
I have a *firm* hold on the affairs of the company.
He walks with *firm* steps.
(d) definite :
I have *firm* belief in socialism.
Are you a man of *firm* principles?
(e) decisive; strong and consistent in attitude and behaviour:
You must be *firm* with your children.

8. FARTHER/FURTHER

farther-adj : more distant in space, direction or time :
He lives at the *farther* end of the street.
Kolkata is *farther* from Delhi than Allahabad is.

Note : *Farther*, as an adverb, means at or to a greater distance in space or time; more remote :

We cannot go any *farther* without resting.
I am looking *farther* forward to the end of the century.

further-adv: (a) (comparative of far) at or to a greater distance or more distant point :
I am too tired to walk any *further* :
She can swim *further* than I can.

(b) more; to a greater degree :
Don't try my patience any further.
I've nothing *further* to say.

(c) in addition; *further* more :
The house is too large for us, and further, it is far from the market.

Note: **1.** Further, as an adjective, means :

(i) later than the one spoken of :
The office will be closed until *further* notice. (i.e. until we inform you that it is open again.)

(ii) more; additional :
I have no further use for this book.
Have you any further questions to ask?

2. Further, as a verb, means to help sth advance or succeed:
This success should further your chances of promotion.

9. FAT/FATE

fat-adj: (a) large in size :
That grocer is a *fat* man.

(b) large in quantity :
He has a *fat* income.
I gave her a nice *fat* cheque.

Note : *Fat* is also used as a noun in the sense of :

1. White or yellow greasy substance in animal bodies under the skin :
This goat has too much *fat* on it.

2. oily substance found in certain seeds :

Fate-n : (a) power believed to control all events in a way that cannot be resisted; destiny :
He had hoped to become President, but *fate* decided otherwise.

(b) person's destiny or future :
I am resigned to my *fate*.

(c) death or destruction :
he met his fate bravely.

Note : Fate, as a verb, means destiny :
He was *fated* to die in abject poverty.
It was *fated* that he would fail.

10. FAUN/FAWN

faun-n : (in Roman myths) God of the fields and woods, with goat's horns and legs, but a human torso :

fawn-v : try to win sb's approval by flattery or by obsequious behaviour:
I am fond of her *fawning* behaviour.

Note : *Fawn,* as a noun, denotes deer less than one year old:
Children are playing with the *fawn*.

11. FAZE/PHASE

faze-v : fluster sb :
She is so calm; nothing seems. O *faze* her.
stage in a process of change or development :
The child is going through a difficult phase.
This is the most exciting *phase* of her career.

Note : *Phase,* as a verb, means plan or carry out sth in stages :
There was a phased withdrawal of troops.
The modernisation of the industry was *phased* over a ten-year period.

12. FEAST/FIST

feast-n : (a) unusually large or elaborate meal :
Will you invite me to your wedding feast?
(b) thing that pleases the mind or the senses with its richness or variety :
Children always enjoy feasts of colours and sounds.

Note : *Feast,* as a verb, means :
1. enjoy a *feast* :
They celebrated by *feasting* all day.
2. provide sb with a *feast* :
I feasted my guests with delicacies.
3. enjoy the beauty of sb/sth :
I *feasted* my eyes upon her lovely face.
He *feasted* his eyes on the beauty of the valley.

fist-n : hand when closed tightly with the fingers bent into the palm:
She struck me with her *fist*.
He clenched his *fists*.

13. FEAT/FEET/FIT

Feat-n : successful completion of sth needing skill, strength or courage:
He showed brilliant *feats* of engineering.
He performed *feats* of valour.
The bridge is a *feat* of engineering.

feet-n : The plural form of foot :
(a) lowest part of leg, below the ankle :
He rose to his *feet*.
(b) measure of length : 12 inches:
They are flying at 20,000 *feet*.

Note: *Foot* is also used to mean the lowest part of sth; base or bottom of sth :
He is standing at the *foot* of the stairs.
Look at the *foot* of the page.

fit-adj : (a) suitable or suited for sb/sth; well -adapted for sb/sth; good enough for sb/sth :
India is a land *fit* for heroes to live in.
The food was not *fit* to eat.
(b) in good health :
He has been ill and is not *fit* for work yet.
(c) suitable and right :
You are not *fit* for the position.

(d) decide or choose :
Do as you think *fit*.
The newspaper did not see *fit* to publish my letter.

Note: There is another *fit*, a noun, that means;

1. sudden attack of epilepsy or other disease with violent movements and loss of consciousness :
He suffered an epileptic *fit*.
2. sudden attack of a minor illness :
He had a *fit* of coughing.
3. sudden burst of laughter, activity, etc :
We were all in *fits* of laughter at her jokes.
4. short period of an intense feeling:
He slapped her in a *fit* of anger.

14. FEEL/FILL

feel-v : (a) perceive sth by touching or by holding in hands:
Can you *feel* the bump on his head?
Feel how rough it is.

(b) sense; be aware of sth physical or emotional:
We all *felt* the earthquake tremors.
I can *feel* a nail sticking into my shoe.

(c) be in the specified physical, emotional or moral state:
How are you *feeling* today?
Are you *feeling* hungry?
She feels cold.

(d) search with hands, *feet*, a stick, etc :
He *felt* in his pocket for some money.

fill-v : (a) make sth full of sth :
He *filled* the hole with sand.
Smoke *filled* the room.

(b) hold a position :
She *fills* the post satisfactorily.

(c) appoint sb to a position :
The vacancy has already been *filled*.

15. FINAL/FINALE

final-adj: (a) coming last; of the end :
This is the *final* chapter of the book.

(b) conclusive; decisive; which cannot be changed :
The judge's ruling is *final*.
I am not coming, and that is *final*.

finale-n : last part of a piece of music or a drama, etc :
Everyone enjoyed the grand *finale* of the pantomime.

16. FINIS/FINISH

finis-n : (at the end of a book) the end :
I have read her book from the very beginning to the *finis*.

Note : *Finis*, a Latin word, is used as a noun in the singular only.Don't use it in the sense of *finis* as a noun. After completing the writing of a book, you can pen *finis* toward the end of the last page.

finis-v : Come or bring 5th to an end :
The term *finishes* next week.
Finish your work.
Finish, as a noun, means :
1. last part or end of sth.
Did you see the finish of the race?
2. state of being *finished* or perfect :
He bought furniture with fine *finish*.
Your manners lack *finish*.

17. FLAIR/FLARE

flair-n : (a) natural ability to do sth well :
He has a real *flair* for languages.
They were impressed by my political *flair*.
He has much *flair* for criminal laws.
(b) original and attractive quality; stylishness :
She showed her usual flair and cunning:

flare-v : (a) burn brightly but briefly or unsteadily :
The candle began to *flare*.
(b) burst into sudden anger or activity :
Tempers *flared* at the conference.
(c) suddenly become angry; reach a more violent state.
She *flares* up at the slightest provocation.
Violence has *flared* up again.

18. FLAK/FLAKE/FLECK

flak-n : (a) severe criticism :
The plans for the new tax have come in for a lot of *flak*.
The Prime Minister has already run into murderous political *flak* over his decision.
(b) guns shooting at enemy aircraft; fire from those guns :
I saw one of the Dakotas hit by *flak*.

flake-n : small thin layer or piece broken off a surface or object; small loose bit :
Scrape off all the loose *flakes* of paint before redecorating.
These are *flakes* of burnt paper from a bonfire.

fleck-n : (a) very small patch or spot of a colour :
There are *flecks* of brown and white on the bird's breast.
There are grey *flecks* in his eyes.
(b) small particle or grain of sth :
There are *flecks* of dust on your coat.

19.FLAX/FLEX

flax-n: plant grown for its fibre and seeds :

flex-v : bend or move a limb, joint or muscle :
Note : *Flex* your knee.
There is another *flex*, a noun. It means *flexible* insulated wire used for carrying an electric current to an appliance.

20. FLEA/FLEE

Flea-n: small jumping insects that feed on blood of humans and animals :

The cat has got *fleas*.
As has been bitten by a *flea*, his arms are itchy.

(a) run or hurry away; escape :
The customers *fled* from the bank when the alarm sounded.

(b) run away from sb/sth :
During the civil war, thousands of people *fled* the country.

21. FLEET/FLIT

fleet-n: (a) group of warships, submarines, etc. under one commander:
(b) group of ships fishing together :
(c) all the warships, submarines, etc. of a country:
(d) group of aircraft, buses, taxis, etc. owned and operated by one organisation or travelling together :

flit-v: fly or move lightly and quickly :
Bees are *flitting* from one flower to another.
He *flits* from one thing to another.
An expression of pain *flitted* across her face.

22. FLOOR/FLOUR

floor-n : (a) surface of a room :
He sat on the *floor*.
(b) number of rooms, etc. on the same level in a building; level or story of a building :
Her office is on the second *floor*.
(c) part of an assembly hall where members sit :
Two members spoke from the *floor*.
(d) right to speak in such an assembly :
The *floor* is yours-you may present your argument.

Flour-n : fine powder obtained by grinding grain and used for making bread, cakes, etc :
Flour is made by grinding wheat.

23. FOOUFULL

fool-n : person who acts unwisely; person lacking in good judgement or sense; idiot; dolt :
Are you a *fool*?

full-adj : (a) completely filled; holding, containing as much or as many as possible :
My cup is *full*.
The drawers are *full* to overflowing.
The dustbin is *full* of rubbish.
(b) crowded; having or containing much or many:
She is *full* of vitality.
The room is full of people.
The lake is *full* of fish.
(c) complete; plentiful :
She gave me *full* information about the case.

Note : *Full* is also used as an adverb in the sense of :

1. exactly; directly :
I hit him *full* in the face.
2. very:
She knows me *full* well.

24. FORT/FORTE

fort-n : building or buildings specially made or strengthened for the military defence of an area :
Where is the Red *Fort*?

forte-n : strong point; thing that sb does particularly well :
Mathematics was never my *forte*.
Cooking is her *forte*.

25. FOUT/FOWL

foul-adj : (a) having a bad smell or taste; dirty and disgusting :
That is a *foul* rubbish dump.
This medicine tastes *foul*.

(b) unpleasant; dreadful :
Do you have a *foul* temper?

(c) obscene and offensive :
Don't use *foul* language.

Note : There is another *foul*, a noun. It means action that is against the rules of a game :
That last *foul* against Ram lost us the match.

fowl-n : domestic cock or hen :
Do you keep *fowls* and goats?

7

First Word of Each Group Beginning With-G

1. GABBLE/GABLE

gabble-v : talk quickly and indistinctly :
Take your time and don't *gabble.*

Note : *Gabble,* as a noun, means fast unintelligible speech.
Do you like her *gabble*?

gable-n : triangular upper part of the side or end of a building, under a sloping roof:

GAFF/GAFFE

gaff-n : stick with an iron hook for pulling large fish out of water:

gaffe-n : social blunder; indiscreet act or remark :
He did not realize what a *gaffe* he had made.

3. GAGGLE/GOGGLE

gaggle-n : (a) flock :
There is a *gaggle* of wild geese in the park.
(b) group of noisy or talkative people:
A *gaggle* of young women visited me last evening.

gaggle-v : look at sb /sth with wide, round, bulging eyes:
He *goggled* at her in surprise.

4. GAIT/GATE

gait-n : manner of walking or running :
She walks with an unsteady *gait.*

gate-n : movable barrier which closes an opening in a wall, etc :
He opened the garden *gate* and went into the street.

5. GAMBLE/GAMBOL

gamble-v : (a) play games of chance, etc. for money:
Do you *gamble* at cards?
(b) spend money by playing such games, etc:
He *gambled* all his winnings on the last race.

Note : *Gamble* is also used as a noun to mean act of gambling; undertaking with a risk of loss and a chance of profit.
Setting up this business was a bit of a *gamble.*

gambol-v: jump or skip about playfully:
Children are *gambolling* in the park.

6. GANTRY/GENTRY

gantry-n: tall metal frame supporting a crane, signals on a railway or motorway, rocket-launching equipment, etc :

gentry-n : people of good social position next below the nobility :
Do you belong to the *gentry*?
He likes the *gentry*.

7. GAOUGOAL

gaol-n : prison :
He was sent to *gaol*?
Did you spend a year in *gaol*?

Note: *Gaol*, as a verb, means put sb in *gaol* :
He was gaoled for six months for his part in the robbery.

goal-n : (a) pair of posts with a crossbar, between which the ball has to be kicked, hit, etc. in order to score:
He headed the ball irito an open goal.
(b) target; object of one's efforts :
What is your *goal* in life?
Their *goal* was to eradicate malaria.

8. GAP/GAPE

gap-n : (a) opening or break in sth, or between two things :
There is a *gap* in the wall.
(b) lapse; unfilled interval of time :
There was a *gap* of ten minutes in our conversation.
(c) separation:
There is a wide *gap* between the opinions of two persons.
There was a *gap* in his education.

gape-v : (a) stare with an open mouth :
What are you *gapping* at?
(b) be or become open wide:
A huge chasm *gaped* before them.

Note: Gape, as a noun, means open-mouthed stare :
There were *gapes* of astonishment on the faces of the spectators.

9. GAUGE/GAZE

gauge-v : (a) measure sth accurately :
It is the duty of weather men to *gauge* rainfall.
(b) make an estimate of sth :
Can you *gauge* the strength of the wind from the movement of the trees?
(c) make a judgement about sth :
I *gauged* that it was not a good moment to speak to her.

gaze-v : (a) look long and steadily at sb/sth in surprise or admiration :
She *gazed* at me in disbelief when I told her the news.
(b) look at sb/sth :
She was the most beautiful woman I had ever *gazed* upon.

10. GEN/GENE

gen-n : information :
Give me the *gen* on this new project.

gene-n : (in biology) unit in a chromosome which controls heredity
What is your dominant *gene*?

11. GENTEEL/GENTLE

genteel-adj : polite or refined in an affected or exaggerated way :
She is too *genteel* for words.
Do you behave in a *genteel* way?

gentle-adj : (a) mild; kind; careful; not rough, violent or severe :
I laud her *gentle* manner.
He is a doctor who is *gentle* with his hands.
(b) (of weather, temperature, etc.) mild; temperate :
A *gentle* breeze is blowing.

12. GERMAN/GERMANE

German-n : (a) a person belonging to *Germany*:
(b) language spoken in *Germany*:
Germans speak *German* language.

Note: *German*, as an adjective, means of *Germany*, its culture, its language or its people :
Tell me something about German traditions.

Germane-adj : relevant :
He remarks are *germane* to the discussion.

13. GHASTLY/GHOSTLY

ghastly : (a) causing horror or fear :
That was a *ghastly* accident.
(b) very bad; distasteful :
His uncle is a *ghastly* man.
That was a *ghastly* error.
(c) ill; upset :
I feel *ghastly*; I should not have eaten so much.
(d) very pale and death-like in appearance:
You look *ghastly*; are you all right?
She had a *ghastly* pallor.

ghostly : like a ghost in appearance or sound; of or being a ghost:
A *ghostly* voice was whispering in his ear.
Ghostly shapes of bats were flitting about in the dark.

14. GILD/GUILD

gild-v : cover sth with gold leaf or gold-coloured paint:
Gild the picture-frame.

guild-n : society of people with similar interests and aims :
He is the President of the film producers *guild*.

15. GILT/GUILT

gilt-n : gold or sth resembling gold applied to a surface in a thin layer:
The paintings are in *gilt* frames.
The *gilt* had been chipped.

guilt-n : (a) condition or fact of having done wrong :
The police established his *guilt* beyond all doubt.
(b) blame or responsibility for wrongdoing :
Find out where the *guilt* lies.
Guilt was written all over her face.

16. GIRD/GUARD

gird-v : (a) surround sth :
Trees *girded* the lake.
(b) clothe sb :
He *girded* himself with armour for the battle.

guard-n : (a) a person, especially a soldier, policeman, etc. who watches over a person or place to prevent escape, danger, etc :
There are security *guards* at the airport.
(b) a group of people, especially soldiers, whose duty is to *guard* sb or sth :
The prisoner was brought in under armed *guard*.
(c) a state of watchful readiness to protect or defend :
There are soldiers on *guard* at the gate.
(d) an apparatus which covers and protects :
Football players often wear shin *guards*.
(e) a position of being ready to defend oneself danger :
Be on your *guard* against pickpockets.

Note : Guard, as a verb, is used in the sense of :
1. to watch over to protect from danger :
The dog *guarded* the house.
2. to keep under control :
You must *guard* your tongue carefully.

17. GLAD/GLADE

glad-adj : (a) delighted; pleased :
I am *glad* she is feeling better.
(b) grateful for sth :
I would be *glad* of your help.
(c) willing and eager to do sth :
I would be *glad* to help you with money.
(d) causing or bringing joy :
She gave me the *glad* news.

glade-n: open space in a forest :
This *glade* is a good picnic spot.

18. GRATE/GREAT

grate-v : (a) rub sth into small pieces; rub small bits off sth :
Grate the carrot into small pieces.
(b) have an irritating effect:
His voice *grates* on my ears.
Her bad manners *grate* on my nerves.
It is your ingratitude that *grates* on me.

Note : There is another *grate* used as a noun to mean fire place:
Put coals in the *grate*.

great-adj : (a) well above average in size, extent or quantity :
People had turned up in *great* numbers.
He lives a *great* distance away.
(b) considerable:
Your advice was of *great* value.
Take *great* care to do it properly.

(c) outstanding; of remarkable ability or quality:
Mahatma Gandhi was a *great* man.

19. GREED/GRID

greed-n : (a) excessive desire for food, especially when one is not hungry:
I detest your *greed*.
(b) excessive and selfish desire for wealth, power, etc.
His *greed* for wealth baffles expression.

grid-n : (a) network of horizontal and vertical lines, bars, etc :
Graph paper is a good example of a *grid*.
(b) national network of electricity supply:
There was no electricity for many hours due to *grid* failure.

20. GREEN/GRIN

green-adj : (a) of colour between blue and yellow; grass-coloured :
It is as *green* as grass.
(b) not yet ripe:
Do you like *green* apples?
He bought *green* bananas.
(c) immature; inexperienced; easily fooled:
She is a girl who is still *green* at her job.
I am not so *green* as to believe that.
He is a *green* young novice.
(d) extremely envious:
I was absolutely *green* when I saw his splendid new car.

grin-v: (a) smile broadly, so as to show the teeth, expressing amusement, foolish satisfaction, contempt, etc :
He *grinned* at me, as if sharing a secret joke.
Don't *grin* at her.
(b) express sth by grinning :
She *grinned* her approval.

Note: *Grin*, as a noun, means act of *grinning*:
He was unhurt; he talked to us with a cheeful *grin*.
With a nasty *grin* on his face, he took out a knife.

21. GREET/GRIT

greet-v: (a) give a conventional sign or word of welcome or pleasure when meeting sb or receiving a guest:
She *greeted* me in the street with a friendly wave of the hand.
(b) receive sth with a particular reaction:
The news was *greeted* with cheering.
This appointment was *greeted* with dismay.

grit-a : (a) tiny hard bits of stone, sand, and so on :
I have got a piece of *grit* in my shoe.
Spread *grit* on the icy road.
(b) quality of courage and endurance:
Do you have enough *grit* to face the crowd?
The soldiers showed that they had plenty of *grit*.
Mountaineering in a blizzard needs a lot of *grit*.

22. GRIM/GRIME

grim-adj : (a) very serious and unsmiling in appearance:
He looked *grim*.
(b) severe:
Her *grim* day-to-day struggle for survival saddened me beyond expression in language.
(c) unpleasant :
Was that a *grim* news?

grime-n : dirt :
His face was covered with *grime* and sweat.

Note: *Grime*, as a verb, is used in the sense of make sb/sth dirty :
Her face was *grimed* with dust.

23. GRIP/GRIPE

grip-n : (a) firm hold; action of *gripping* :
He took a *grip* on the rope.
I released my *grip* and he ran away.
(b) way or power of *gripping* :
Tyres give good *grip* on the road.
(c) force that disables :
People are in the *grip* of disease.

Note: *Grip*, as a verb, means :
1. take and keep a firm hold of sb /sth :
The little boy *gripped* his mother's hand.
2. seize the attention, imagination of sb :
Children were *gripped* by fear.
The audience was *gripped* by the play.

gripe-v : feel or cause sudden sharp pain in the stomach or intestines:
She has a *gripping* pain in the stomach.
Take this medicine when your stomach *gripes*.

Note : There is another *gripe*, a verb. It means complain about sb/sth; grumble habitually :
He keeps *griping* about having no money.

24. GULF/GULP

gulf-n : (a) part of the sea almost surrounded by land:
Where is the *Gulf* of Mexico?
What is the importance of the Persian *Gulf*?
(b) deep hollow in the ground; chasm; abyss :
A yawning *gulf* was opened up by the earthquake.
(c) area of difference :
The *gulf* between the two leaders cannot be bridged.

gulp-v : swallow quickly or greedily :
Don't *gulp* your food.
He *gulped* down a cup of tea.

Note : *Gulp*, as a noun, is used to mean :
1. act of *gulping* :
Don't swallow anything with loud *gulps*.
2. mouthful of sth liquid :
He had a *gulp* of cold milk.
He emptied the glass at a *gulp*.

8

First Word of Each Group Beginning With-H

1. HACK/HECK

hack-v : (a) strike heavy cutting blows at sth/sb :
He *hacked* at the branch until it fell off.
(b) kick sth roughly:
Hack the ball.
I *hacked* his shin.

Note : There is another *hack*, a noun. It means :

1. person paid to do hard and uninteresting work, especially as a writer:
He is a publisher's *hack*.
Are you a *hack* journalist?
2. horse for ordinary riding or one that may be hired:
A *hack* is generally used to draw a tonga.

heck-n : (used to express mild annoyance or surprise or for emphasis), hell :
Oh *heck*, I am going to be late.
We had to wait a *heck* of a long time.

2. HAIL/HALE

Hail-v: (a) call out to attract attention:
He *hailed* a taxi.
(b) enthusiastically acknowledge sb/sth as sth:
People *hailed* him as a hero.
The book was *hailed* as a masterpiece.
(c) originate from:
Where do you hail from?
She *hails* from Hyderabad.

Note: There is another *hail*, a noun, used in the sense of:

1. frozen rain falling in a shower:
I saw big *hails* during the rainfall.
2. thing coming in great numbers and with force:
He was killed in a *hail* of bullets.

hale-adj: This word is used in the idiom *hale* and hearty.
It means strong and healthy:
Are you parents *hale* and hearty?

3. HAIR/HARE/HEIR

hair-n : one of the fine thread-like strands that grow from the skin of people and animals:
We have *hair* grown on our head.

hare-n : fast-running animal that lives in fields, like a rabbit, but larger, with long ears and a divided upper lip :
The story of *hare* and tortoise is world famous.

heir-n : person with the legal right to receive property, etc. when the owner dies :
He is *heir* to the throne.

. HALF/HUFF

half-n : either of two equal or corresponding parts into which a thing is divided :
Two *halves* make a whole.
The seond *half* of the book is more exciting than the first.

huff-n: fit or bad temper or annoyance :
He went off in a *huff.*

. HALL/HAUL

hall-n : (a) space or passage on the inside of the main entrance or front door of a building :
Leave your hat in the *hall.*
(b) building or large room for meeting, meals, concerts, etc :
Where is the dance *hall*?

haul-v : pull or drag sth with effort or force :
We *hauled* the car out of the mud.
Elephants were *hauling* logs.

. HAPLESS/HOPELESS

hapless: unlucky; unfortunate :
Who is your *hapless* hero?
She is *hapless* but not hopeless.

hopeless: (a) showing lack of hope :
I can't bear to see her *hopeless* tears.
(b) giving no cause for *hope* :
My position is *hopeless.*
According to the doctors, it is a *hopeless* case.
(c) very bad or unskilled :
I'm *hopeless* at maths.

. HARD/HERD

hard-adj : (a) solid; firm; not soft or yielding to touch or easily cut:
Their bodies were *hard* and muscular after much training.
(b) not easy; difficult to do or understand or answer :
It was a *hard* task.
She found it *hard* to decide.
(c) though; requiring much effort :
We must take a *hard* look at our finances.
Some *hard* bargaining is called for.
(d) energetic; showing much effort :
Are you a *hard* worker?
(e) harsh; forceful; violent :
Don't use *hard* words.

Note: *Hard* is also used as an adverb in the sense of :
1. with great effort, energy or concentration; strenuously:
You must try *hard* to succeed.

2. with difficulty :
Our victory was *hard* won.
3. heavily; severely :
It is raining *hard*.
4. at a sharp angle .
Turn *hard* left.

herd-n : number of animals, especially cattle, feeding or staying together:
Where is your *herd* of cows?

Note: The term the *herd* means mob; large number of people :
He preferred to stick with the *herd* so as not to be noticed.

8. HARRY/HURRY

harry-v: (a) annoy sb with repeated requests, questions, etc; harass :
I was *harried* by press reporters wanting a story.
He set to work *harrying* people for donations.
(b) raid and plunder repeatedly :
Dacoits *harried* that village.

hurry-n : need or wish to get something done quickly; eager haste:
What is the *hurry*? Stay for a little longer.
In his *hurry* to leave, he forgot his passport.
There is no *hurry*, so do it slowly and carefully.

Note: *Hurry*, as a verb, is used in the sense of :
1. rush; do sth or move quickly :
Don't *hurry*; there is plenty of time.
It is no use trying to make her *hurry*.
2. make sb to sth or move quickly :
We are late; I must *hurry* you.
They *hurried* her into hospital.
I was *hurried* into making an unwise decision.
3. hasten the process of sth :
A good meal should never be *hurried*.
4. do sth more quickly:
Hurry up and get ready-we are waiting.

9. HART/HEART

hart-n : adult male of deer; stag :

heart-n : (a) hollow muscular organ that pumps blood through the body
He has *heart* disease.
His *heart* stopped beating and he died soon after-wards.
(b) part of the body where the heart is:
She pressed my hand against her *heart*.
(c) centre of a person's thought and emotions; ability to feel emotion :
She knew it in her *heart*.
He has a kind *heart*.
The President captured the *hearts* of the nation.
(d) enthusiasm:
Put more *heart* into your work.
(e) central, innermost or most important part of sth :
Get to the *heart* of the matter.
Let me know the *heart* of the subject.

(f) beloved person ':'
Is she your dear *heart*?

10. HASTE/HEIST

haste-n : quickness of movement:
He went off in great *haste*.
Make *haste*, all of you, and get ready.

heist-n : robbery; burglary:

11. HAUNT/HUNT

haunt-v : (a) (of ghosts) visit a place regularly:
It is a *haunted* house.
People say that a spirit *haunts* the deserted house.
(b) be in a place very often:
This is one of the cafes I used to *haunt*.
(c) return repeatedly to the mind of sb :
The memory still *haunts* me.

hunt-v : (a) chase wild animals, etc. and try to kill or capture them:
Let us go *hunting*.
They had gone to the forest to *hunt* wild birds.
(b) search for; try to find :
Police are *hunting* an escaped criminal.
He was *hunting* for a lost book.

12. HAVEN/HEAVEN

haven : place of safety or rest; refuge:
Criminals will not find a safe *haven* here.
This town is a *haven* for foreign tourists.

heaven-n : (a) place believed to be the home of God and the angels, and of good people after death :
Do you want to ascend into the *heaven*?
(b) place or state of very great happiness:
She was in *heaven* when her boyfriend kissed her.
Sitting here with you is *heaven*.

Note: 1. *Heaven* is also used in the sense of God; providence:
It was the will of heaven.
2. The term the *heavens* means the sky, as seen from the Earth:
Rain fell from the *heavens* all day.

13. HEAL/HEEL/HILL

heal-v : (a) become healthy again :
The wound *healed* slowly but steadily.
(b) make easier to bear; cause sth to end :
Time *heals* all sorrow.

heel-n : (a) back part of the human foot :
(b) part of a boot or shoe supporting this :
She wears high-*heel* sandles.
(c) dishonourable man; rogue; villain :
Is he a *heel*?

hill-n: natural elevation on the Earth's surface, not as high or rugged as a mountain :
His house is on the side of a *hill*.

14. HEAP/HIP

heap-n : (a) number of things or mass of material lying piled up :
It is a *heap* of books.
The building was reduced to a *heap* of rubble.
(b) plenty; great number or amount:
She has been to our house *heaps* of times.
I have got *heaps* to tell you.
Note: *Heaps*, plural of heap, must be used in the sense at (b) above:

hip-n : part of either side of the body below the waist where the bone of a person's leg is joined to the trunk:
He stood with his hands on his *hips*.
She is quite wide in the *hips*.

15. HEAT/HIT

heat-n : (a) hotness; high temperature :
Feel the *heat* of the Sun's rays.
This fire does not give out much heat.
(b) hot weather :
Never go out in the *heat* of the rays.
He was suffering from the *heat*.
(c) intense feeling of anger or excitement :
He spoke with considerable *heat*.
I abused him in the *heat* of the argument.
That topic generated a lot of *heat*.

hit-v: (a) strike sb/sth with a blow, etc :
She *hit* me on the head with a book.
(b) come against sth/sb with force :
The lorry *hit* the lamp-post with a crash.
(c) have a bad or sudden effect on; affect; cause to suffer:
The rent increase will *hit* the poor.
(d) encounter; experience sth :
If you go now, you are likely to *hit* the rush hour.
Note: Hit, as a noun, means :
1. person or thing that is very popular; success:
He is a *hit* with young women.
His new film is quite a *hit*.
2. make a very favourable impression on sb :
He has made quite a *hit* with her.
3. act of hitting; blow or stroke:
That was a clever *hit*.
4. sarcastic comment made to or about sb :
That last remark was a *hit* at you.

16. HEROIN/HEROINE

heroin-n : narcotic drug made from morphine, used medically to cause sleep or relieve pain, or by drug addicts:
Use of *heroin* is dangerous.

heroine-n : heroine or protagonist :
The *heroine* in the films deserves an award.

(a) woman who is admired by many for her noble qualities or bravery:
She died a *heroine.*
Rani Laxmibai of Jhansi was a real *heroine.*

(b) chief female character in a play, story, etc :
Tell me the name of the *heroine* of the novel.

17. HEW/HUE

hew-v: chop or cut sth/sb with an axe, etc :
He *hewed* his enemy to pieces.

heu-n: colour; variety or shade of colour:
There are birds of many different *hues.*

18. HISTORIC/HISTORICAL

historic: famous or important in history :
This is a *historic* occasion.
The Taj Mahal is a *historic* building.
The Prime Minister made a *historic* speech about communal harmony.

historical: (a) concerning past events :
These are *historical* records.

(b) based on the study of history :
It is a *historical* fact.
We have no *historical* evidence of it.

19. HOARD/HORDE

hoard-n : carefully collected and guarded store of money, food or other treasured objects :
Let me know where your *hoard* is.

Note: Hoard, as a verb, means collect sth and store it away:
He *hoarded* food during the famine, and was severely punished.

horde-n : very large group; huge crowd; throng:
There were *hordes* of people at the jumble sale.
Hordes of tourists were going to Kashmir.

20. HOBBY/HUBBY

hobby-n : favourite activity that a person does for pleasure and not as his regular business:
His *hobby* is stamp-collecting.

hubby-n : husband:
She is lucky to have such a handsome *hubby.*

21. HOLE/WHOLE : ***ALSO REFER TO P. 233-234***

hole-n : (a) cavity; sunken or hollow place in a solid mass or surface.
The prisoner escaped through a *hole* in the wall.

(b) animal's burrow:
That is a rabbit *hole.*

(c) awkward or different situation:
He is in a bit of a *hole.*

whole-adj : (a) entire; complete:
The *whole* town was destroyed by the earthquake.
Tell me the *whole* truth.

(b) intact; not broken, damaged or injured:
After the party, there was not a glass left *whole.*

Note: *Whole,* as a noun, is used in the sense of :
1. thing that is complete in itself :
A *whole* is greater than any of its parts.
2. all that there is of sth :
He spent the *whole* of the year in prison.

22. HOLLY/HOLY

holly-n : evergreen shrub with hard shiny sharp-pointed leaves and, in winter, red berries:
Are you fond of *holly*?

holy-adj: (a) associated with God or with religion:
Have you read the *holy* scriptures?
(b) regarded as sacred:
Where is the nearest *holy* ground?
(c) devoted to the service of God; morally and spiritually pure:
My grandfather is a *holy* man.
I live a *holy* life.

23. HOOF/HOOP

hoof-n: horny part of the foot of a horse, a deer or an ox :
A horse-shoe is nailed to the horse's *hoof*.

hoop-n: circular band of metal, wood, etc :
The barrel is bound with iron *hoops*.

24. HOP/HOPE

hop-v: (a) move by jumping on one foot:
Do you know how to *hop*?
(b) move by jumping with both or all feet together:
Several frogs were *hopping* about on the lawn.

Note : **1.** *Hop,* as a noun, means :
(i) act of *hopping;* short jump:
(ii) short flight or one stage in a long-distance flight:
We flew from Kolkata to Delhi in one *hop*.
(iii) informal dance party:
Are you coming to the *hop* tonight?
2. There is another *hop,* a noun. It refers to a climbing plant with flowers growing in clusters. Dried flowers of this plants are used for giving bitter flavour to beer:

hope-n: (a) desire for sth to happen, combined with the expectation that it will:
I have pinned all my *hopes* on her.
Don't give up *hope* yet.
(b) person thing or circumstance that encourages hope:
You are my last *hope;* if you can't help, I am ruined.

Note: *Hope,* as a verb, is used in the sense of desire and expect sth or feel confident about sth :
I have not heard from him for weeks but I am still *hoping* for a letter.

25. HUMAN/HUMANE

human-adj : of or characteristic of man:
There was a terrible loss of *human* life.
This food is not fit for *human* consumption.

humane-adj: having or showing sympathy, kindness and understanding:
He is a *humane* person.

9

First Word of Each Group Beginning With-I

1. IDEAL/IDYLL

ideal-adj : satisfying one's idea of what is perfect; most suitable :
He is the *ideal* husband for her.

Note: *Ideal*, as a noun, means :

1. person or thing regarded as perfect:
He is looking for a job, but has not found his *ideal* yet.
2. standard of perfection:
He finds it hard to live up to his *ideals*.

idyll-n : short piece of poetry or prose that describes a happy and peaceful scene or event, especially of rural life :
Tell me something about an *idyll* of rural India.

2. IDLE/IDOL

idle-adj : (a) doing or having no work; not employed :
Lakhs of people are *idle* in the country.
(b) not active or in use :
The factory machines lay *idle* during the workers' strike.
(c) lazy; avoiding work :
Are you an *idle* student?
(d) worthless; useless :
It is *idle* to expect help from her.

idol-n: (a) image of a God, used as an object of worship :
He bought an *idol* this forenoon.
(b) person or thing that is greatly loved or admired :
As an only child, he was the *idol* of his parents.

3. ILL/EEL

ill-adj : (a) sick; physically or mentally unwell :
She was taken *ill* suddenly.
(b) bad; not good :
He has an *ill* health.
(c) harmful; intending harm :
What are the *ill* effects of this drug?
(d) unkind; resentful :
I bear you no *ill* will.
There is no *ill* feeling between the two friends.
(e) not favourable:
As *ill* luck would have it, he could not pass the examination.

Note: *Ill*, as a noun, means :
1. harm; evil :
I wish you no *ill*.
2. misfortune; problem :
What are the various *ills* of life?

idol-n : a long thin snake-like fish :

4. IMAGINABLE/IMAGINARY

imaginable : which can be imagined :
Give me every bit of information *imaginable*.
We had the greatest difficulty *imaginable* getting here in time.

imaginary : existing only in the mind or in imagination; not real:
These are your *imaginary* fears.
Don't harbour fears of *imaginary* dangers.

5. IMPART/IMPORT

impart-v : (a) give a quality to sth :
Her persence *imparted* an air of elegance to the function.
(b) revel sth; make known :
I have no news to *impart* to you.

import-v : bring sth from a foreign country into one's own country :
We *import* most of our raw materials.
They have *import*ed these cars from Japan.

Note: **1.** *Import*, as a noun, means imported goods, services, etc :
We should restrict expensive foreign *imports*.
2. There is another *import*, a verb, used in the sense of mean or convey sth to sb :
What does it *import* to you?
What did these developments *import* to them?
3. There is still another *import* used as a noun in the sense of importance or significance :
It is a matter of great *import*.
What is the hidden *import* of his speech?

6. IMPASSABLE/IMPOSSIBLE

impassable : impossible to travel on or over :
The roads have been made *impassable* by the fallen trees.

impossible : (a) not possible; which cannot be done:
It is virtually *impossible* to predict the future accurately.
It is an almost *impossible* task.
(b) very difficult to bear; hopeless :
It is an *impossible* situation.

7.IMPERIAL/IMPERIOUS

imperial-adj : of an empire or its ruler :
Where is the *imperial* place?
He was in the *imperial* service.

imperious-adj: proud and arrogant; expecting obedience; domineering :
She is *imperious* by nature.
I totally dislike your *imperious* gesture.
All his *imperious* orders were obeyed.

8. IMPOSTOR/IMPOSTURE

impostor-n : person pretending to be sb else, usually in order to deceive others :
Is he an *impostor*?
This person is not Dr. Dinesh Datta, but an *impostor*.

imposture-n : action of deliberately deceiving by pretending to be sb else:
He makes a living by lying and *imposture*.
Don't indulge in *imposture*.

9. IMPRUDENT/IMPUDENT

imprudent-adj : not wise or discreet; not prudent :
It would be *imprudent* of you to resign from your present job before you are offered another.
It would be *imprudent* of you to make enemies of those who can help you.

impudent-adj : very rude and disrespectful :
Is he an *impudent* child?
I am tired of his *impudent* questions.

10. INAPT/INEPT

inapt-adj: not relevant, appropriate or useful :
She did not like your *inapt* remarks.

inept-adj. (a) completely unskilful at sth :
I have never heard anyone so *inept* at making speeches.
His *inept* handling of a minor problem turned it into a major crisis.
(b) said or done at the wrong time; not appropriate or tactful :
He took offence at your *inept* remarks.

11. INCITE/INSIGHT

incite-v : (a) persuade sb to do sth by making him very angry or excited:
People *incited* the workers against the government.
(b) create or cause sth :
They *incited* a riot in the town.

insight-n : (a) deep understanding; ability to see into the true nature of sth :
He is a person of great *insight*.
I have deep *insight* into human nature.
She showed *insight* into human character.
(b) instance of this :
This book is full of remarkable *insights*.
(c) sudden perception or understanding of the true nature of sth:
She was given an unpleasant *insight* into what life would be like as his wife.
I gained an *insight* into the problem.

12. INCREDIBLE/INCREDULOUS

incredible : (a) impossible to believe :
It is an *incredible* story.
You have no basis for this *incredible* suggestion.
(b) amazing or fantastic :
She earns an *incredible* amount of money.
Are you an *incredible* actor?

incredulous : showing disbelief; not willing or able to believe :
Did you notice her *incredulous* smiles?

13. INDOOR/INDOORS

indoor-adj : carried on or situated inside a building; used in or suitable for:
We have an *indoor* swimming pool.
She is fond of *indoor* games.

indoors-adv : in or into a building :
As he was out of sorts, he stayed *indoors*.
We were kept *indoors* all week by bad weather.

14. INDUSTRIAL/INDUSTRIOUS

industrial : (a) of or engaged in industry :
They are *industrial* workers.
We need *industrial* development.
(b) having many well-developed industries :
Kolkata is an *industrial* city.
Can you name the *industrial* areas of India?

industrious: diligent; hard-working :
Are you an *industrious* student.

15. INFLAMMABLE/INFLAMMATORY

inflammable: (a) that can be set on fire :
Petroleum is highly *inflammable.*
(b) easily excited or aroused :
He is a man with an *inflammable* temper.

inflammatory: (a) tending to make people angry of excited :
He made *inflammatory* speeches against the government.
Your *inflammatory* remarks annoyed her.
(b) of, being or tending to produce inflammation :
He suffered from an *inflammatory* condition of his lungs.

16. INGENIOUS/INGENUOUS

ingenious : (a) clever at finding new or simple solutions for complex problems :
I am *ingenious* at solving difficult crossword puzzles.
He has an *ingenious* mind.
(b) orginal in design and well-suited to its purpose :
These *ingenious* gadgets are in great demand.
(c) very clever and original :
He adopted an *ingenious* method to overcome his financial difficulty :

ingenuous: innocent; open; not attempting to deceive or conceal :
Her expression was frank, *ingenuous,* and engaging.
Her *ingenuous* smile pleased me beyond expression.

17. INGRESS/EGRESS

ingress-n : going in; entrance :
It is a means of *ingress.*

egress-n : going out; exit :
Where is the *egress*?

18. INTOLERABLE/INTOLERANT

intolerable: too bad to be borne or endured :
I don't know what made her wife *intolerable.*
Don't indulge in *intolerable* behaviour.
There was *intolerable* noise in the room.
I cannot bear such *intolerable* remarks.

intolerant: not tolerant :
He was *intolerant* of other people's weaknesses.
Don't support *intolerant* regimes.

19.IRK/ARC

irk-v : annoy; be tiresome to sb :
It *irks* me to see money being wasted.
It *irked* him that she had thought of it first.

arc-n : (a) part of the circumference of a circle or some other curved line:
I use an *arc* lamp while studying.
(b) thing with this shape :
Have you seen the *arc* of a rainbow?

20. ITCH/EACH

itch-a : (a) feeling of irritation on the skin, causing a desire to scratch:
Do you feel an *itch*?
(b) restless desire or longing :
She cannot resist the *itch* to travel.
Do you have an *itch* for adventure?

Note: *Itch*, as a verb, means :
1. have or cause an *itch* :
Scratch where is *itches.*
Are your mosquito bites still *itching*?
(b) feel a strong restless desire for sth :
Pupils are *itching* for the lesson to end.
I was *itching* to get away.

each-adj: everyone considered individually :
Each day passed without any news.
There are trees on *each* side of the road.

Note: 1. *Each,* as a pronoun, means every individual member:
Each of them phoned to thank me.
Each of us has a company car.
I shall see *each* of you separately.
2. *Each,* as an adverb, means everyone seperately :
The books are 10 rupees *each.*

10

First Word of Each Group Beginning With-J

1. JEALOUS/ZEALOUS

jealous-adj. : (a) feeling or showing fear or resentment of possible rivals in love or affection :
Her *jealous* looks annoy me.
(b) feeling or showing resentment of sb's achievements, etc; envious :
He is *jealous* of my tremendous success.
(c) possessive; anxiously protective of one's rights, belongings, etc :
I am *jealous* of my privileges.
You should keep a *jealous* eye on your property.

zealous-adj. : full of zeal; eager :
Mahatma Gandhi was a *zealous* anti-racist.
I am *zealous* for liberty and freedom.
He is *zealous* to please this employer.

2. JEEP/ZIP

jeep-n : small sturdy motor vehicle with four-wheel drive :
I like to ride a *jeep*.

zip-n : (a) vigour; energy :
He is full of *zip*.
(b) device for locking together two toothed metal or plastic edges by means of a sliding tab, used for fastening articles of clothing, bags, etc :
Zip of this bag is not working properly.
(c) short sharp sound as of a bullet going through the air :
The bullet *zipped* through the air.

3. JEST/ZEST: ***ALSO REFER TO P. 243***

jest-n : joke; thing done or said to cause amusement :
He did it in *jest*.

Note : *Jest*, as a verb, means make jokes; speak or act without seriousness :
Don't *jest* about such important matters.

zest-n : (a) gusto; great enjoyment or excitement :
She entered into my plans with tremendous *zest*.
(b) quality of having added interest, charm, flavour, etc :
The element of risk gave an added *zest* to the adventure.

4. JINK/ZINC

jink-v : move quickly or suddenly with sharp turns, usually to avoid being caught; dodge :
Don't try to *jink* me.
The thief *jinked* as soon as he saw the police.

zinc-n : a blush white metal used in the production of other metals and to place (= cover) metal objects with a protective surface :
Printing blocs are generally made of *zinc*.

5. JOG/JUG

jog-v : (a) push or knock sb/ sth slightly :
Don't *jog* me.
(b) run slowly and steadily for a time, for physical exercise :
He goes *jogging* every evening.

Note : *jog*, as a noun, means :
1. nudge; slight push, knock or shake :
He gave the pile of tins a jog and they all fell down.
2. spell of jogging as exercise :
Are you coming for a *jog* tomorrow morning?

jug-n : (a) deep vessel, with a handle and a lid, for holding and pouring liquids :
Pour milk from the *jug*.
(b) amount of liquid contained in a jug.
He spilled a whole *jug* of juice.

6. JUDICIAL/JUDICIOUS

judicial : (a) of or by a court of law; of a judge or of judgement :
There was a *judicial* inquiry into the police firing.
(b) impartial; able to judge things wisely :
He is a man with a *judicial* mind.

judicial : showing or having good judgement and sense :
You should make *judicious* use of your time and money.

7. JUT/JUTE

jut-v : stand out from sth; be out of line :
The balcony *juts* out over the garden.
His chin *juts* out rather a bit.

jute-n : fibre from the outer skin of certain tropical plants, used for making rope, etc :
There are many *jute* mills in Kolkata.

11

First Word of Each Group Beginning With-K

1. KEEL/KILL

keel-n : timber or steel structure along the bottom of a ship :
They have begun to lay down the *keel.*

Kill-v : (a) cause death or cause the death of sb/sth :
Careless driving *kills.*
Cancer *kills* thousands of people every year.

(b) cause pain to sb :
My feet are *killing* me.

(c) bring sth to an end :
His behaviour outraged her and killed their friendship.

(d) cause sth to fail or be rejected :
Lack of funds *killed* our project.
The play was *killed* by bad services.

Note : *Kill,* as a noun, means :

1. act of killing :
The lion made only one *kill* that day.

2. animal or animals killed :
The hunters brought their *kill* back to camp.
The female lions make the majority of *kills.*

2. KEEN/KIN

keen-adj : (a) eager; enthusiastic :
He is a *keen* swimmer.
I am not *keen* to meet her.

(b) intense; deep; strong :
He took a *keen* interest in domestic affairs.
He has a *keen* desire to go abroad.

(c) highly developed :
Dogs have a *keen* sense of smell.

kin-n : one's family and relatives :
All his *kin* were at the wedding.
We are near *kin.*

3.KEEP/KIP

keep-v : (a) remain or stay :
He has the ability to *keep* calm in an emergency.
Please *keep* quiet-I am trying to get some work done.
The notice said, "*keep* off the grass."

(b) do sth repeatedly or frequently :
Keep talking amongst yourselves, I shall be back in a minute.
Keep going until you reach a large round about.

(c) delay or detain sb :
You are an hour late; what *kept* you?

(d) retain :
You can *keep* that book I lent you; I don't want it back.
Here is a ten-rupee note; you can *keep* the change.

(e) own and manage :
His father *kept* a grocer's shop for a number of years.

(f) not reveal :
Can you keep a secret?

Note : *Keep*, as a noun, means cost of providing food and other necessities of life :
It is the time you got a job and started paying for your *keep*.
Do you earn your *keep*?

kip-n : sleep :
Did you have a *kip* last night?

Note : *Kip*, as a verb, means lie down to sleep :
Could I *kip* here tonight?
Kip down on the floor.

4. KNACK/NECK

Knack-n : (a) skill at performing some special task; ability :
I have the *knack* of getting things done.
He has the *knack* for combining colours and paterns.

(b) habit of doing sth :
My car has a *knack* of breaking down just when I need it most.

neck-n : part of the body that connects the head to the shoulders :
He wrapped a scraf round his *neck*.

5. KNAVE/NAVE

Knave-n : dishonest man; man without honour :
Don't rely on him too much; he is a *knave*.

nave-n : long central part of a church where the congregations sits :

6. KNEAD/NEED

knead-v : press and stretch bread dough, etc. with the hands to form a firm smooth paste :
Knead the dough into a ball.

need-v : require sb/sth; want :
Do you *need* any help?
Don't go - I may *need* you.

Note : *Need*, as a noun, is used to mean :

1. necessity :
There is no *need* for you to start yet.
I feel a *need* to talk to you about it.

2. adversity; poverty; misfortune :
She helped me in my hour of *need*.

7. KNIT/NEAT

Knit-v : (a) make a garment, etc. by forming yarn into connecting loops :
Do you know how to *knit*?
She *knitted* a sweater.
She often *knits* while reading.
(b) unite firmly or closely :
The broken bones have *knitted* well.
The two groups are *knitted* together by common interests.

neat-adj : (a) tidy; done carefully; arranged in an orderly way :
His clothes are *neat*.
He is a *neat* worker.
(b) simple and elegant :
She wears a *neat* dress.
(c) having a pleasing appearance or shape :
She has a *neat* figure.
(d) efficient; skilful; economical with time and effort :
What is the *neat* way of doing the job?
He gave a *neat* summary of the financial situation.

8. KOOK/COOK

Kook-n : peculiar, eccentric or crazy person :
That man is a kook.

cock-v : (a) prepare food :
Where did you learn how to *cook*?
(b) falsify; alter sth secretly or dishonestly so as to deceive :
He was sent to prison for *cooking* the accounts books.
(c) be planned; happen as a result of plotting :
What is *cooking* up here?

Note : Cook, as a noun, means person who *cooks* food :
He is employed as a *cook* in a hotel.
I am not much of a *cook*.

12

First Word of Each Group Beginning With-L

1. LABEL/LEVEL

label-n : (a) piece of paper, cloth, metal, etc. on or beside an object and describing its nature, name, owner, destination, etc :
Put a *label* on your luggage.

(b) descriptive word or phrase applied to a person, group, etc :
I am not willing to accept the *label* of anarchist.

Note : *Label*, as a verb, means :

1. describe or classify sb/sth :
He is work is difficult to *label* accurately.
He was not going to be *labelled* mad.
His behaviour is *labelled* deviant.

2. put a *label* on sth :
This is a machine for *labelling* milk bottles.

level-n : (a) line or surface parallel to the horizon; such a surface with reference to its height :
This place is 1000 metres above sea *level*.
The water rose until it was on a *level* with the river banks.

(b) position on a scale of quantity, strength, value, etc. :
What is the *level* of alcohol in blood?
Levels of unemployment vary from region to region.

(c) relative position in rank, class or authority :
There were discussions about budget proposals at Cabinet *level*.
I always take part in high-*level* negotiations.

Note : 1. *Level*, as an adjective, means :

(i) flat; not sloping :
Find *level* ground for the table.
Add one *level* tablespoon of sugar.

(ii) of the same height, standard or position on a scale :
The two pictures are not qui te *level*–that one is higher than the other.

2. *Level*, as a verb, means :

(i) make sth *level*, equal or uniform :
Steps should be taken to *level* social differences.
The ground should be *levelled* before you plant a lawn.

(ii) demolish :
The town was *levelled* by an earthquake.

(iii) aim a gun, etc :
The hostage had a rifle *levelled* at his head.

(iv) bring a charge etc. against sb :
People *levelled* criticism at the government.

2. LAG/LEG

lag-v : go too slow; fail to keep pace with others :
As he became tired, he *lagged* far behind the rest of the walkers.
Production *lagged* and unemployment rose.

Note : *Lag,* as a noun, means period of time separating two events, especially an action and its effect; delay :
There was a *lag* of several seconds between the lightning and the thunder.
There will be a one-year *lag* between the time I pen this book and its publication.

leg-n : (a) one of the limbs of an animal's or a person's body used for standing and walking :
He has long *legs.*
(b) section of a journey :
The last *leg* of our trip was the most tiring.
(c) one of the supports of a chair, table, etc :
This is a chair with one *leg* missing.

3. LALR/LIAR/LYRE

lair-n : (a) sheltered place where a wild animal regularly sleeps or rests; den :
This zoo has a large *lair* for wild horses.
(b) person's hiding place :
The dacoit's *lair* was an old farm in the hills.

liar-n : person who tells lies habitually :
Are you a good *liar?*
He is a bad *liar.*

lyre-n : musical instrument with strings, played by plucking with fingers :
Do you know how to play on a *lyre?*

4. LARK/LURK

lark-n : (a) bit of adventurous fun :
The boys did not mean any harm–they were only having a *lark.*
They stole the car for a *lark,* but now they are in trouble.
(b) unpleasant or irritating type of activity :
I don't much like this queuing *lark.*

Note : 1. *Lark,* as a verb, means behave playfully or irresponsibly :
It is against your own interest to *lark* about.
2. There is another *lark,* a noun. It means any of several small songbirds, especially the sky *lark* :
Do you have a lark?

lurk-v : (a) be or stay hidden :
Somebody is *lurking* in the bushes.
A suspicious looking man is *lurking* in the shadows.
(b) wait near a place trying not to attract attention :
He is usually *lurking* somewhere near the restaurant.
(c) linger in the mind without being clearly shown :
I have a *lurking* suspicion that he belongs to a very notorious gang.

5. LAST/LUST

last-adj. : (a) coming after all others in time or order :
December is the *last* month of the year.
(b) most recent :
She visited me *last* night.
I thought his *last* book was one of his best.
(c) least likely or suitable :
She is the *last* person to trust with a secret.
(d) final :
This is his *last* hope of winning.
This is our *last* bottle of milk.

Note : 1. *Last,* as an adverb, means :
(i) after all others :
He came *last* in the race.
That counter ranks *last* in industrial output.
(ii) most recently; on the occasion before the present time :
I saw her *last* in Kuala Lumpur two years ago.
We *last* defeated them in 1992.
2. *Last,* as a verb, means :
(i) endure :
The war *lasted* five years.
She will not *last* long in that job - it is too tough.
How long do you think this fine weather will *last*?
(ii) be adequate or enough :
We have enough food to last five days.
(iii) be strong enough to survive or endure sth :
He is very ill and probably will not *last* the night.
3. *Last,* as a noun, means :
(i) person or thing that is last or mentioned last :
These are *last* four apples.
We invited Gita, Rita and Sita - the *last* being Rana's sister.
(ii) consistently, until the last possible moment :
He died protesting his innocence to the *last*.

lust-n : (a) strong sexual desire :
You should curb your *lust*.
Did you gratify your *lusts*?
(b) intense desire for sth or enjoyment of sth :
He has a *lust* for power.

Note : *Lust,* as a verb, means feel a strong desire for sb/sth :
He *lusts* after girls.
He *lusted* for revenge.

6. LATH/LATHE

lath-n : thin narrow strip of wood :
Laths are used in making false ceiling.
machine that shapes pieces of wood, metal, etc. by holding and turning them against a fixed cutting tool :

lust-n : This factory has computerised *lathe*.

7. LATHER/LEATHER

lather-n : white foam or froth produced by soap or detergent mixed with water :
You should work up a *lather* on your face before shaving.

leather-n : material made by tanning animal skins :
This sofa is covered in real *leather*.
Do you wear *leather* shoes?

8. LAUNCH/LUNCH

launch-v : (a) put sth into motion :
We *launched* a missile into the outer space.
(b) put sb/sth into action; set going :
We *launched* an attack against the enemy.
He is *launching* his son on a career in banking.

Note : 1. *Launch*, as as noun, means process of putting into motion, a ship, spacecraft or new product :
The *launch* of our new saloon received immense media coverage.
2. There is another *launch*, a noun. It means large motor boat :
Do they have a *launch*?

lunch-n : (a) meal taken in the middle of the day :
She has gone for *lunch*.
(b) light meal taken at anytime :
We shall have a *lunch* after the show.

Note : Lunch, as a verb, means eat *lunch* :
Where do you usually *lunch*?

9. LEA/LEE

lea-n : area of open grassland; meadow :
Many children are playing in the *lea*.

lee-n : part or side of sth providing shelter against the wind :
They took shelter in the *lee* of a hedge.

10. LEAD/LID

lead-n : (a) example; guidance given by going first or in front :
He is the chief trouble-maker; the others just follow his *lead*.
(b) first place or position :
I took the *lead* from him.
(c) principal part in a play, etc; person who plays this part :
He plays the *lead* in the new East West hit.
(d) piece of information or evidence that might provide the solution to a problem; clue :
The police are investigating an important new *lead*.

Note : Lead, as a verb, means :
1. show the way :
He *led* the guest to his room.
2. guide :
Let him *lead* the blind man across the street.
3. influence actions or opinions of sb :
What *led* you to this conclusion?
Don't be *led* astray by him.

lid-n : hinged or removable cover for a box, pot, etc :
Where is the *lid* of the box?

11. LEAF/LEAP/LIP

leaf-n : (a) one of the parts of a plant :
Sweep up the dead *leaves*.
(b) sheet of paper :
Give me a loose *leaf* of paper.

Note : *Leaf*, as a verb, means turn over the pages of a book, etc. quickly; glance through sth :
While he is waiting, he *leafs* through a magazine.

leap-v : (a) jump vigorously :
She *leapt* into the water.
Some monkeys can *leap* five metres from one tree to another.
My heart *leapt* for joy at the news.
(b) rush :
I *leapt* into my car.
He *leapt* to the telephone.
(c) accept sth eagerly :
She *leapt* at the chance to go to America.

Note : *Leap*, as a noun, means :

1. vigorous jump :
   He crossed the garden in five *leaps*.
2. rapid increase or change :
   There was a *leap* in prices of vegetables.
   There was a *leap* in the number of people out of employment.

lip-n : either of the fleshy edges of the opening of the mouth :
She kissed me on the *lips*.

12. LEAK/LEEK/LICK

leak-n : (a) hole, crack, etc :
There is a *leak* in the roof.
(b) accidental or deliberate disclosure of secret or confidential information :
This is the latest in a series of damaging *leaks*.
(c) act of urination :
He has gone for a *leak*.

Note : *Leak*, as a verb, means :

1. allow liquid or gas to get in or out wrongly :
   This boat *leaks* like a sieve.
   Air *leaked* out of the balloon.
2. reveal information :
   I don't know who *leaked* this to the press.

leek-n : vegetable related to the onion but with wider green leaves above a long white bulb :
Chop *leeks* to make a sauce.

lick-v : (a) pass the tongue over sb/sth :
Don't *lick* your fingers.
(b) (of flames) touch lightly.
Flames are beginning to *lick* the furniture.

13. LEASE/LEES

Lease-n : contract by which the owner of land, a building, etc. allows another person to use it for a specified time in return for rent :
They took out a *lease* on a holiday home.
When does the *lease* expire?

lees-n : sediment at the bottom of a bottle of oil, etc. dregs :
Don't shake the bottle or you will disturb the *lees*.

14. LEAVE/LIVE

leave-v : (a) go away from :
Leave this at once.
I am *leaving* for Paris next week.
(b) cease to live at a place, work for an employer, etc :
My secretary has threatened to *leave*.
Many children *leave* school at 16.
(c) allow sb/sth to remain :
Leave the door open.
Don't *leave* her waiting outside in the rain.
(d) Neglect or fail to take or bring sth :
He has *left* his gloves on the bus.
(e) cause sth to remain as a result :
The accident *left* a scar on her leg.
(f) hand over sth and then go away :
Did the postman *leave* anything?
Someone *left* this note for you.
(g) entrust sth to another person :
You can *leave* the cooking to me.
(h) have sb remaining alive :
He *leaves* a widow and two children.

Note : There is another leave, a noun. It means :
1. time absent from duty or work :
She was granted 90 days' maternity *leave*.
I was on ten days' sick *leave*.
2. official permission to be absent :
He was given *leave* to visit his mother.
3. permission :
She has my *leave* to see him.

live-v : (a) remain alive :
He is not likely to *live* through the night.
How long do elephants *live*?
(b) *reside* :
Where do you *live*?
He *lives* abroad.
(c) survive; remain in existence :
The memory will *live* in my heart for ever.

Note : 1. There is another *live* pronounced *laiv*. It is an adjective. It means :
(i) having life :
These are *live* fish.
(ii) actual, not pretended :
We saw real *live* lion.

(iii) burning :
Don't touch the *live* coals.
(iv) not yet exploded or lit :
That is a *live* bomb.
The soldiers have several rounds of *live* ammunition.
(v) of interest or importance at the present time :
Rampant corruption in government offices is very much a *live* issue.

2. *Live,* as an adverb, means broadcast, played or recorded at an actual performance, etc. without being edited :
This show is going out *live.*

15. LEND/LAND

lend-v : (a) give or allow use of sth temporarily :
Can you *lend* me hundred rupees?
(b) contribute or add sth to sth :
His presence *lent* dignity to the occasion.
A little garlic *lends* flavour to a sauce.

land-n : (a) solid part of the earth's surface :
They travelled over *land* for ten kilometres.
(b) ground or soil as used for a particular purpose :
Do you have arable *land*?

Note : *Land,* as a verb, means :

1. go on *land* from a ship :
We *landed* at Bombay.
2. bring an aircraft down to the ground :
The pilot managed to *land* the damaged plane safely.
3. come down to the ground :
We shall be *landing* at Delhi airport shortly.
4. succeed in obtaining sth against strong competition :
He *landed* a good job.

16. LESSEN/LESSON

lessen-v : (a) become less :
The pain was already *lessening*.
(b) reduce sth :
You should *lessen* your expenses.
How to *lessen* the risk of fire?

lesson-n : (a) thing to be learnt by a pupil :
The first *lesson* in driving is how to start the car.
(b) period of time given to learning or teaching :
My yoga *lesson* begins in ten minutes.
She gives piano *lessons*.
(c) experience from which one can learn :
His courage is a *lesson* to us all.
We are still absorbing the *lessons* of this disaster.
Let this be a *lesson* to you, never to play with matches.

17. LICENCE/LICENSE

licence-n : (a) official document showing that permission has been given to own, use, or do sth :
He has a *licence* to practise as a doctor.
Do you have a driving *licence*?
(b) permission :
Don't give them *licence* to enter the place at will.

license-v : give a licence to sb/sth :
This ship is *licensed* to sell kerosene.

18. LION/LOIN

lion-n : (a) large powerful flesh-eating animal :
(b) brave or famous person :
He is a literary *lion*.

loin-n : side and back of one body between the ribs and the hip-bone :

19. LOAD/LODE

load-n : (a) thing that is being carried or to be carried :
He carried a *load* of sand.
(b) amount of work that a motor, an engine, etc. is required to do :
(c) amount of electric current supplied by a dynamo or generating station :
This powerful machine needs heavy *load*.
(d) weight of responsibility, worry, grief, etc :
I have a heave *load* of work to do.

Note : *Load*, as a verb, means :

1. put a *load* in or on sth/ sb :
They *loaded* a lorrywith bricks.

2. receive a *load* :
The boat is still loading.

3. put film in a camera or ammunition into a gun :
Be careful, that gun is *loaded*.

20. LOAN/LONE

loan-n : (a) thing that is lent, especially a sum of money :
Give me a *loan* of fifty ruppes.
(b) lending or being lent :
May I have the *loan* of your car?

lone-adj : solitary; without companion :
They made an attack on the town's *lone* hospital.

21. LOATH/LOATHE

loath-adj : unwilling; reluctant :
He seemed somewhat loath to depart.

loathe-v : (a) feel great hatred or disgust for sb/sth :
Do you *loathe* the smell of garlic?
(b) dislike sth greatly :
I *loathe* having to go to these conferences.

22. LOB/LOBE

Lob-v : send or strike a ball in a high arc :
She *lobbed* the ball over her opponent's head to the back of the court.

Lobe-n : lower soft part of the outer ear :
The *lobe* of your ear is the flat, soft piece at the bottom.
The bullet pierced the *lobe* of the lung.

23. LOCAL/LOCALE

Local-adj : (a) belonging to a particular place or district :
Tell me something about the *local* news.
She is a *local* girl.
(b) (medical) affecting a particular place; not general :
Is the pain *local*?

Note : Local, as a noun, means :
1. inhabitant of a particular place or district :
The *locals* tend to be suspicious of strangers.
2. public house, near one's home :
Which is your *local*?

Locale-n : scene of events, operations, etc :
The director is looking for a suitable *locale* for his new film.

24. LOOSE/LOSE

loose-adj : (a) freedom from control; not tied up, packed or contained in sth :
He carried his coins *loose* in his trouser pocket.
That dog is dangerous; don't leave it *loose*.
(b) vague; not exact :
Don't indulge in *loose* thinking.
(c) physically slack :
He has *loose* skin.
She has loose bowels. (=She suffers from diarrhoea.)
(d) (talk, behaviour, etc.) not sufficiently controlled :
I detest your *loose* talk.
He leads a *loose* and dissolute life.
Is she a *loose* woman?

lose-v : (a) have sb/sth taken away by accident, misfortune, death, etc :
He *lost* a leg in an accident.
He *lost* both his sons in the war.
She has just *lost* her husband.
(b) no longer have or maintain :
I have *lost* interest in her.
I warn you, I am rapidly *losing* patience.
(c) become unable to find :
I have *lost* my keys.
He *lost* his wife in the crowd.
(d) fail to obtain or catch sth :
His words were *lost* in the applause.
(e) be no longer understood by sb :
I am afraid you have *lost* me.
(f) elude; escape from sb/sth :
The dacoits managed to *lose* the police in the darkness.
(g) fail to win; be defeated :
They *lost* the match.
They *won* the battle but *lost* the war.
We *lost* the resolution in the Parliament.

(h) forfeit sth :
The Socialist Party candidate *lost* his deposit.

(i) waste, time, etc :
He *lost* ten minutes through having to change a tyre.
There is no time to *lose*.

(j) become poorer as a result of sth :
You will *lose* nothing by telling the truth.
We *lost* a lot on that deal.
Poetry *loses* something in translation.

(k) cause sb to be without or forfeit sth :
His carelessness lost him the job.
Such behaviour will *lose* you everyone's sympathy.

(l) (watch or clock) go too slowly by an amount of time :
A good watch neither gains nor *loses*.
This clock *loses* five minutes a day.

25. LOP/LOPE

lop-v : cut branches, twigs, etc. off a tree :
He *lopped* several twigs off the tree.

lope-v : run fairly fast with long bounding strides :
The tiger *loped* off into the jungle.

Note : *Lope*, as a noun, means *long* bounding step or stride :
The thief moved at a steady *lope*.

26. LUNG/LUNGE

lung-n : either of the two breathing organs in the chest of man and other animals :
Many women died of *lung* cancer.
I have good *lungs*.

lung-n : sudden forward movement of the body; thrust :
When he makes a *lunge* at you, run.

Note : *Lunge*, as a verb, means make a *lunge* :
He *lunged* wildly at his opponent.
She *lunged* out with a knife.

13

First Word of Each Group Beginning With-M

1. MAGNATE/MAGNET

magnate-n : wealthy and powerful landowner or industrialist :
He is an industrial *magnate*.

magnet-n : (a) piece of iron which can attract iron :
The pin was extracted with a *magnet*.
(b) person or thing that has a powerful attraction :
This disco is a *magnet* for young people.

2. MAIL/MALE

mail-n : (a) official system of collecting, transporting and delivering letters and parcels :
Send the letter by *airmail*.
The letter is in the *mail*
(b) *letters*, parcels, etc. sent by post :
Post office workers sort the *mail*.
The office *mail* is opened in the morning.
(c) letters, parcels, etc. delivered or collected at one time :
I want this letter to catch the afternoon *mail*.

Note : *Mail*, as a verb, means send sth to sb by post :
I shall *mail* it to you tomorrow.

male-adj : (a) of the sex that does not give birth to offspring :
It is a *male* horse.
(b) (of a plant) having flowers that contain pollen- bearing organs and not seeds :

Note : Male, as a noun, means *male* person, animal, etc :

3. MAIN/MANE

main-adj : principal; chief; most important :
My *main* concern is the welfare of the poor.
What is the *main* thing to remember about her?
There is another *main*, a noun. It means :

1. principal pipe bringing water or gas, or principal cable carrying electric current, from the source :
The *main* exploded and set fire to the house.
2. source of water, gas, electricity supply to a building or an area :

My new house is not yet connected to the *mains*. The electricity supply has been cut off at the *mains*.

Note : Remember that *mains*, plural form of *main*, must be used in the sense at (b) above. Besides, It must be preceded by the definite article the :

mane-n : long hair on the neck of a horse, lion, etc :
Mane of this horse is beautiful.

4. MALL/MOLL/MAUL

mall-n : street or covered area with rows of shops, closed to traffic :
That is a shopping *mall*.

moll-n : woman companion of a gangster :
Is she a *moll*?

maul-v : (a) handle sb/sth roughly or brutally :
Her novel has been badly *mauled* by the critics.
(b) injure (a person or an animal) by tearing his or its flesh :
He died after being *mauled* by a tiger.

5. MANAGE/MENAGE

manage-v : (a) be in charge of sth; run :
Can you *manage* a shop?
She *manages* the finances here.
(b) keep in order; control :
Can you *manage* children well?
He is good at *managing* his accounts.
(c) cope with sth; succeed in doing sth :
I just cannot *manage* on ₹ 400/ - a week.
He will not be able to *manage* the job without help.
(d) succeed in producing, achieving or doing sth :
As I have not been learning Hindi for long, I can only *manage* (i.e. speak) a few words.
Despite his disappointment, he *managed* a smile.

menage-n : household :
An expert housewife runs a *menage* efficiently.

6. MANNER/MANOR

manner-n : (a) way in which a thing is done or happens :
The *manner* of his death is suspicious.
Do it in a business like *manner*.
I objected in a forceful *manner*.
(b) way of behaving towards others :
He has an aggressive *manner*.
I don't like her *manner* - she is very hostile.
(c) Social behaviour :
You have no *manners* at all.
It is bad *manners* to stare at people.
(d) (of person or thing) sort; kind :
What *manner* of man is he?

Note : *Manners*, not manner, must be used in the sense at (c) above :

manor-n : area for which a particular police station is responsible (It is a slang.) :

7. MANSION/MENTION

mansion-n : large and stately house :
Who is the owner of that *mansion*?

mention-v : refer to sth/ sb; say the name of sth/ sb; write or speak about sth/sb briefly :
They *mentioned* you as a good source of information.
Did you *mention* it to the police?
Did she *mention* when she would arrive?

Note : *Mention,* as a noun, means reference to sb/sth :
He made no *mention* of your request.
Did the function get a mention in the paper?

8. MANTLE/MANTEL/MENTAL

mantle-n : (a) loose sleeveless cloak :
He was wearing a *mantle.*
(b) covering :
The hills are with a *mantle* of snow.
(c) the responsibilities of an important job, etc :
Who will assume the *mantle* of supreme power?

mantel-n : (a) structure of wood, marble, etc. above and around a fireplace :
Round a fireplace there is usually a *mantelpiece* of tiles of bricks, on top of which one can stand a clock or ornaments.
(b) shelf projecting from the wall above a fireplace :

mental-adj : (a) of, in or to the mind :
Make a *mental* note of this information.
This experience caused him much *mental* suffering.
(b) mad :
You must be *mental* to drive so fast.

9. MARBLE/MARVEL

marble-n : type of hard limestone used for building and sculpture :
These steps are made of *marble.*

marvel-n : (a) wonderful or miraculous thing; thing causing astonishment :
It is a *marvel* that he escaped unhurt.
(b) person or thing that is surprisingly good, pleasing, etc :
Her room is a *marvel* of neatness and order.
He is a *marvel* of patience.
(c) wonderful results :
The doctor's treatment has worked *marvels,* the patient has recovered completely.

Note : 1. *Marvels,* plural of *marvel,* must be used in the sense at (c) above :
2. *Marvel,* as a verb, means be very surprised :
We *marvelled* at her boldness.
They *marvelled* at the maturity of such a young child.
I *marvel* that he agreed to do something so dangerous.

10. MARE/MERE

mare-n : female horse or donkey :

mere-adj : nothing more than; no better or more important than :
She is a *mere* child.
He is not a *mere* boxer; he is world champion.

Note : There is another *mere*, a noun. It means pond; small lake :
Children are playing in the *mere*.

11. MARK/MARQUE/MURK

mark-n : (a) stain, spot, line, etc :
Who made these dirty *marks* on my new book?
(b) noticeable spot or area on the body :
This scar is her main distinguishing *mark*.
(c) written or printed symbol; figure, line, etc. made as a sign or an indication of sth :
Put a *mark* in the margin to show the omission.
(d) visible trace; sign or indication :
Those are *marks* of old age.
Please accept this gift as a mark of our respect.
(e) number or letter used as an *assessment* of sb's work or conduct :
She got 80 *marks* out of 100 for Geography.
He got a poor mark in English.

Note : 1. Mark, as a verb, means :
(i) make a *mark* on sth :
Prices are *marked* on the goods.
His face is *marked* by smallpox.
(ii) denote or indicate sth :
His death *marked* the end of an era.
There will be ceremonies to *mark* the President's birthday.
(iii) give *marks* to :
I have thirty examination papers to *mark* tonight.
(iv) show sth by putting a *mark* :
She *marked* me present.
Why have you *marked* the sentence wrong?
(v) be a distinguishing feature of sth :
He writes in a style *marked* by precision and wit.
These are qualities which mark the novel as quite exceptional.
(vi) pay attention to sth; note carefully :
Mark carefully how it is done.
2. There is another *mark*, a noun. It means unit of money in Germany :
Give me a ten-*mark* note.

marque-n : famous or particularly good make or brand :
Do you like the Mercedes *marque*?

murk-n : darkness; gloom :
He was peering through the *murk*.

12. MARROW/MORROW

marrow-n : (a) soft fatty substance that fills the hollow parts of human or animal bones :
It was so cold that he felt frozen to the marrow.
(b) essential part; inner meaning :
What is the *marrow* of his statement?

morrow-n : the next day after the present or after any given day :
They wondered what the *morrow* had in store for them.

13. MARRY/MERRY

marry-v : (a) take sb as a husband or wife :
They *married* when they were young.
She did not *marry* until she was over forty.
(b) (of clergyman or civil official, etc.) join in marriage at a ceremony :
Which priest is going to *marry* them?
They were *married* by her father, who is a priest.
(c) combine sth successfully with sth else :
This is a training that *marries* well with the needs of the job.
He *marries* wit with scholarship in his writing.

merry-adj: (a) happy and cheerful; full of joy and gaiety.
She wished me a *merry* Christmas.
(b) slightly drunk :
They were already *merry* after only two glasses of wine.

14. MARSHAL/MARTIAL

marshal-v : arrange sb/sth in proper order; gather :
The children were *marshalled* into straight lines.
Marshal the relevant facts about the case.

Note : There is another *marshal*, a noun. It means :
(a) officer of high rank :
He is a Field-*Marshal* in the army.
(b) official responsible for arranging or controlling crowds at certain public events :
Marshal was called to control the crowed.

martial-adj : of or associated with war :
I am fond of *martial* music.

15. MASH/MESH

mash-n : (a) grain, bran, etc. cooked in water until soft, used as food for animals :
Children eat *mash-food* gladly.
(b) boiled potatoes crushed into a soft mass :
Are you fond of *mash* ?

mesh-n : material made of a network of wire, thread, etc.
There is a wire *mesh* on the front of the chicken coop.
These stockings are made of fine silk *mesh*.

16. MASK/MASQUE/MUSK

mask-n : (a) covering for the face worn as disguise :
The bank robber was wearing a stocking *mask*.
(b) likeness of a face carved in wood, ivory, etc. or made of plastic, card, etc :
The child was wearing a gorilla *mask*.
(c) thing that hides the truth; pretence :
Her sociable manner is really a *mask* for a very shy nature.
He conceals his worries behind a *mask* of non-chalance.

Note : *Mask*, as a verb, means :
1. cover with a *mask* :
The thief *masked* his face with a stocking.

2. disguise; conceal sth :
He *masked* his fear by a show of confidence.
Will this perfume *mask* the unpleasant smell?

masque-n : (a) verse drama with music and dancing :
(b) this theatrical form :

musk-n : strong-smelling substance produced in glands by male-musk deer, used in the manufacture of perfume :
Musk is used in making perfume.

17. MASSAGE/MESSAGE

massage-n : act of rubbing and pressing the body with the hands to relieve or prevent stiffness or pain in muscles, joints, etc :
The doctor recommended *massage* for my back pain.
Give her a relaxing *massage*.

message-n : (a) information, news, request etc. sent to sb in writing, speech, by radio, etc :
We have had a *message* to say that his father is ill.
The ship sent a radio message for help.
(b) statement of political, moral or social significance made by a prophet, writer, book, etc :
This is a film with a *message*.

18. MAST/MUST

mast-n : (a) upright post of wood or metal used to support a ship's sails :
(b) tall pole :
(c) tall steel structure for the aerials of a radio or T.V. transmitter :
(a) indicating obligation :
I *must* go to the bank to get some money.
(b) indicating advice or recommendation :
I *must* ask you not to do that again.
(c) drawing a logical conclusion :
You *must* be hungry after your long walk.
They *must* be twins.
He *must* have known what she wanted.
(d) indicating insistence :
You *must* put your name down for the team.

Note : 1. *Must*, as a noun, means thing that must be done, seen, heard, etc :
Her new novel is a *must* for all lovers of crime fiction.
2. There is another *must*, a noun. It means - grape juice before fermentation has changed it into wine :
Is *must* good for health?

must-v : (modal)

19. MEAD/MID

mead-n : alcoholic drink made from fermented honey and water :
The middle of :
She was here from *mid* April to *mid* August.

20. MEAL/MILL

meal-n : (a) occasion when food is eaten :
He was present at all family *meals*.
Breakfast is the first *meal* of the day.

(b) food eaten on such an occasion :
He eats a big *meal*.
She ate a *meal* of vegetables.

mill-n : (a) machinery or apparatus for grinding grain into flour :
(b) machine for grinding or crushing a solid substance into powder :
(c) building fitted with machinery for processing materials of certain kinds :
He is the owner of a paper *mill*.

21. MEDAL/MEDDLE

medal-n : flat piece of metal which commemorates an event, etc. or is an award to sb for bravery, sporting achievement, etc :
He was awarded a *medal* for meritorious services.

meddle-v : (a) interfere in sth that is not one's concern :
I did not *meddle* in your affairs.
(b) handle sth that one ought not to, or about which one has no specialised knowledge :
He *meddled* with my books.
Don't *meddle* with the electrical wiring; you are not an electrician.

22. MEET/METE

meet-v : (a) come face to face with sb; come together :
Did you *meet* him yesterday?
(b) come together formally for discussion, etc :
The Cabinet *meets* regularly.
The debating society *meets* on Fridays.
(c) experience sth unpleasant; encounter :
He *met* his death five days ago.
(d) be introduced to sb; make acquaintance of sb :
I know Ram by sight, but we have never *met*.
She is an interesting young woman, would you like to *meet* her?
(e) go to a place and await the arrival of a person, train, etc :
Will you *meet* me at the airport?
I shall *meet* your bus.
(f) come into contact with sth; touch; join :
His hand *met* hers.
These trousers will not *meet* round my waish any more.
(g) fulfil a request, demand, etc; satisfy :
I can *meet* her needs.
Can you *meet* all their objections?
(h) pay sth :
I shall *meet* all her expenses.

Note : 1. *Meet*, as an adjective, means suitable; appropriate :
It is not a meet place to live in.
Your remarks were not meet.

2. *Meet*, as a noun, means :
(i) gathering of riders and hounds at a fixed place for fox-hunting :
(ii) sporting contest where many competitors gather :
Did you visit the athletic *meet*?

mete-v : give or administer (punishment, rewards, etc.) :
justice was *meted* out to the offenders.
The magistrate *meted* out severe penalties.

23. METAL/METTLE

metal-n : any of a class of mineral substance, such as iron, gold, etc :
Various *metals* are used to make the parts of this machine.

mettle-n : quality of endurance or courage :
Are you a man of *mettle*?
She showed her *mettle* by winning in spite of her handicap.

24. MIGHT/MITE

might-v : (a) indicating permission :
Might I make a suggestion?
(b) indicating possibility :
He *might* get her in time, I cannot be sure.
This ointment *might* help to clear up your rash.
(c) asking for information :
How long *might* that take?
(d) used to make polite requests or appeals :
You *might* just (i.e. Please) call in at the library for me.

Note : There is another *might*, a noun. It means great strength or power :
Do you fear the military *might* of the enemy?
I pushed the rock with all my *might*.

mite-n : very small or modest contribution or offering :
I offered a *mite* of comfort to her.
Give your *mite* to a good cause.

Note : The term *mite*, an adverb, means somewhat; a little :
This curry is *mite* too hot for me.

25. MINER/MINOR

miner-n : person who works in a mine underground :
People say that you are a *miner*.

minor-adj : smaller, less serious, less important, etc :
He suffered *minor* injuries.
She had a *minor* role in the play.

Note : *Minor*, as a noun, means person under the age of full legal responsibility (18 in India) :
Is your sister a minor?

26. MINISTER/MINSTER

minister-n : (a)a political person at the head of government department or ministry :
Name the Prime *Minister* of Japan.
(b) person, usually of lower rank than an ambassador, representing his government in a foreign country :

Note : There is another *minister*, a verb. It means give active help or service to sb/sth :
Nurses are *ministering* to the needs of the sick and wounded.

minster-n : large or important church :
Tell me the way to York *Minister*.

27. MIXER/MIXTURE

mixer-n : (a) device for mixing things :
It is a cement *mixer*.
(b) person able or unable to mix easily with others :
He is a good *mixer*.

mixture-n : (a) mixing or being mixed :
(b) thing made by mixing :
Give me a cough *mixture*.
The city was a *mixture* of old and new buildings.
(c) (chemistry) combination of two or more substances which do not alter their composition :
Air is a *mixture*, not a compound, of gases.

28. MOAT/MOTE

moat-n : Jeep wide ditch filled with water, dug round a fort, castle, and so on :
The *moat* round the Red Fort is five metres deep.

mote-n : speck; small particle, usually of dust :
Remove *mote* from your coat.

29. MOB/CROWD

mob-n : (a) large disorderly crowd, especially one that has gathered to attack or cause mischief :
The fans rushed onto the pitch in an excited *mob*.
The police faced a *mob* throwing bricks and petrol bombs.
(b) gang of criminals :
Whose *mob* are you with?

crowd : (a) large number of people gathered together in the open :
Police had to break up the *crowd*.
I punished my way through the *crowd*.
A *crowd* had already collected outside the embassy gates.
(b) audience; mass of spectators :
My speech attracted a large *crowd*.
The *crowd* cheered the winning team.
(c) group; company :
I don't associate with the *crowd*.
(d) people in general :
He moved with the *crowd*.

Note : *Crowd*, when used in the sense at (d) above, must be preceded by the definite article *the*.

30. MOD/MODE

mod-n : young person wearing neat and fashionable clothes :
His son is a *mod*.

Note : Mod, as an adjective, means up-to-date and smart in dress.
I found him *mod*.
He is a *mod* young man.

mode-n : (a) way or manner in which sth is done :
Tell me something about the *mode* of his life.
What is the *mode* of transport to get there?
The level of formality determines the precise *mode* of expression.
(b) style or fashion in dothes, art, drama, etc :
What is the latest *mode* of clothes?

31. MODAL/MODEL

modal-n : (in grammar) verb that is used with another verb (not a *modal*) to express possibility, permission, obligation, etc. (can, could, may, might, must, shall, should are a few of the modals) :

Note : *Modal*, as an adjective, denotes relating to mode or manner.
What are the *modal* verbs?

model-n : (a) a small representation of sth original :
This is the *model* of the proposed new airport.

(b) particular design or type of product :
All this year's new *models* are displayed at the motor show.
This is the most popular *model* in our whole range.

(c) pattern; system used as a basis for a copy :
Our constitution provided a *model* that other countries followed.

(d) person or thing regarded as excellent of his/its kind and worth imitating :
His handling of the complicated case showed a *model* of tact.
Are you a *model* student?

(e) person employed to display clothes, hats, etc. to possible customers, by wearing them :
She is one of the country's top *models*.
That is a fashion *model*.

Note : Model, as a verb, means :

(i) take sb/sth as an example for action, plans, etc. :
She *models* herself on her favourite novelist.

(ii) work as a *model*; display clothes etc. by wearing them :
She earns a living by modelling.

32. MOP/MOPE

mop-n : (a) tool consisting of a bundle of thick strings or a piece of sponge fastened to a long handle for clearing floors :
He cleaned the floor with a *mop*.

(b) mass of thick, untidy hair :
Look at the *mop* of her curly red hair.

Note : *Mop*, a verb, is used in the sense of :

1. clean with a mop :
Mop the floor.

2. wipe with a handkerchief to remove sweat, tears, etc :
Mop your brow with a handkerchief.
Mop tears from your face.

mope-v : (a) feel very unhappy :
I always see him moping about.

Note : *Mope*, as a noun, means person who *mopes* :
Stop being a *mope*.

33. MORAL/MORALE

moral-adj : (a) ethical; concerning principles of right and wrong behaviour :
I have strong *moral* fibre.
I challenged his actions on *moral* grounds.
Can you tell me something about the decline of *moral* standards?

(b) based on people's sense of what is right and just :
He had the *moral* courage which enables a man to stand alone.

She showed tremendous *moral* courage.
It is our *moral* obligation to help the earthquake victims.

(c) good or virtuous; following standards of right behaviour :
I lead a *moral* life.
Are you a *moral* person?

(d) teaching or illustrating good behaviour :
This is a *moral* story.

Note : **1.** *Moral*, as a noun, means :

(i) practical lesson that a story, an event or an experience teaches :
What is the *moral* of this story?

(ii) principles of right and wrong; standards of behaviour :
You cannot question my *morals*.
She is a woman of loose *morals*.
Steps should be taken to end the corruption of public *morals*.

2. Morals, plural form of *moral*, must always be used in the sense at (b) above.

morale-n : state of confidence, enthusiasm, determination, etc. of a person or group a t a particular time :
The *morale* of our soldiers was good.
I did my best to boost her *morale*.

34. MYSTIC/MYSTIQUE

mystic : (a) of hidden meaning or spiritual power, especially in religion :
Name a few *mystic* rites and ceremonies.

(b) of or based on mysticism :
Are you a follower of a *mystic* religion?

(c) causing feelings of awe and wonder :
What is *mystic* beauty?

Note : Mystic, as a noun, means person who tries to be united with God, the Greatest, and through that, reach truths beyond human understanding :
Is he a *mystic*?

mystique : quality of sth which is not fully known about or understood but is seen to be admirable or special :
What is the *mystique* surrounding doctors?
She says that there is a certain *mystique* about eating oysters.

14

First Word of Each Group Beginning With-N

1. NAB/NOB

nab-v : catch sb doing wrong; seize :
He was *nabbed* by the police for speeding.
upper class, important or high-ranking person :
He acts as if he is one of the *nobs.*
That lady is truly a *nob.*

Note : There is another *nob,* a noun. It means head :
She hit him on the *nob.*
He has a bald *nob.*

2. NAFF/NAP/NAPE

naff-adj : lacking taste or style; worthless; unfashionable :
Your suit is pretty *naff.*
short sleep, especially during the day :

nap-n : He takes a quick *nap* after lunch.
back part of the neck :
She kissed me on the *nape* of my neck.

3. NATIONAL/NATIONALISTIC

national : of a nation; common to or characteristic of a whole nation :
He sells both *national* and local newspapers.
We must highly value our *national* characteristics.
It made the headlines in the *national* news papers.
Our leaders wear *national* dress to impress the common people.

Note : *National,* as a noun, means citizen of a particular nation :
He is an American *national* working in India.

nationalistic : of or showing great love of one's country :
It is an attempt to arouse *nationalistic* passions against the foreigners.

4. NAUGHTY/KNOTTY/NATTY

naughty : (a) disobedient; bad; causing trouble :
He is a terribly *naughty* child.
Don't be a *naughty* boy.

(b) shocking or intended to shock people through mild indecency :
That was your *naughty* joke.
Don't use *naughty* words.
Is that a *naughty* play?

knotty : (a) difficult; puzzling :
I know how to solve a *knotty* problem.
Answer to his *knotty* question.
(b) (of timber) full of *knots* :
It is *knotty* board.

natty : (a) smart and tidy; neat :
These *natty* new uniforms are for police-women.
Children are fond of *natty* dress.
(b) clever; well thought out :
What is the *natty* solution to her problem?

5. NAVAL/NAVEL

naval-adj : of a navy; of warships :
He is a *naval* officer.

navel-n : in human beings, small hollow in the middle of the belly where the umbilical cord was attached at birth :

6. NAVVY/NAVY

navvy-v : unskilled manual labourer who works on a building site, etc :
He earns his livelihood by working as a *navvy*.
The poor man is only a *navvy*.

navy-n : country's warships and their crews :
There were naval exercises involving five *navies*.
He is an officer in the Indian *Navy*.

7. NEAT/NIT

neat-adj : (a) tidy; done carefully; arranged in an orderly way :
I have small, *neat* writing.
Do you wear *neat* clothes?
This is not a *neat* household.
(b) liking to keep order and do things carefully :
(c) (of clothes) simple and elegant :
Put on a *neat* uniform.
(d) having a pleasing shape or appearance :
Do you have a *neat* figure?
(e) efficient; skilful :
This is the *neat* way of doing the job.
I found a *neat* solution to the problem.

nit-n : (a) egg of a louse or other parasitic insect :
(b) stupid or foolish person :
people say you are a *nit*.

8. NOBBLE/NOBLE/NOVEL

nobble-v : (a) tamper with (a race horse) so that it is less likely to win a race :
(b) influence or get the favour of sb, especially by unfair or illegal means :
He *nobbled* the judge before the trial.
(c) catch (a criminal) :
The police *nobbled* the murder accused.

noble-adj: (a) belonging to the aristocracy by birth or rank :
Are you a man of *noble* birth?
I belong to a family of *noble* descent.

(b) having or showing an excellent character; not petty or mean :
It was *noble* of you to accept a lower salary to help the company.
I highly admire your *noble* sentiments.

(c) splendid; impressive in appearance, size, etc :
She is a woman with a *noble* bearing.
He resides in a *noble* building.

novel-n : book-length story in prose about either imaginary or historical characters :
This is one of his historical *novels*.

Note : There is another *novel*, an adjective, used in the sense of new and strange; of a kind not known before :
I adopted a *novel* method to solve the knotty problem.

9. NOD/NODE

nod-v : (a) move the head down and then up again quickly to show agreement, or as a greeting or command :
She *nodded* to me as she passed.
He *nodded* in agreement.

(b) indicate by *nodding* :
Our chairman *nodded* his approval.
I *nodded* him a welcome.
She *nodded* to me to leave the room.

(c) let one's head fall forward when drowsy or asleep :
The old lady sat *nodding* by the gas fire.

Note : *Nod*, as a noun, means act of *nodding* the head :
I gave her a *nod* as I passed.

node-n : (a) knob on a root or branch :

(b) point on the stem of a plant where a leaf or bud grows out :

(c) hard swelling, e.g., on a joint in the human body :

10. NODDLE/NOODLE

noddle-n : head :

noodle-n : fool :

Note : There is another *noodle*, a noun. It refers to long thin strip made of flour and water, or flour and egg paste, and used in soups, with sauces, and so on :
Chinese food is often served with rice or *noodles*.

11. NOHOW/KNOW-HOW

nohow-adv : in no way; not at all :
He could not fix it *nohow*.

know-how-n : practical knowledge or skill in an activity :
We have the facilities and *know-how* to produce long-range missiles and rockets.

12. NOISY/NOSEY

noisy-adj : (a) making or accompanied by a lot of noise :
I totally dislike *noisy* games.
Take the *noisy* children out of the room.
Don't be so *noisy*.

(b) full of noise :
I cannot remain in a *noisy* classroom even for ten minutes.
I cannot work in here - it is far too *noisy*.

nosey-adj : over-curious; rudely inquisitive :
I have always found her unbearably *nosey.*
Who are you? Don't be so *nosey.*

13. NONE/NUN

none-pron : not one; not any :
He had four parrots - *none* of them is alive now.
None of the guests wants to stay.
None of them has come back yet.
None of the six women members was present at the meeting.

Note : *None,* as an adverb, is used in the sense of :

1. not at all :
After hearing her talk on computers, I am afraid I am *none* the wiser.
He is *none* the worse for falling into the river.

2. not very :
The salary they pay me is *none* too high.

nun-n : woman living in a convent, usually after taking religious vows :
After her husband's health, she became a *nun.*

14. NOOSE/NOSE/NOUS

noose-n : loop in one end of a rope, with a knot that allows the loop to be tightened as the other end of the rope is pulled :
The condemned prisoner is facing the hang man's noose (i.e. is waiting to be hanged).

nose-n : (a) part of the face above the mouth, used for breathing and smelling :
She gave me a punch on the *nose.*
He has a long, thin and sharp *nose.*

(b) sense of smell :
The police have a dog with a good *nose.*

(c) an ability to detect or find sth :
He is a reporter with a *nose* for news.
Do you have a *nose* for scandal?

Note : *Nose,* as a verb, means :

1. go forward slowly; cause sth to go forward slowly :
I *nosed* the car into the garage.
The plane *nosed* into the hanger.

2. pry into or search sth :
Two reporters are *nosing* around for racy news.
Don't *nose* into my affairs.

3. discover sth by searching :
That reporter can *nose* out a news story anywhere.

nous-n : commonsense; resourcefulness :
None of them had the *nous* to shut the door when the fire broke out. You cannot do anything thoroughly unless you possess plenty of *nous.*

15. NOZZLE/NUZZLE

nozzle-n : spour or end piece of a pipe, etc., through which a stream of air or liquid is directed :
Do you need a *nozzle*?

nuzzle-v : press or rub sb/sth gently with the nose :
The horse *nuzzled* his shoulder.
She *nuzzled* my cheek.

16. NUT/NUTS

nut-n :
(a) fruit consisting of a hard shell with a kernel inside it that can be eaten :
Children are fond of chocolate with fruits and *nuts*.
(b) small piece of metal with a hole through the centre, used for screwing onto a bolt to secure it :
(c) head of a person :
She cracked her *nut* on the ceiling.
(d) foolish, eccentric or mad person :
He drives like a *nut* - he will kill himself one day.
(e) person very interested in sth; fanatic :
He is a movie *nut*.

nuts-adj : very much in love with sb; very enthusiastic about sth :
She is very beautiful and attractive. I am *nuts* about her.

17. NYMPHOMANIA/NYMPHOMANIAC

nymphomania : excessive and uncontrollable sexual desire in women :
She is a patient of *nymphomania*.

nymphomaniac : woman suffering from nymphomania :
You must always avoid a *nymphomaniac* woman.

15

First Word of Each Group Beginning With-O

1. OAR/ORE

oar-n : long pole with a flat blade, pulled by hand in order to drive a boat through the water :
Do you now how to pull on *oar*?

ore-n : rock, earth, mineral, etc. from which metal can be obtained :
West Bengal is rich in *ores*.

2. OBJECT/ABJECT

object-n : (a) solid thing that can be seen and tracked :
Where are the plastic *objects*?

(b) person or thing to which sth is done or some feeling or thought is directed :
He is an *object* of pity.
This temple is the main *object* of his interest.

(c) purpose; thing aimed at; intention :
His one *object* in life is to earn as much money as possible.

Note : *Object*, as a verb, means :

1. protest; say that one is not in favour of sb/sth :
I *object* to the plan on the ground that it is too expensive.
I *object* to being treated like this.
2. give sth as a reason for opposing sb/sth :
I *objected* that she was too young for the job.

abject-adj : (a) hopeless; wretched :
He is living in *abject* poverty.

(b) despicable; contemptible; lacking all pride :
You are an *abject* coward.

3. ODD/ADD

odd-adj : (a) strange; unusual; peculiar :
She gets *odder* as she grows older.
He wears rather *odd* clothes.

(b) extra; surplus; left over :
He made a cushion out of *odd* bits of material.

(c) a little more than :
This hall has five hundred *odd* seats.
It will cost you hundred rupees *odd*.

(d) occasional; not regular or fixed :
You shold weed the garden at *odd* times.
Do you have an *odd* minute to help me with this?

add-v : (a) put sth together with sth else so as to increase the size, number, amount, etc :
Many words have been *added* to this edition of the dictionary.
This was an *added* disappointment.

4. OFFICIAL/OFFICIOUS

official-adj : (a) of or concerning a position of authority or trust :
Don't talk about my *official* powers.
I passed orders in my *official* capacity.
(b) said, done, etc. with authority; recognised by authority :
There was an *official* announcement about his appointment as the director general of police.
(c) formal :
The document has been written in an *official* style.
I had to attend an *official* dinner last evening.

Note : *Official* is also used as a noun in the sense of person who holds a public office :
Most of the government *officials* are corrupt as well as inefficient.

officious-adj : too ready or willing to give orders, offer advice, or use one's authority; bossy and interesting :
People are tired of being pushed around by *officious* civil servants.

5. OFFSET/UPSET

offset-v: balance sth; compensate for sth :
He put up his prices to *offset* the increased cost of materials.

Note : There is another *offset*, a noun. It means method of printing in which ink is transferred from a metal plate to a rubber surface and then onto paper :
Offset printing is the order of the day.

upset-v : (a) cause sth to become overturned or spilt :
A large wave *upset* the boat.
(b) disrupt :
Fog *upset* the train timetable.
How were your arrangements for the weekend *upset*?
(c) cause sb to feel distressed :
He was *upset* at not being invited to the dinner.
The sight of physical suffering always *upsets* me.
(d) cause sb to feel ill by disturbing his digestion :
Garlic often *upsets* her stomach.

Note : *Upset*, as a noun, means :

1. upsetting or being upset :
Last minute changes caused a great deal of *upset*.
He had a major emotional *upset*.

2. stomach disorder :
He is in bed with a tummy *upset*.

6. OFFSTAGE/UPSTAGE

offstage : not on the stage; not visible to the audience :
At this point in the play, most of the actors are *offstage*.

upstage : (a) at or towards the back of a theatre stage :
Where is the *upstage* door?

(b) snobbish :
They are much too *upstage* for us.

7. OFT/OPT

oft-adv : often :
It is an *oft*-told tale.
That was an *oft*-repeated warning.

opt-v : choose; decide to do sth :
He *opted* to go to Paris rather than to Cairo.
Fewer students are *opting* for science courses nowadays.

8. OPPOSITE/APPOSITE

opposite : (a) facing; having a position on other side of sb/sth :
You will find the word on the *opposite* page.
Anita and Sunita sat at *opposite* ends of the table.

(b) facing a specified person or thing :
Smoke is coming out of the house *opposite.*

(c) contrary; entirely different :
He turned and walked in the *opposite* direction :

Note : 1. *Opposite,* as a preposition, means :

(i) on the other side of a specific area from sb/sth:
I sat *opposite* to her during the meal.
The bank is *opposite* the post office.
Put the wordrobe in the comer *opposite* the door.

(ii) (of actors) taking part in a play, film, etc. as the partner of sb :
She had always dreamed of appearing *opposite* Hemadri Datta.

2. *Opposite,* as a noun, means word or thing that is as different as possible from sth :
Hot and cold are *opposites.*
Light is the *opposite* of heavy.

apposite : (of a remark, etc.) very appropriate for a purpose or an occasion:
He made an *apposite* comment on our proposal.
I found her speech wholly *apposite* to the current political situation in the country.

9. ORDINAL/CARDINAL

ordinal-adj : (of a number) showing order or position in a series :
I passed the M.A. (English) examination from Kolkata University securing a high first division and standing *first* in order of merit.

Note : *Ordinal* is also treated as a noun :
First, second and third are *ordinals.*

cardinal-n, adj : Whole number representing quantity, e.g. 1,2, 3, etc :

Note : 1. *Cardinal,* as an adjective, means most important; chief; fundamental :
Can you name a few *cardinal* virtues?
What are the *cardinal* facts of the case?

2. There is another *cardinal,* a noun. It means any of a group of senior Roman Catholic priests who elect the Pope :

10. ORDINANCE/ORDNANCE

ordinance-n : order; rule or law made by a government or an authority :
The new government passed many an *ordinance.*
The Government of India is likely to promulgate an *ordinance*, nationalising all steel industries.

ordnance-n : (a) military supplies and materials :
Our *ordnances* are of very high quality.
(b) government service dealing with these :
There are *ordnance* depots in the country, dealing with military supplies and materials.

11. OUTGOING/OUTGOINGS

outgoing-adj : (a) leaving; going out :
The *outgoing* tenant will soon leave for abroad.
(b) leaving office, a political post, etc :
What is the name of the *outgoing* president of your party?
The *outgoing* government did nothing for the poor.
(c) friendly and sociable :
She is very *outgoing.*
He has an *outgoing* personality.
He has never been an *outgoing* kind.

outgoings-n : amount of money spent; expenditure :
What are your monthly *outgoings* on food and rent?

12. OUTWARD/OUTWARDS

outward-adj : (a) (of a journey) going out or away from :
He got lost on the *outward* journey.
(b) of or on the outside :
Don't be deceived by the *outward* appearance of things.
To all *outward* appearances, the child seems very happy.
(c) in, or relating to, one's expressions or actions :
She gives no *outward* signs of the sadness she must feel.
An *outward* show of confidence concealed his nervousness.

outwards-adv: (a) towards the outside :
The two ends of the wire must be bent *outwards.*
(b) away from home or from the point from which one started :
The train is travelling *outwards* from Delhi.

13. OVERHEAD/OVERHEADS

overhead-adj : above one's head; raised above the ground :
Where is the *overhead* railway?
Don't touch the *overhead* wires.

Note : Overhead is also used as an adverb to denote above one's head; in the sky :
Look at the stars *overhead.*
Hundreds of birds are flying *overhead.*

overheads-n : regular expenses involved in running a business, etc :
Heavy *overheads* reduced his profits.
Take suitable steps to reduce your *overheads.*

14. OVERT/COVERT

overt-adj : done or shown openly or publicly; not secret or hidden :
There were *overt* acts of violence during the riot.
There was *overt* hostility between those two young men.

covert-adj : concealed; secret; not open :
Tell me something about the *covert* activities of a spy.
She took offence at your *covert* glances.

Note : There is another *covert*, a noun. It means area of thick low bushes, trees, etc. in which animals, especially hunted animals, hide :

15. OVOID/AVOID: *ALSO REFER TO P. 16*

ovoid-ad : egg-shaped :
I have an *ovoid* table.

Note : *Ovoid*, as a noun, means an egg-shaped object :

avoid-v : (a) keep oneself away from sb/sth:
Don't *avoid* me.
(b) stop sth happening; prevent :
You must always try to *avoid* accidents.

16. OWE/AWE

owe-v : (a) be in debt to sb :
She *owes* me five hundred rupees
He *owes* ten thousand rupees to his father.
(b) recognise sb/sth as the cause or source of sth; be indebted to sb/sth for sth :
I *owe* my success to my wife.
He *owes* his success more to luck than to ability.
(c) be under an obligation to sb; give sth as a duty to sb :
You must *owe* loyalty to your employer.
(d) feel gratitude to sb in return for a service, favour, etc :
I *owe* my teachers and parents a great deal.
He *owes* a lot to his parents and children.

awe-n : feeling of respect combined with fear or wonder :
Her first view of the Taj Mahal at Agra filled her with *awe*.
I lived in *awe* of my father until I was at least twenty.
He always held his parents in *awe*.

Note : *Awe*, as a verb, means fill sb with awe :
Children were *awed* by the solemnity of the occasion.
They were *awed* into silence by the sternness of my voice.

16

First Word of Each Group Beginning With-P

1. PACK/PECK

pack-n: (a) number of things wrapped or tied together for carrying :
He carried his belongings in a *pack* on his back.
(b) group of wild animals that hunt together:
Wolves hunt in *packs*.
(c) group of dogs kept for hunting :
They are a *pack* of thieves.
Your statement is a *pack* of lies.

Note : *Pack*, as a verb, means:
(a) put sth into a container; fill with sth :
Haven't you *packed* your suitcase yet?
Pack these books into a box.
(b) be able to be put into a container for transport or storing :
This dress *packs* easily.
These clothes will not all *pack* into one suitcase.
(c) fill, crowd or cram sth with sb/sth :
This book is *packed* with highly useful information.
Chanting fans *packed* the stadium.

peck-v : (a) strike sth with the beak :
Hens feed by *pecking*.
Birds are *pecking* at the window.
(b) get or make sth by striking with the beak :
The birds *pecked* a hole in the sack.
(c) kiss sb lightly and hurriedly :
She *pecked* me on the cheek.

Note: *Peck*, as a noun, means :
1. stroke made by *pecking* :
2. mark made by *pecking* :
The parrot gave me a sharp *peck* on the finger.
3. hurried kiss :
She gave her aunt a quick *peck* on the cheek.

2. PADDLE/PEDAL/PEDDLE

paddle-n: (a) short oar with a broad blade at one end or both ends, used to move a canoe through the water :
(b) instrument shaped like a *paddle*, used for beating, mixing or stirring food :

Note: **1.** *Paddle*, as a verb, means :
(i) move through the water using a *paddle* :
We *paddled* the canoe slowly upstream.

(ii) row a boat with ligth easy strokes.
We *paddled* from place to place in a canoe.
They were *paddling* a boat in the river.

2. There is another *paddle*, a verb, used in the sense of :

(i) walk with bare feet in shallow water :
He was *paddling* at the water's edge.
It was too cold for *paddling*.

(ii) move feet or hands gently in water :
She *paddled* her toes in the water.

pedal-n : level that drives a machine when pressed down by the foot or feet :

Note : *Pedal*, as a verb, means :

1. use a pedal or *pedals* :
You should *pedal* rapidly to make the machine run smoothly.

2. move by pedalling; ride :
Don't *pedal* fast.
He pedalled along the canal.
Her legs were aching from *pedalling* too fast.

peddle-v : (a) go from house to house to sell goods; be a pedlar :

(b) offer (idea, gossip, etc.) to individual people:
She is in the habbit of *peddling* malicious gossip.
He tried to *peddle* his crazy plan to other party members.

3. PAIL/PALE

pail-n : bucket :
Bring me a *pail* of water.

pale-adj : (a) having little colour; having less colour than usual :
She has a *pale* complexion.
He turned deathly *pale* at the news.
He went *pale* with anger.

(b) not bright or vivid :
She has *pale* blue eyes.

(c) dim, faint :
I left home in the *pale* light of dawn.

Note : **1.** *Pale*, as a verb, means :

(i) become pale :
He *paled* with shock at the news.

(ii) become less important in comparison with sth :
Her beauty *pales* beside her mother.
Their other problems *paled* into insignificance beside this latest catastrophe.

2. There is another *pale*, a noun. It means :

1. pointed piece of wood forming part of a fence; stake :

2. fence or boundary :

4. PAIN/PANE

pain-n : (a) physical suffering or discomfort :
Do you suffer from acute back *pain* ?
He was screaming with *pain*.

(b) mental distress:
His harsh words caused her much *pain*.

(c) annoying or boring person :
She has been complaining again - she is a real *pain*.
We have missed the last bus - what a *pain*?

Note : *Pain*, as a verb, means cause *pain* to sb :
My foot is still *paining* me.
It *pains* me to have to tell you that your father is excessively angry with you.

pane-n : single sheet of glass in a window:
Who has smashed the *pane* in the window?
Clean the window *panes*.

5. PAIR/PARE

Pair-n : (a) two things of the same kind, usually used together :
I need a *pair* of gloves.
(b) object consisting of two parts joined together :
He bought a *pair* of spectacles.
This is a *pair* of scissors.
These trousers cost ₹ 876/- a *pair*.
(c) two persons closely connected or doing sth together :
They are a happy *pair*.

pare-v : (a) Trim sth by cutting away the edges :
Pare your fingernails.
The gardener *pared* the hedge.
(b) cut away the skin or outer covering from sth; peel :
Pare an apple.

6. PAN/PEN

pan-n : (a) wide flat container used for cooking food :
This is a frying *pan*.
(b) amount contained in a *pan* :
Give them a *pan* of hot tea.

pen-n : (a) instrument for writing with ink, consisting of a pointed piece of split metal, a metal ball, etc., fixed into a metal or plastic holder :
This is my fountain *pen*.
(b) writing, especially as a profession :
He lives by his *pen*.

Note : **1.** *Pen* is also used as a verb in the sense of write (a letter, etc.) :
She *penned* a few words of thanks.
I shall *pen* you a letter next week.
2. There is another pen, a noun. It means :
1. small piece of land surrounded by a fence, especially for keeping cattle, sheep, poultry, etc :
This is a cattle *pen*.
2. bomb-proof shelter for submarines :
3. *Pen*, as a verb, means shut sb / sth in, or as if in, a pen :
Pen up the chickens for the night.
She feels *penned* in by her life as a house wife.

7. PANDER/PONDER

pander-v : try to satisfy (a vulgar, weak or immoral desire, or sb having this); gratify sth/ sb :

Newspapers are *pandering* to the public love of scandal.
He *panders* to his children's slightest whims for something.

ponder-v : think about sth carefully, and for a long time, in trying to reach a decision; consider :
You have *pondered* long enough; it is time to decide.
I *pondered* over the incident.
They *pondered* many a things.

8. PANEL/PENAL

panel-n : (a) separate part of the surface of a door, wall, ceiling, etc :
There were glass *panels* in the front door.
This is a ceiling with carved *panels*.
(b) piece of metal forming a section of the body work of a vehicle :
(c) strip of material inserted into a garment:
(d) group of people chosen to take part in a discussion, quiz, etc. with audience :
What were the questions answered by the *panel* of experts ?
(e) list of persons chosen to serve on a jury :
The interviewing *panel* consists of five members.

penal-adj : (a) relating to or used for punishment, especially law :
He was punished according to *penal* laws.
(b) punishable by law :
Theft is a *penal* offence.

9. PAP/PEP

pap-n : (a) soft or semi-liquid food suitable for babies or invalids :
(b) undemanding, trivial or worthless reading matter :
I don't read such *pap*.
Can you bear to read such *pap*?

pap-n : vigour; feeling of liveliness :
He is full of *pep*.

Note :
1. *Pep*, as a verb, means make sb/sth feel more lively or energetic; stimulate sb/sth:
A walk in the fresh air will *pep* you up.
There was a lovely music to *pep* up the party.
2. The expression *pep* talk means talk intended to improve morale, especially by encouraging the listener or listeners to work harder, try to win, etc :
The team was given a *pep* talk on the morning of the big match.

10. PAPER/PEPPER/PAUPER

paper-n : (a) substance made in thin sheets from wood pulp or rags and used for writing, printing, etc :
Give me a sheet of *paper*.
(b) newspaper :
Where is today's *newspaper*?
(c) official documents showing sb's identity, nationality, etc :
Immigration officials will ask to see your *papers*.
(d) pieces of paper which have been written on :
My desk is always covered with *papers*.

(e) set of examination questions on a particular subject :
The geography *paper* was difficult.
Was the Hindi *paper* easy?

(f) written answers to examination questions :
She spent the evening marking examination *papers*.

(g) article or essay read to an audience of academics or specialists :
I read a *paper* at a medical conference on the results of my research.

pepper-n : (a) hot-tasting powder made from the dried berries of certain plants and used for flavouring food :
Give me a dash of *pepper*.

(b) garden plant with large green, yellow or red hollow seed pods; capsicum :
I relish a salad of green *peppers*.

pauper-n : very poor person :
She died *pauper*.
He is a *pauper*.

11. PARCH/PERCH

parch-v : (a) make sth very dry and hot:
It is very difficult to pass through a *parched* desert.

(b) make sb very thirsty:
Give me a glass of cold water - I am *parched*.

perch-n : (a) place where a bird rests:

(b) high seat or position:
I watched the game from my *perch* on top of the wall.

Note : Perch is also used as a verb to denote :

1. (of a bird) come to rest or stay:
The birds *perched* on the television aerial.

2. (of a person) sit on sth high or narrow:
He *perched* on the edges of his seat.
He *perched* dangerously on a high ledge.

3. place sth in a high or dangerous position :
There is a hut *perched* at the edge of the cliff.
He *perched* a beret on the side of his head.

12. PARISH/PERISH

parish-n : area within a diocese, having its own church and clergyman :
He is the vicar of a large rural *parish*.
Are you a *parish* priest?

perish-v : die; be destroyed :
Thousands of people *perished* in the earthquake.

13. PARK/PERK

park-n : (a) public garden or recreation ground :
The children have gone to play in the *park*.

(b) enclosed area of grassland, usually planted with trees :

Note: *Park*, as a verb, means :

1. stop and leave a vehicle in a place for a time:
Where can we *park* the car?
You cannot *park* in this street.

2. leave sb/sth in a place for a time :
Park your luggage here while you buy a ticket.

perk-n : (a) money or goods received as a right in addition to one's pay; perquisite :
His *perks* include a car provided by the firm.
(b) advantage or benefit of a particular job, one's position, etc:
One of the *perks* is the use of the official car park.

14. PARRY/PERRY

parry-v: (a) turn aside or ward off (a blow or an attack) by using one's own weapon or one's hand to block it:
I *parried* his sudden attack.
(b) avoid having to answer sth :
He *parried* the awkward question.

perry-n : drink made from the fermented juice of pears:

15. PARSE/PURSE

parse-v: (a) describe the grammatical form and function of a word, giving its part of speech, case, and so on :
(b) divide a sentence into parts and describe them grammatically:
Do the exercise in *parsing*.

purse-n: (a) small bag for money:
Her *purse* was stolen from her handbag.
(b) sum of money collected and given as a gift or prize :
A *purse* of ten thousand rupees was presented to the winner of the boxing match.

16. PARSON/PERSON

parson-n : (in the Church of England) parish priest; vicar or rector :
Is he a *parson*?

person-n : (a) human being as an individual with distinct characteristics :
You are just the *person* we need for the job.
Here she is - the very *person* we were talking about.
(b) (especially known or unspecified) human being :
A certain *person* told me everything about your character.
Any *person* found leaving rubbish in front of a temple will be severely dealt with.

17. PART/PERT

part-n : (a) some but not all of a thing or number of things :
The early *part* of my life was spent in London.
They spent *part* of their holiday in Kolkata.
Parts of the book are very interesting.
The film is good in *parts*.
(b) distinct part of a human or animal body or of a plant :
What are the delicate *parts* of the body?
Which *part* of your hand hurts?
(c) area or region of a country, town, etc :
Which *parts* of West Bengal have you visited?
Which *part* of Delhi do you come from?
(d) member of sth :
Work as *part* of the team.
We would like you to feel that you are *part* of the family.

(e) division of a book, etc., as much as is published at one time :
The book was published in twenty weekly *parts*.

(f) each of several equal portions of a whole :
Divide the cake into four *parts*.

(g) person's share in an activity; role :
You must do your *part*.
I had no *part* in the decision.

(h) role played by an actor in a film, play, etc :
He played the *part* of Ram.

Note : *Part*, as a verb, is used in the sense of :

1. go away or separate from :
Let us *part* as friends.
She has *parted* from her husband.

2. divide or form separate parts :
Her lips *parted* in a smile.
The crowd *parted* to let us through.
The clouds *parted* and the Sun shone through.

3. separate along a line and comb the hair away from it :
He *parts* his hair in the middle.

pert-adj : (of a girl or young woman) cheeky; not showing respect :
Don't be so *pert*.
Helen is a *pert* young miss.

18. PASSABLE/POSSIBLE

passable : (a) clear of obstructions and therefore able to be driven on :
The mountain roads are not *passable* until late spring.

(b) that can be crossed :
The Yamuna is *passable*.

(c) fairly good but not excellent; adequate :
He possesses a *passable* knowledge of English language.

possible : (a) which can be done :
Come as quickly as *possible*.
It is not humanly *possible* to lift the weight.

(b) which can exist or happen:
Are you insured against all *possible* risks?

(c) which is reasonable or acceptable :
What is the *possible* solution to the dispute?

Note : *Possible*, as a noun, is used in the sense of person who is suitable for selection :
They interviewed twenty persons of whom four were *possibles*.

19. PAST/PASTE/PEST

past-adj : (a) gone by in time:
The time for discussion is *past*.

(b) gone by recently; just finished or ended :
I have seen little of her in the *past* few weeks.
The *past* month has been a difficult one for him.

Note : 1. *Past*, as a noun, denotes :

1. time that has gone by :
I have been there many times in the *past*.

2. things that happened in an earlier time; past events :
Don't regret the *past*.
We cannot change the *past*.
3. person's past life or career, especially one that is discreditable :
We know nothing of his *past*.
She is a woman with a *past*.

2. *Past*, as a preposition, means :
1. after; later than sth :
It is half *past* two.
It is ten *past* eleven.
It was *past* midnight when I got home.
2. older than:
He is an old man *past* seventy.
She is *past* her twenties.
3. on the far side of sth; from one side to the other of sth :
You can see the temple *past* the station.
I walked *past* the school.
He hurried *past* me without stopping.
4. beyond the limits of sth/ doing sth :
It is quite *past* my comprehension.
He is *past* working.
I am *past* caring what she does.
5. beyond the age of sth/ doing sth :
I am *past* playing with dolls.
He is long *past* retirement age.

paste-n : moist soft mixture:
She mixed the flour and water to a *paste*.

Note : *Paste,* as a verb, means put paste on sth :
They *pasted* posters onto the wall.

pest-n : (a) annoying person or thing :
That child is an absolute *pest*.
(b) insect or animal that destroys plants, food, etc :
Those are garden *pests*.

20. PASTOR/PESTER

pastor-n : minister, especially of a non-conformist church :

pester-v : annoy or disturb sb, especially with frequent requests :
Beggars *pestered* him for money.
She *pestered* him with requests for help.
They *pestered* me to join in the scheme.

21. PAT/PET

pat-v : (a) tap sb/sth gently with the open hand or with a flat object :
I *patted* the child on the head.
(b) put sth in the specified position or state by patting :
She *patted* her hair into shape.
He *patted* his face dry with a towel.

Note: 1. *Pat* is also used as a noun in the sense of gentle lap with the open hand or with a flat object :

She gave the child a *pat* on the head.
I gave her an affectionate *pat* on the knee.

2. There is another *pat*, an adverb. It means at once and without hesitation :
His answer came *pat*.

3. *Pat*, as an adjective, means appropriate; exactly right :
I unfailingly gave my *pat* reply.
It is a complex question and her answer was too *pat*.

(a) tame animal or bird kept as a companion and treated with care and affection :
They have many *pets*, including two cats.

(b) person treated as a favourite:
Who is your *pet* ?
She is *pet* of mine.

(c) thing that is given special attention :
What is your *pet* project?

(d) kind or lovable person :
His daughter is a perfect *pet*.
Be a *pet* and post this letter for me.

22. PATROL/PETROL

patrol-v : go round to check that all is secure and orderly or to look for wrongdoers, an enemy or people who need help:
Police *patrol* the streets at night.

Note : *Patrol*, as a noun, means :

1. action of patrolling:
The army make hourly *patrols* of the area.

2. person, group of people, vehicle, etc. that patrols an area:
Where is the police *patrol*?

petrol-n : inflammable liquid obtained from petroleum by a refining process:
There was an increase in the price of *petrol*.
Fill the car up with *petrol*.

23. PATTER/POTTER

patter-n : rapid and often glib speech used by a comedian, conjuror or salesman :
You have to learn to resist the sales *patter*.
He gave the usual *patter* about water-tight boxes.
The conjuror kept up a steady *patter*.

Note : **1.** *Patter*, as a verb, means :

(i) say or repeat (prayers, etc.) in a rapid mechanical way :

(ii) talk quickly or glibly :
Will you please stop *pattering* ?

2. There is another *patter*, a noun. It means sound of quick light steps or taps :
We heard a *patter* of rain on the roof.
Did you hear the *patter* of footsteps on the corridor?

3. This *patter* is also used as a verb in the sense of make sound of quick light taps or steps :
Ram was *pattering* on the window panes.
Dead leaves *pattered* against the walls.
I heard her feet *pattering* about upstairs.

potter-v : Work or move in a leisurely or aimless way :
I love to *potter* in the garden.

Note : *Potter* is also used as a noun in the sense of person who makes earthenware posts by hand :
Is he a *potter*?

24. PAUNCH/PUNCH

paunch-n : fat stomach, especially a man's :
You are getting quite a *paunch*.

punch-n : (a) tool or machine for cutting hole in paper, leather, metal, etc :
(b) tool for forcing nails beneath a surface :
(c) tool for stamping designs on surfaces :

Note : 1. *Punch*, as a verb, means make a hole in sth with a *punch*; perforate sth :
He *punched* a few train tickets.
Punch holes in a sheet of paper.

2. There is another *punch* used as a verb in the sense of strike sb/sth hard with the fist :
I *punched* her on the chin.

3. *Punch*, as a noun, means :
(i) blow given with the fist :
Give him a hard *punch* on the nose.
(ii) ability to give such a blow effectively :
He is a boxer with a strong *punch*.
(iii) effective force or vigour :
She made a speech with plenty of *punch*.

25. PEACE/PEACH/PIECE

peace-n: (a) state of freedom from war or violence :
We should live together in *peace* with one another.
After years of fighting, people longed for *peace*.

(b) period of *peace* :
We want a lasting *peace*.
After a brief *peace*, fighting broke out again.

(c) treaty ending a war:
Peace was signed between the two countries.

(d) state of calm or quiet :
Their activities threaten world *peace*.
For your own *peace* of mind, you should find out what happened.
I just want to be left in *peace*.

peach-n: (a) round juicy fruit with yellowish-red skin and a rough stone:
Those were the best *peaches* I ever tasted.

(b) very attractive young woman :
She is a real *peach*.

(c) sth that is exceptionally good or attractive of its kind :
That was a *peach* of a shot.

piece-n : (a) any of the parts of which sth is made :
The table is made of five *pieces*.
He lost one of the *pieces* of his model engine.

(b) any of the portions into which sth breaks :
The pot shattered into many *pieces*.
He tore the paper to *pieces*.

(c) single instance or example of sth :
She gave me a *piece* of sound advice.
It is a fine *piece* of work.
(d) essay or newspaper article:
Did you read her *piece* in today's paper?
(e) coin:
Give me a five-rupee *piece*.
(f) woman or girl :
She is nice little *piece*.
Do you know the *piece* he was with last night?

26. PEAK/PEEK/PICK/PIQUE

peak-n : (a) pointed top, especially of a mountain :
The plane flew over the snow-covered *peaks*.
(b) the mountain itself :
The climbers made camp half-way of the *peak*.
(c) any shape, edge or part of sth that narrow to a point :
He reached the *peak* of the roof.
(d) the pointed part of a cap :
(e) point of highest intensity, value, achievement, etc :
Traffic reaches a *peak* between 8 and 10 in the morning.
She is at the *peak* of her career.

Note: There is another peak, a verb, used in the sense of reach the highest point or value :
Demand for electricity *peaks* in the evening.
Toy sales *peaked* just before Dussehra, and are now decreasing.

peek-v : look quickly and often secretively at sth :
Don't *peek* at my diary.
He was *peeking* over the wall.

Note: *Peek,* as a noun, means quick, often sly, glance :
He took a *peek* at what was hidden in the cup-board.

pick-v : (a) choose or select sth :
You can *pick* whichever you like.
(b) pluck, gather or remove from the place where they grow :
I bought flowers freshly *picked* from the garden.
(c) remove small pieces of matter from sth in order to clean it :
Pick your nose.
Did you *pick* your teeth today?
(d) remove sth from a surface:
He *picked* the books off the floor.
He *picked* a hair from the collar of his coat.
(e) make a hole in sth:
The child was *picked* a hole in his apron.
(f) take up (grain, etc.) into the bill :
Chickens are *picking* com.
(g) eat in very small amounts or without appetite :
Sparrows *picked* at the crumbs.

Note : There is another *pick,* a noun. It means :

1. choice; right of selecting:
The winner has the first *pick* of the prizes.

2. the best example of sth :
What is the *pick* of the new season's fashions?

pique-v : (a) offend; hurt the pri~e or self-respect of sb :
He was *piqued* to discover that he had not been invited.
She seemed rather *piqued*.
(b) arouse (a person's interest or curiosity) :
Her curiosity was *piqued*.
Note: *Pique*, as a noun, means feeling of hurt or annoyance; resentment:
When he realised nobody was listening to him, he left the room in a fit of *pique*.

27. PEAL/PEEL/PILL

peal-n : (a) loud ringing of a bell or a set of bells with different notes:
(b) loud burst of sound:
She broke into *peals* of laughter.
There was a *peal* of thunder.
Note: *peal*, as a verb, means :
1. sound in a peal :
The nearby temple bells *pealed* a few minutes ago.
2. cause bells to ring or sound loudly :
They *pealed* the bells to celebrate victory.

peel-v : (a) take the skin of :
Peel a banana.
Would you *peel* me an orange?
(b) be removed :
The label will *peel* off if you soak it in water.
(c) cause (skin, etc.) to be removed:
Peel away the outer layer of the wall.
I found her *peeling* potatoes.
(d) have a skin or outer layer come off :
These oranges *peel* easily.
Note : *Peel* is also used as a noun in the sense of outer covering or skin of fruit, vegetables, etc :
Give me some grated lemon *peel*.

pill-n: (a) small ball or flat round piece of medicine made to be swallowed whole:
He has to take six *pills* a day until he recovers.
(b) oral contraceptive; artificial hormone in *pill* form taken regularly to prevent conception:
She has gone on the *pill*.
Note: *Pill*, when used in the sense at
(b) above, must be preceded by the definite article the.

28. PEAR/PEER

pear-n : sweet, juicy yellow or green fruit with a rounded shape that becomes narrower towards the stalk:
Let me taste a *pear*.

peer-n : (a) person who is equal to another in rank, status or merit :
It will not be easy to find his *peer*.
You will be judged by your *peers*.
(b) person who is the same age as another :
He does not spend enough time with his *peers*.

(c) (In Britain) male member of one of the ranks of nobility (e.g. duke, earl, baron, marquis, viscount) : He is a life *peer*.

Note : *Peer,* as a verb, means look closely or carefully:
She *peered* at me over her spectacles.
He was *peering* over the wall.

29. PEARL/PURL

pearl-n : (a) small, hard, round, silver-white or bluish-grey lustrous mass that forms inside the shells of oysters and is of great value as a gem :
Let me have a string of *pearls*.
She was wearing a *pearl* necklace.
(b) very precious or highly valued thing:
She is a *pearl* among women.

purl-n: stitch in knitting that produces ridges on the upper side :
She knitted a sweater in *purl*.

30. PEEP/PIP

peep-v : (a) look quickly and slyly or cautiously at sth :
Don't *peep* at the secret documents.
He was caught *peeping* through the keyhole.
(b) appear through a narrow opening:
Daylight was *peeping* through the curtains.
(c) appear slowly or partly:
The moon *peeped* out from behind the clouds.

Note: 1. *Peep* is also used as a noun to mean short, quick look, especially a secret or sly one:
He had a *peep* through the window.
She took a *peep* at the baby asleep in her cot.
2. There is another *peep,* used as a noun in the sense of short, weak sound made by mice, young birds, etc., squeak:
3. *Peep,* as a verb, means make a *peep* :
short, high-pitched sound used as a time-signal on the radio or telephone; bleep:
At the second *pip,* the time will be 8.45 exactly.
Wait until you hear the *pips* and then put in more money.

Note: There are three others *pips,* all nouns. Each of them has altogether different meanings :

1. pip-n : seed, especially of a lemon, a grape, a pear, an orange or an apple:

2. pip-n : feeling of annoyance or bad temper:
She gives me the *pip*.
His dirty jokes gave everybody the *pip*.

3. pip-n : 1. any of the spots on playing cards, dice and dominoes:
2. star on the shoulder strap of anarmy officer's uniform:

31. PERSONAL/PERSONNEL

personal: (a) of or belonging to a particular person rather than a group or an organisation:
This car is for my *personal* use only.
I made a *personal* donation to the fund.

(b) private; not of one's public or professional life :
Her *personal* life is a mystery to her colleagues.
Please leave us alone-we have something *personal* to discuss.

(c) done or made by a particular person :
The Prime Minister made a *personal* appearance at the function.
I shall give the matter my *personal* attention.

(d) done or made for a particular person :
We offer a *personal* service to our customers.
Will you do it for me as a *personal* favour?

(e) critical of a person's faults:
Try to avoid making *personal* comments.
The argument was becoming too personal.

personnel: people employed in one of the armed forces, a firm or a public office; staff :
Army *personnel* are not allowed to leave the base without permission.
We have advertised for extra security *personnel*.
We had not got the *personnel* to cope with the work.

32. PIER/PYRE

pier-n : (a) structure of wood, iron, etc. built out into the sea, lake, river, etc. so that boats can stop and take in or put down passengers or goods:
(b) one of the pillars supporting an arch or a span of a bridge:

pyre-n: large pile of wood, etc. for burning a dead body as part of a funeral ceremony:

33. PLAIN/PLANE

plain-adj : (a) clear; easy to see, hear, or understand :
The markings along the route are quite *plain*.
He made his annoyance *plain*.

(b) frank and direcet; not trying to deceive:
She gave a *plain* answer to my question.

(c) ordinary and simple; not decorated or luxurious :
He was wearing a *plain* but very elegant dress.

(d) not beautiful or good looking :
Those are a few *plain* bits of furniture.
From a rather *plain* child, she had grown into a beautiful woman.

Note: There is another *plain*, a noun, used to denote large area of flat land; prairie :
There is a vast, grassy *plain* behind the temple.

plane-n : (a) vehicle with wings and one or more engines, which can fly through the air :
We travelled by *plane*.
The *plane* is about to land.
We brought the goods on the *plane*.

(b) any flat or level surface:

(c) surface such that a straight line joining any two points in it touches it at all points :

(d) level of thought, existence or development:
They seem to exitst on a different spiritual *plane*.
This species has reached a higher *plane* of development.

I tried to lift the conversation onto a more elevated *plane*.

Note: Plane is also used as an adjective to mean completely flat; level:
It is very easy to walk on a *plane* surface.

34. PLAIT/PLATE

plait-v : weave or twist (three or more lengths of hair, straw, etc.) under and over one another to make one rope-like length:
She was *plaiting* her hair.

Note : *Plait* is also used as a noun in the sense of form made by plaiting.

plate-n: (a) dish made of earthenwa re of china, from which food is served or eaten:
Where is the dinner *plate*?

(b) contents of a plate :
Give me a *plate* of vegetable soup.

(c) thin, flat sheet of metal, glass, etc :
Those are steel *plates*.

Note: Plate is also used as a verb to denote *cover another metal with a thin layer*, especially of gold or silver:
This is a copper tray *plated* with silver.
These are gold *plated* dishes.

35. POISE/POSE

poise-n: (a) graceful and balanced control of bodily position or movement:
She received me with incredible *poise* for one so young.
He was moving with the assured *poise* of a ballet dancer.
She walks with a good *poise* of the body.

(b) quiet, dignified self-confidence and self-control:
I can safely assert that she is a woman of great *poise*.

Note : *Poise* is also used as a verb in the sense of be or keep sth balanced or suspended:
He *poised* the javelin in his hand before throwing it.
The eagle *poised* in mid-air ready to swoop on prey.

pose-v: (a) sit or stand in a particular position in order to be painted, drawn or photographed:
He had to *pose* wearing a laurel wreath.
The artist asked her to *pose* for him.

(b) behave in an unnatural or affected way in order to impress people:
Step *posing* and tell me what you really think.

(c) claim or pretend to be sb/sth:
She *poses* as an expert on old coins.
The detective *posed* as a mourner at the victim's funeral.

(d) cause sth to arise; create or present:
Winter *poses* particular difficulties for the elderly.
Heavy traffic *poses* a problem in many an old town.

Note: *Pose*, as a noun, denotes:

1. position in which a person poses or its posed.
   She adopted an elegant *pose*.
2. unnatural of affected way of behaving, intended to impress people: His concern for the poor is only a *pose*.

36. POOL/PULL

pool-n: (a) small area of still water:
After the rainstorm, there were *pools* on the roads.
(b) shallow patch of water or other liquid lying on a surface:
The body was lying in a *pool* of blood.
(c) place in a river where the water is deep and there is not much current:

Note: 1. There is another *pool*, a noun, used in the sense of :
(i) common fund of money:
People pay small sums of money each week into football *pools* in the hope of winning a big prize.
(ii) common supply of funds, goods or services which are available to a group of people to be used when needed:
There is a *pool* of cars used by the firm's salesmen.
(iii) group of people available for work when required:
There is a *pool* of doctors available for emergency work.
We have a typing *pool* in the office.
2. *Pool*, as a verb, means put (money, resources, etc.) into a common fund :
They *pooled* their savings and bought a new car.
If we *pool* our ideas, we may find a solution to the problem.

pull-v: (a) use forece on sth in order to move it towards oneself:
You push and I shall *pull*.
(b) use this force on sth; tug :
She *pulled* me by the ears.
(c) draw sth; cause sth to move:
The horse was *pulling* a heavy cart.
Pull your chair up to the table.
Pull the plug out.
(d) remove sth; draw sth out:
He *pulled* a tooth.
(e) attract sb sexually:
He can still *pull* the girls.

Note: *Pull*, as a noun, denotes:
(a) act of pulling; tug:
A *pull* on the rope will make the bell ring.
I felt a *pull* at my sleeve and turned round.
(b) physical force or magnetic attraction found in nature:
The tides depend on the *pull* of the moon.
(c) force that influences a person's behaviour, career, etc :
Tell me something about the *pull* of the wandering life.
(d) influence over the people :
He has a lot of *pull* with the managing director.
(e) action of inhaling smoke from a cigarette, pipe, etc :
She took a long *pull* at her cigarette.
(f) prolonged effort (in walking, etc.) :
It was a long *pull* to the shore.
It was a hard *pull* up to the mountain hut.

37. POVERTY/PUBERTY

poverty-n: (a) state of being poor :
He lives in *poverty*.
She had been worn down by *poverty* and prolonged illness.
(b) scarcity or lack; existing in too small amounts :
His work was criticized for its *poverty* of imagination.
They were handicapped by *poverty* of resources.
(c) poor quality; state of being inferior :
They were recognisable by the *poverty* of their dress.

puberty-n : stage at which a person becomes physically able to become a parent; maturing of the sexual functions :
Have you reached the age of *puberty*?

38. PRACTICE/PRACTISE

practice-n: (a) actual doing of sth :
We should put the plan into *practice*.
His idea did not work in *practice*.
(b) regularly repeated exercise done in order to improve one's skill:
I help her with her music *practice*.
Skating is just a matter of *practice*.
Playing the piano well requires a lot of *practice*.
I began the *practice* of holding regular meetings.
(c) way of doing sth that is common or habitual:
Paying bills promptly is good financial *practice*.
It is the *practice* in India to drive on the left.
(d) thing done regularly; habit or custom:
I had coffee after dinner, as is my usual *practice*.
(e) work of a doctor or lawyer:
She has retired from *practice*.
He is a doctor working in general *practice*.

practise-v: (a) do sth repeatedly or regularly in order to improve one's skill:
I need to *practise* my English before I visit England.
You should *practise* throwing the ball into the net.
(b) make sth part of one's behaviour by doing it regularly:
You should *practise* economy.
(c) work as a doctor or lawyer:
Does he still *practise*?
She *practise* homoeopathic medicine.

39. PRAY/PREY

pray-n : offer thanks, make request known, etc :
We *prayed* for the dying man.
They *prayed* to God for an end to their sufferings.
We *prayed* that she might recover soon.

prey-n : (a) animal, bird, etc. hunted and killed by another for food:
The lion stalked its *prey* through the long grass.
(b) person who is exploited or harmed by another; victim:
She was easy *prey* for dishonest salesmen.

Note: *Prey* is also used as a verb to mean:

1. trouble sb greatly:
Fear of punishment *preyed* on his mind.

2. hunt or catch as prey:
   Hawks were *preying* on small birds.
3. make sb one's victim; exploit or attack :
   A trickster has been *preying* on rich widows for a long time.
   The villagers were *preyed* on by bandits from the hills.

40. PREMIER/PREMIERE

premier-adj : first in importance, position, etc :
Our company has achieved a *premier* position in the electronics field.
They are the *premier* exporters of tea.

Note: There is another *premier,* a noun, used in the sense of Prime Minister:
Can you name the *premier* of Nepal?

premiere-n : first public performance of a play or showing of a film:
The film had its world *premiere* in Kolkata.

Note : *Premiere* is also used as a verb to denote perform a play or show a film to the public for the first time:
The film was *premiered* in Hyderabad.

41. PRESCRIBE/PROSCRIBE

prescribe: (a) advise or order the use of :
Don't exceed the *prescribed* dose.
The doctor *prescribed* some pills to help me sleep.

(b) declare with authority that sth should be done or a rule is to be followed :
The law *prescribes* heavy penalties for this offence.
Army regulations *prescribe* how rifles must be carried.

proscribe: state officially that sth is dangerous or forbidden:
The sale of narcotics is *proscribed* by law.

42. PRINCIPAL/PRINCIPLE

principal-adj: first in rank or importance; chief; main:
What is your *principal* aim in life?
Who are the *principal* members of the government.
The Ganga is one of the *principal* rivers of India.

Note: *Principal* is also used as a noun in the sense of :
1. person with the highest authority in an organisation:
   Who is the *principal* of your college?
2. (finance) money lent or invested on which interest is paid; capital sum:
   You should repay *principal* and interest within seven days.
3. person for whom another acts as his agent:
   I must consult my *principals* before agreeing to your proposal.

principle-n : (a) a truth or belief that is accepted as a base for reasoning or action:
Democracy is based on the *principle* of free speech.
One of the *principles* of this book is that definitions are in simple language.

(b) a moral rule or set of ideas which guides behaviour:
He resigned on a matter of *principle.*
I follow the *principle* that "Prevention is better than cure."

(c) strong belief in, and practice of, honourable behaviour :
Our principal is a man of *principle.*

(d) (a statement of) the way in which natural objects and forces work in the universe, especially as it affects the workings of, e.g. a machine:
Archimedes' *principle* is that "when a body is immersed in a liquid, apparent loss in weight is equal to weight of liquid displaced."
A bicycle and a motorcycle are built on the same *principle.*

43. PRIVATE/PRIVET

private-adj : (a) personal; of, belonging to or for the use of one particular person or group only:
This is my own *private* chair which no one else is allowed to use.
Those fields are *private* property.

(b) secret; not to be revealed to others:
I am not going to tell you about it; it is *private..*
That is my *private* opinion.

(c) not liking to share thoughts and feelings with others:
He is a rather *private* person.

(d) with only a small number of participants:
I would like a *private* chat with you.

(e) quiet and free from intruders:
Let us find some *private* spot where we can discuss the ma tter.

(f) undisturbed by others; alone together:
Let us go upstairs where we can be a bit more *private.*

(g) having no official position or job:
He is acting as a *private* individual in this matter.

(h) not connected with one's work on official position:
People are fascinated by the *private* lives of our politicians.

privet-n: evergreen bush with small leaves and small white flowers, often used for garden hedges:
That is a *privet* hedge.

44. PROBE/PROVE

probe-n : (a) thorough and careful investigation of sth :
There was a *probe* into the disappearance of government funds.

(b) tool for examining a place which cannot be reached otherwise, especially a thin implement with a blunt end used by a doctor for examining a wound.

Note: Probe is also used as a verb. It means :

(a) explore or examine sth with, or as if with, a probe:
He *probed* the swelling anxiously with his finger.
Search lights *probed* the night sky.

(b) investigate or examine sth closely:
She tried to *probe* my mind to find out what I was thinking.
The journalist was *probing* into several financial scandals.

prove-v: (a) show that sth is true or certain by means of argument or evidence:
Prove that he is guilty.
Can you *prove* it to me?
I shall *prove* to you that the witness is not speaking the truth.

(b) turn out to be sth; be seen or found to be sth :
The old methods *proved* best after all.
He *proved* himself to be a better driver than the world champion.
The task *proved* to be more difficult than we had thought.

45. PUT/PUTT

put-v : (a) move sth/sb away from oneself :
She *put* the book on the table.
Did you *put* sugar in my tea ?
She *put* her arm round my shoulders.
Put the baby to bed.

(b) fit or fix sth to sth else :
Put a new lock on the front door.

(c) thrust sth :
I *put* a knife between his ribs :

(d) write on mark sth on sth :
Put your name here.
He *put* his signature to the doucment.

(e) cause sb/sth to be in the specified condition :
Your decision *puts* me in an awkward position.
The incident *put* him in a bad mood.
The injury to his back will *put* him out of action for several weeks.

(f) rate or classify :
I *put* her in the top rank of modem writers.
I don't *put* him among the greatest historians.
As a writer I would *put* him on a par with Ram.

(g) express or state sth :
He *put* it very tactfully.
That was very well *put*.

putt-v: (in golf) hit the ball with a light stroke, so that it rolls across the ground into or nearer to the hole:
You need to practice *putting* the ball.

Note: *Putt* is also used as a noun to denote *putting* stroke:
She took three *putts* from the edge of the green.

46. PUTTEE/PUTTY

puttee-n : long narrow strip of cloth that is wound round the leg from the ankle to the knee for protection and support, especially as part of an army uniform:

putty-n : Soft paste a mixture of chalk powder and linseed oil, which is used for fixing glass in window frames, etc. and becomes hard when it has set:

Note: Putty, as a verb, means fill (a hole, gap, etc.) with putty :
Let him *putty* the hole.

17

First Word of Each Group Beginning With-Q

1. QUAIL/QUELL/COIL

quail-n : small bird, similar to a partridge :

Note : *Quail*, as a verb, means feel or show fear; flinch.
His heart *quailed*.
She *quailed* at the prospect of addressing such a large crowd.

quell-v : put an end to sth; suppress :
The government *quelled* the rebellion.
I *quelled* her fears.

coil-v : wind or twist (oneself/ sth) into a continuous circular or spiral shape :
He *coiled* a length of wire.

Note : *Coil*, as a noun, denotes :

1. length of rope, etc. wound into a series of loops :
   He bought a *coil* of flex.
2. single ring or loop of rope, etc :
   Look at the *coil* of her hair.
3. length of coated wire wound in a spiral to conduct an electric current :

2. QUARK/QUIRK

quark-n : (physics) : any of several very small parts of which elementary particles are thought to consist :
As many as eighteen types of *quark* are possible according to a theory.

quirk-n : (a) habit or action that is peculiar to sb/sth :
He had a strange *quirk* of addressing his wife as Deviji.
One of his *quirks* is sleeping with his socks on.

(b) accident; coincidence :
By a *quirk* of fate, they were in the same plane.
By one of those *quirks* of fate, both died within a few days of each other.

3. QUARRY/QUERY

quarry-n : (a) animal or bird that is being hunted :
The hunters lost sight of their *quarry* in the forest.

(b) person or thing that is being looked for or pursued eagerly:
It took the police several days to track down their *quarry*.

Note : 1. There is another *quarry*, a noun, used in the sense of place where stone, slate, etc. is extracted from the ground :
Thousands of people are working in the local *quarries*.

2. *Quarry* is also used as a verb to mean :
   (i) search with great effort for information, etc :
   He was *quarrying* in old documents for historical evidence.

query-v : (a) ask sb a question or questions :
The minister was *queried* about his plans for the industry.
(b) express doubt about sth :
I *query* whether she can be trusted.
He *queried* the amount charged.

Note : *Query* is also used as a noun to denote question :
He did not answer my *queries*.

4. QUEER/QUIRE

queer-adj: (a) different from what is expected; strange, especially in an unpleasant way :
The curry had a *queer* taste.
His behaviour seemed *queer*.
I think he has gone a bit *queer* in the head.
(b) causing doubt or suspicion :
There is something *queer* about him.
I heard some very *queer* noises in the garden.
(c) unwell; faint :
I woke up feeling rather *queer*.

quire-n : twenty-four sheets of paper :
Shoppeers sell paper by the *quire*.

5. QUIET/QUITE

quiet-adj : (a) with little or no sound; not noisy or loud :
Be *quiet*, please.
Keep the children *quiet*.
(b) with little or no movement or disturbance :
The roads are usually *quiet* in the afternoon.
Business is *quiet* at this time of the year.
(c) without excitement, activity or interruption :
He lives a *quiet* life.
I have a *quiet* evening at home.
Their wedding was very *quiet*.
(d) gentle; not forceful :
She is a lady of a *quiet* disposition.
(e) (of colours) not bright; unobtrusive :
The cloth has a *quiet* shade of blue.
(f) not expressed loudly; restrained :
They had a *quiet* laugh about your dress.
Her manner concealed *quiet* resentment.

Note: *Quiet*, as a noun, means state of being quiet; tranquillity :
They live in peace and *quiet*.

quite-adv: (a) fairly; not very; to some extent:
He plays *quite* well.
She sang *quite* a long song.
(b) completely; entirely:
The theatre was not *quite* full.
I *quite* agree with her.
He has *quite* recovered from his illness.

18

First Word of Each Group Beginning With-R

1. RABBLE/RUBBLE

rabble-n : (a) mob; disorderly crowd:
The police fired tear-gas to disperse the *rabble*.
(b) The common people; the lowest social classes:
Don't hate the *rabble*.

rabble-n : bits of broken stones, rocks or bricks :
The explosion reduced the building to a pile of *rubble*.
This is a road built on a foundation of *rubble*.

2. RACK/RAKE

rack-n : framework for holding things or for hanging things on :
Where is the hat *rack*?
There is another *rack*, a verb, used to mean cause agony to sb:
He was *racked* with fever.
A coughing fit *racked* her whole body.
Her voice was *racked* by sobs.

rack-n : long handled tool with a row of prongs at the end for drawing together fallen leaves, etc :

Note : There is another *rake*, a noun, used in the sense of man, especially a rich and fashionable one, who lives a wild, immoral life :
Too much wealth has made him a total rake.

3. RAFT/RAPT

raft-n : flat floating structure of logs, barrels, etc. tied together, used as a substitute for a boat :
We used a *raft* to cross the river.

Note: 1. *Raft*, as a verb, means carry (people or goods) on a raft :
Who will *raft* us across the river?
2. There is another *raft*, a noun, used to denote large number or amount :
She got a *raft* of presents.

rapt-adj : so intent or absorbed that one is unaware of other things; spellbound:
She listened to me with *rapt* attention.
He was *rapt* in contemplation.

4. RAIN/REIGN/REIN

rain-n : (a) condensed moisture of the atmosphere falling as separate drops; fall of these drops :
Don't go out in the *rain*.
The crops need *rain*.

(b) great number of things falling like a *rain* :
The police fired a *rain* of bullets into the crowd.

Note : *Rain*, as a verb, means :

1. fall as *rain* :
   It *rained* hard all day.
2. fall like *rain* on sb/sth:
   People *rained* blows on the thief.
3. flow or come down in large quantities :
   Tears *rained* down her rosy cheeks.

reign-n : period of rule of a king or queen:
People were very happy during the *reign* of Akbar, the Great.
The revolution was followed by a *reign* of terror.

Note : *Reign*, when used as a verb, denotes :

1. rule; be king, queen or regent:
   The king *reigned* over the country for twenty years.
2. be dominant; prevail :
   Silence *reigned* in her house.
   Peace *reigned* in ancient India.
   Chaos *reigns* supreme in your office.

rein-n: (a) long narrow strap fastened to the bit of a bridle and used to guide and control a horse :
He pulled at the *reins*

(b) means of control:
He assumed the *reins* of government last month.

Note : *Reins*, plural of *rein*, must always be used in the sense at (b) above.

5. RAISE/RAZE/RAZZ

raise-v : (a) cause to rise; lift or move sth to a higher level:
Raise your hand.
She *raised* her hat to me.
He *raised* his eyes from his work.

(b) increase the amount or volume or heighten the level of sth :
I shall *raise* your salary.
Don't *raise* your voice.
You should *raise* standards of service.

(c) cause sth to appear or arise:
Your comments *raised* suspicion in people's minds.
The horses' hooves *raised* a cloud of dust.
Your dirty joke *raised* a blush on her rosy cheeks.

(d) bring sth up for discussion or attention; put forward:
The book *raises* many important issues for our consideration.
I am gald you *raised* that point.

(e) get in contact with sb; find sth :
I cannot *raise* her on the phone.

(f) manage to obtain; bring or collect sth together :
We shall *raise* funds for charity.

(g) bring up (a child, etc) :
He was *raised* by his uncle on a farm.
It is difficult *raising* a family on a small income.

raze-v : destroy (a building, etc.) completely :
Two buildings were *razed* to the ground.

razz-v : ridicule; make fun of sb :
Children were *razzing* the beggar.

6. RAND/REND

rand-n : unit of money in the Republic of South Africa:

rend-v : (a) split; tear sth apart focibly :
Don't *rend* you garments.
The tiger *rends* its prey to pieces.
Loud cries *rend* the air.

(b) pull or wrench sb/sth violently:
Children were *rend* from their mother's arms by the brutal soldiers.

7. RANT/RENT

rant-v : speak loudly, violently or theatrically :
He ranted at me about my mistakes.
This actor *rants* his lines.

rent-n : regular payment made for use of land, premises, telephone, etc; sum paid in this way:
He owes me one month's *rent*.
He is two months behind with the *rent*.
Non-payment of rent can mean eviction.
Rents are going up again.

Note: 1. *Rent* is also used as a verb to denote:
(i) pay for the occupation or use of (land, premises, telephone, etc.) :
We *rented* this house five months ago.
(ii) allow sb to occupy or use :
Will you *rent* me this television?

2. There is another *rent*, a noun, used to mean tom place in cloth, etc; tear; split:
The Sun shone through a *rent* in the clouds.
There is a *rent* in your shirt.

8. RAP/RAPE/WRAP

rap-n : (a) sound of a smart, quickly blow or knock:
There was a *rap* on the door.

(b) chatter; rapid talk :
I don't want to listen to your *rap*.

Note : Rap as a verb, denotes :
1. strike sth quickly and smartly :
She *rapped* my neck.
2. knock or tap lightly and quickly :
He *rapped* on the table and called for silence.
Who *rapped* at the door?
3. rebuke or reproach sb :
I *rapped* him publicly for his indiscreet remarks.
4. talk or chatter rapidly :
She has been *rapping* for a long time.

rape-v : commit the crime of forcing a woman or girl to have sexual intercourse against her will :

Note : 1. *Rape* is also used as a noun in the sense of :

(i) act of raping; being raped:
Is *rape* on the increase?
Her *rape* had a profound psychological effect on her.

(ii) act of violently interfering with sth :
The *rape* of beautiful landscape by developers should be stopped.

2. There is another *rape*, a noun. It means plant grown as food for farm animals and for its seed, from which oil is made :
That is a field of *rape*.
Where is the oilseed *rape*?

wrap-v: (a) cover or enclose sth :
I have *wrapped* the parcels and they are ready to be posted.

(b) wind or fold round sb / sth as covering or protection :
Wrap a scarf round your neck.

9. RAPTURE/RUPTURE

rapture-n : intense delight :
He was gazing in *rapture* at the girl he loved.
His face was shining with *rapture*.

rupture-n: (a) instance of breaking apart or bursting :
The *rupture* of a blood vessel is very harmful.
See if you can open it without suffering a *rupture*.

(b) instance of ending of friendly relations :
There are deep *ruptures* within the party.

(c) (medical) swelling in the abdomen caused when some organ or tissue breaks through the wall of its retaining cavity :

Note: *Rupture*, as a verb, means :

1. break or burst:
He has a *ruptured* spleen.
He *ruptured* himself lifting a heavy box.

2. end :
There is the risk of *rupturing* relations between the two countries.

10. RAT/RATE

rat-n : (a) rodent that looks like, but is larger than, a mouse :

(b) disloyal person, especially one who deserts a cause in times of difficulty :
He has changed sides; he is a dirty *rat*.

(c) unpleasant or despicable man :
People call him a *rat*.

rate-n : (a) standard of reckoning obtained by expressing the quantity or amount of one thing in relation to another :
He can walk at the *rate* of two kilometres an hour.

(b) measure of value, charge or cost:
What is the monthly *rate* of pay of a maid?
Surveys are offered at reasonable *rates*.

(c) speed of movement, change, etc; pace :
At the *rate* you work, you will never finish.
He drives at a dreadful *rate*.
Her pulse *rate* dropped suddenly.
(d) tax on land and buildings paid to local authorities:

Note : There is another *rate*, a verb, used in the sense of :

1. estimate the worth or value of sb/sth :
   She is highly *rated* as a novelist.
   I don't *rate* this play at all.
   What do you *rate* his income at?
2. regard/sb/sth as; consider:
   Do you *rate* me among your friends?
   I *rate* her among my fast friends.
3. value property in order to assess rates:
   This house is *rated* at forty thousand rupees per annum.
4. rank :
   That task *rates* low on my priority list.
5. be worthy of sth; deserve:
   Your joke did not *rate* a laugh.

11. RATIONAL/RATIONALE

rational: (a) able to reason:
Man is a *rational* being.
Are you *rational*?
(b) sensible; not foolish or absurd; reasonable :
What is the *rational* solution to the problem?
Panic destroys *rational* thought.
(c) lucid or sane:
Despite her recent stroke, she is quite *rational*.
No *rational* person would go to work in his pyjamas.

rationale : fundamental reason for or logical basis of sth :
What is the *rationale* behind your decision?
I don't understand the *rationale* of your argument.
We discussed the *rationale* for taking children to the rural area.

12. RAVEL/REVEL/REBEL

ravel-v : separate into threads, become untwisted; fray :
Bind the edge of the rug, so that it may not *ravel*.

revel-v : (a) make merry; celebrate noisily:
They were *revelling* until dawn.
(b) take great delight in sth:
She was *revelling* in her newfound freedom.
They *revel* in wielding power.

Note : *Revel* is also used as a noun to denote noisy celebrations :
We were holding midnight *revels*.

rebel-n : (a) person who fights against, or refuses to serve, the established government:
Do you support the *rebel* forces?
The *rebels* made regular attacks on the railways.
Rebel groups controlled a small mountain area.

(b) person who resists authority or control:
She has always been a bit of a *rebel*.
Is he a *rebel*?

Note : *Rebel* is also used as a verb to denote :

1. fight against or resist the established government :
Don't *rebel* against the government.
2. protest strongly :
He finally *rebelled* against his strict upbringing.
Such treatment would make anyone *rebel*.

13. REACH/RICH

reach-v : (a) stretch out hand in order to touch, grasp or take sth :
I *reached* for my gun.
He *reached* across the table for the jam.

(b) extend to sth; be able to stretch up, out, etc. and touch sth :
My fleet can hardly *reach* the pedals.
Her hair nearly *reached* down to her waist.

(c) communicate with sb, especially by telephone :
I *reached* her at home on 66....
I cannot *reach* him by phone,

(d) achieve sth; attain :
We can never *reach* perfection.
They *reached* a decision about the matter.
YQUwill know better when your *reach* my age.

Note: *Reach* is also used as a noun to denote extent to which a hand, etc. can be stretched out :
He is a boxer with a long *reach*.

rich-n : (a) having much money or property; wealthy:
Are you a *rich* man?
India is a *rich* country?

(b) valuable or expensive; splendid or luxurious :
She was wearing *rich* clothes.

(c) producing or having large supply of sth :
Oranges are *rich* in vitamin C.
India is very *rich* in minerals.
That play is *rich* in humour.

Note : The expression the *rich* means rich people :
Take from the *rich* and give to the poor.

14. READ/REED/RID

read-v : (a) be able to understand the meaning of :
Do you know how to. *read* and write well?

(b) discover or find out about sb/sth by reading :
I *read* about her in today's paper.
I *read* that you had resigned.

(c) study a subject at a school, college, etc :
I *read* for a degree in physics.

(d) interpret; learn the significance of sth :
She tried her best to *read* my mind.
A gypsy *read* my palm.
Doctors can *read* symptoms correctly.
How do you *read* the present political situation in the country?

(e) convey meaning which may not be intended :
Silence must not always be *read* as consent.

(f) have a certain wording:
The sign *reads* keep left.
The Prime Minister's statement *reads* as follows...

(g) give a certain impression :
The story *reads* well.
The poem *reads* like a translation. .

(h) (of corrections in text) replace (one word, etc.) with another :
For neat in line 4, *read* nest.

Note : 1. *Read*, as a noun, means:

(i) period or act of reading:
Can I have a *read* of that timetable?
He had a long *read* of the paper.

(ii) (with an adjective) writer, book, etc, that is interesting to *read* :
This author is a very good *read*.
Your novel is a bad *read*.

2. Read, as an adjective (preceded by an adverb), means having knowledge gained from *read*ing:
She is a well-*read* person.
He is widely *read* in the classics.

reed-n : any of various types of grass-like plants growing near water :

rid-n : make sb / sth free from sb / sth unpleasant or unwanted:
We must do our best to *rid* the country of famine.
Can you *rid* the house of mice?

15. REAM/RIM

ream-n : twenty quires, or 480 (often 500) sheets of paper :

rim-n : (a) edge or border of sth that is approximately circular :
He broke the *rim* of a cup.
This is a pair of spectacles with gold *rims*.

(b) outer edge of a wheel on which the tyre is fitted:

16. REAP/REEF/RIP

reap-v : (a) cut and gather (a crop, etc.) as harvest :
They *reaped* a field of wheat. .

(b) receive sth as a result of one's own or other's actions:
She *reaped* the reward of years of study.
He *reaped* the fruits of his actions.

reef-n : ridge or rock, sand, etc. at or near the surface of the sea :
The ship was wrecked on a coral *reef*.

Note : There is another *reef*, a noun, used to mean part of the top or bottom of a sail that can be rolled or folded to reduce the area exposed to the wind :

rip-v : (a) divide or make a hole in sth by pulling sharply :
I have *ripped* my trousers.
He *ripped* a piece of cloth into two.

(b) open sth by pulling sharply :
I *ripped* open a letter.

(c) (of material) become torn :
Be careful with that dress; it *rips* easily.

Note : Rip, when uses as a noun, means :

1. uneven or ragged tear or cut :
   There is a big *rip* in my sleeve.
2. stretch of rough water in a river or the sea :

17. REEK/RICK

reek-v : (a) smell unpleasantly of sth :
His breath *reeked* of garlic.
Your room *reeked* of cheap perfume.

(b) strongly suggest sth unpleasant or suspicious :
Their actions *reek* of corruption.

Note : *Reek*, as a noun, denotes strong bad smell :
I cannot stand the *reek* of tobacco.

rick-n : large stack of hay, straw, com, etc. which is built up in the open and covered to protect it from rain :

Note : 1 There is another *rick*, a noun, used to denote slight sprain or strain:

2. *Rick*, as a verb, means sprain or strain (a joint, etc.) slightly:
   How did you *rick* your wrist?

18. REFUGE/REFUSE

refuge-n : shelter or protection from danger, trouble, pursuit, etc :
This is a place of *refuge*.
He sought *refuge* from the storm.
Do you seek *refuge* in silence?
Books are a *refuge* of the lonely.

refuse-v : say or show that one is unwilling to give, accept, grant or do sth :
I *refused* to dine with her.
She *refused* his proposal of marriage.
He was *refused* admittance.

Note : *Refuse* is also used as a noun in the sense of waste or worthless material; rubbish:
These are kitchen *refuse*.

19. REST/WREST

rest-v : (a) be still or asleep; stop moving or working :
Lie down and *rest* for an hour after lunch.

(b) (of a look, etc.) be directed steadily at sb/sth:
His eyes *rested* on her face.

(c) (of a subject under discussion) be left without further investigation or pursuit :
The matter cannot *rest* there, I demand an apology.

(d) be burried :
May he *rest* in peace.

Note : 1. *Rest* is also used as a noun in the sense of period of sleep or inactivity as a way of regaining strength :
Take a *rest* from all your hard work.
Sunday is a day of *rest*.

2. There is another *rest*, a noun, used to mean :
   (i) the remaining part; the remainder of some amount:
   Take what you want and throw the *rest* away.
   (ii) the remaining individuals or members; the others:
   Her hat was red, like the *rest* of her clothes.
   While we play tennis, what will the rest of you do?
   He spent the *rest* of his life in prison.
   The *rest* of us were allowed to go home.

wrest-v: (a) take sth away from sb violently:
I *wrested* the gun from his grasp.
Wrest the knife from her.
(b) obtain sth from sb/sth by a hard struggle:
The police *wrested* a confession from the accused.
They are trying to *wrest* control of the firm from me.

20. REVIEW/REVUE

review-n : (a) act of re-examination or re-consideration :
The terms of the contract are subject to review.
(b) report or survey past events or a subject :
Put up the monthly *review* of progress.
(c) published report that assesses the merits of a book, film, etc :
The book got splendid *reviews*.

Note: *Review,* when used as a verb, means :
1. re-examine or reconsider sth :
   The government is *reviewing* the situation.
2. survey; go over past events in one's mind :
   Did you *review* your successes and failures?
3. write a *review* for publication:
   Our book was favourably *reviewed*.
   She *reviews* for The Kolkata Times.

revue-n : theatrical entertainment consisting of a mixture of dialogue, song and dance, especially of a topical and satirical nature:
She acted in a political *revue*.

21. RIFE/RIPE

rife-adj : (a) (of bad things) widespread; common:
This is an area where crime is *rife*.
Bribery and corruption in the government service are *rife*.
(b) full of (sth bad) :
The country was *rife* with rumours of war.

ripe-adj : (a) (of fruit, grain, etc.) ready to be gathered and used, especially for eating:
Are the mangoes *ripe* enough to eat yet?
Harvest the *ripe* com.
The pears are heavy and *ripe*.
(b) (of a person's age) advanced :
He lived to a *ripe* old age.
(c) Ready; fit; prepared:
The land, west of the airport is *ripe* for development.

22. RIGHT/RITE/WRITE

right-adj: (a) morally good; required by law or duty :
Do what is *right* and honourable.
(b) true or correct :
What is the *right* time?
(c) most suitable; best in view of the circumstances:
She is the *right* person for the job.
Are you on the *right* road?
Is this the *right* way to the airport?
(d) complete; real:
She is a *right* old witch.

Note: 1. *Right*, as an adverb, means :
(i) exactly; directly:
She was sitting *right* beside me.
(ii) completely; all the way:
Go *right* to the end of the road.
(iii) correctly; properly; satisfactorily:
Nothing seems to be going *right* for me at the moment:
Have I guessed *right* or wrong?
(iv) immediately:
I must answer that phone, but I shall be *right* back.

2. *Right,* as a noun, denotes:
(i) what is good, just, honourable, etc :
She did *right* to tell me the truth.
Do you know the difference between *right* and wrong?
(b) proper claim to sth, or authority to do sth :
What *right* have you to do that?
(c) thing one may do or have by law:
Everyone has a *right* to a fair trial.

rite-n : religious or some other solemn ceremony:
Everyone performs religious *rites*.

write-v : (a) make letters or other symbols on a surface with a pen or pencil:
Write on both sides of the paper.
Don't *write* in the margin.
(b) (of a pen, pencil, etc.) be capable of being used for writing:
My new pen *writes* well.
(c) work as an author or journalist by *writing* about sth or for a newspaper, etc :
He gave up his job in the factory in order to *write*.
I *write* about politics for a newspaper.
(d) *write* and send a letter to sb :
Write to me often while you are away.
She *wrote* to thank me.

23. RING/WRING

ring-n : (a) small circular band of precious metal worn on the finger :
She was wearing a diamond *ring*.
Where is your engagement *ring*?
(b) combination of people working together, especially secretly :
What has happened to the spy *ring*?

They are a *ring* of dealers controlling prices at an antiques auction.

Note : 1. *Ring* is also used as a verb to mean :

(i) surround sb/sth:
A high fence *ringed* the prison camp.
They were *ringed* about with enemies.

(ii) make a circular mark round sth :
Ring the correct word with your pen.

2. There is another *ring*, a verb, used to denote:

(i) make a clear resonant sound:
Will you answer the telephone if it *rings*?
The buzzer *rang* when the meal was ready.

(ii) cause (a bell, etc.) to sound:
Ring the fire alarm.

(iii) produce a certain effect when heard :
Her words rang hollow.
His story may seem incredible, but it *rang* true.

(iv) make a bell sound to call, warn, etc. sb :
Ring for the maid.
Someone is *ringing* at the door.

(v) telephone sb :
I shall *ring* her tonight.

3. The *ring* (at 2 above) is also used as a noun to mean :

(i) act of *ringing* a bell; sound of a bell :
There was a *ring* at the door.

(ii) loud clear sound:
Did you hear the *ring* of happy voices?

(iii) tone or feeling of a particular kind :
That has a *ring* of truth about it.

(iv) telephone call :
I shall give you a *ring* tomorrow.

wring-v : (a) twist and squeeze sth in order to remove liquid from it :
He *wrung* the clothes before putting them on the line to dry.

(b) remove from sth in this way:
Wring the water out of,your wet bathing costume.

(c) extract or obtain sth from sb with effort or difficulty:
Wring the water out of your wet bathing costume.
I managed to *wring* a promise out of her.

(d) have a deep effect on sb's heart or soul, causin sb to feel great sadness and pity :
The plight of the refugees really *wrung* my heart.

24. RISK/RISQUE

risk-n : (a) possibility of meeting danger or suffering harm, loss, etc :
Is there any *risk* of the bomb exploding?
What are the *risks* of the enterprise?
There is no *risk* of her failing.
Always avoid a task involving a high degree of *risk*.

(b) person or thing insured or represnting a source of risk:
He is a poor *risk*.
All the people, who know their secret, represent a security *risk*.

Note : *Risk* is also used as a verb to denote:
1. expose sb / oneself to danger :
   Don't *risk* your health.
2. accept the possibility of sth :
   Why did you *risk* failure?
   Don't *risk* getting caught in a storm.

risque-adj : (of a story, remark, item of clothing, etc.) slightly indecent :
He took offence at your *risque* remarks.
He was talking in a *risque* manner.

25. ROAST/ROOST

roast-v : (a) cook in an oven, or over or in front of a fire :
Roast some potatoes.
(b) expose sb/sth/oneself to the heat of a fire, the Sun; etc :
We are going to lie in the Sun and *roast* ourselves for one week.
Roast your toes in front of the fire.

roost-n : place where birds perch or settle for sleep :
One of the main *roosts* is on top of the Town Hall.

26. ROB/ROBE/ROVE

rob-v : (a) take illegally:
He was *robbed* of his cash and cheque-book.
He *robbed* her of her share.
(b) deprive sb/sth of what is expected or normal:
Those cats *robbed* me of my sleep.

robe-n : (a) long loose outer garment:
Many Arabs wear long flowing *robes*.
(b) such a garment worn as a sign of rank or office, or for a ceremony:
They were wearing convocation *robes*.
The king was wearing coronation *robes*.

Note: *Robe,* when used as a verb, denotes dress sb / oneself in a robe, etc :
He was *robed* in a ceremonial gown.
The priest was *robed* in his ceremonial dress.

rove-v : roam; wander without intending to reach a particular destination:
Bands of hooligans were *roving* round the streets.

27. ROGUE/ROUGE

rogue-n : (a) dishonest or unprincipled man:
You are not a *rogue*.
They are all cheats and *rogues*.
(b) mischievous person :
He is a charming *rouge*.
(c) wild animal driven or living apart from the herd :
People are scared of the *rogue* elephant.

rouge-n : (a) reddish cosmetic for colouring the cheeks :
Does she use *rouge*?
(b) fine red powder used for polishing metal:
The jeweller bought a packet of *rouge*.

28. ROLE/ROLL

role-n : (a) actor's part in a play:
He plays a variety of *roles*.
She played the leading *role* in the play.
What is the title *role in* the play?

(b) function or importance of sb/sth:
What is the key *role* of the teacher in the learning process?
What is the *role* of the University in modem society?
He had played a major *role* in the formation of the Union Cabinet.

roll-n : (a) cylinder made by turning flexible material over and over on itself without folding it :
Wallpaper is bought in *rolls*.
He sold a *roll* of film.

(b) person or thing with this shape :
He is a man with *rolls* of fat around his stomach.

(c) official list or register, especially of names :
Let me see the electoral *roll*.
The teacher was calling the *roll* in our class.

Note : *Roll*, when used as a verb, denotes :

1. move on wheels or rollers or by turning over and over :
The ball *rolled* down the hill.
The coin fell and *rolled* away.
2. casue sth to move in this way :
Roll it over and look at the other side.
They were *rolling* barrels across a yard.
3. turn on an axis, over and over, or round and round :
He *rolled* his eyes strangely.
He was *rolling* a pencil between his fingers.
4. wrap or cover sb/sth in sth :
He *rolled* himself in his blanket.
5. sway or rock helplessly :
She was *rolling* with laughter.
He was *rolling* drunk.

29. ROOT/ROUTE/ROUT

root-n : (a) part of a plant that keeps it firmly in the soil and absorbs water and food from the soil :
This is a plant with very long *roots*.

(b) family ties, feelings, etc. that attach a person emotionally and culturally to the society or community where he grew up and/or lives or where his ancestors lived :
She has no real *roots* in this area.
They are totally cut off from their peasant *roots*.
People are again searching for their *roots*.
Many Americans have *roots* in Europe.

(c) source or basis:
The *root* of the problem is lack of trust.
Money is often said to be the *root* of all evil.

Note : *Root,* as a verb, denotes:

1. send down *roots* and begin to grow:
   This type of plant *roots* easily.
2. plant sth :
   Root the cuttings in peat.
3. cause sb to stand fixed and unmoving:
   He stood *rooted* to the spot.
   Fear *rooted* him to the spot.
4. establish sth deeply and firmly:
   Her love for me is deeply *rooted.*
   This is a story firmly *rooted* in reality.

route-n : way taken or planned to get from one place to another:
We drove home by a roundabout *route.*

Note : *Route,* as a verb, means send sth by a specified route :
This flight is routed to Kolkata *via* Patna.

rout-n : utter defeat ending in disorder:
After our fourth goal, the match became a *rout.*
The terrified army fled in *rout.*

Note: *Rout,* as a verb, means defeat sb completely; make sb retreat in confusion:
The Prime Minister resigned after his party was *routed* in the election.

19

First Word of Each Group Beginning With-S

1. SAC/SACK

sac-n : bag-like part of an animal or plant:
The honeybee carries honey in a honey *sac*.

sack-v : dismiss sb from a job; fire:
He was *sacked* for incompetence.

Note: 1. Sack, as a noun, means dismissal from a job :
He got the *sack* for petty thieving.
Sack, when used in this sense, must be preceded by the definite article the.

2. There are two other *sacks*, one of which is a noun and the other a verb:
(i) *Sack*, as a noun, means any large bag of strong material used for storing and carrying.
The *sack* split and the rice poured out.
(ii) *Sack*, as a verb, denotes steal or destroy property :
It is wrong to *sack*.

2. SAG/SAGE

sag-v: (a) sink or curve down in the middle under weight or pressure :
The tent began to *sag* as the canvas became wet.
(b) hang loosely and unevenly :
Your skin starts to *sag* as you get older.

Note: Sag, as a noun, means extent to which sth sags; sagging :
There is a *sag* in the seat of the chair.

sage-n: very wise man :
Rabindranath Tagore was a *sage*.

Note : 1. *Sage* is also used as an adjective to mean wise or wiselooking:
He is a *sage* judge.

2. There is another *sage*, a noun, used to mean plant with fragrant, greyish-green leaves used to flavour food :
Do you use *sage* in cooking?

3. SAIL/SALE

sail-n : (a) sheet of canvas spread to catch the wind and drive a ship or boat along:
Hoist the *sails*.
(b) voyage or excursion on water for pleasure :
They went for a *sail*.

Note : *Sail*, as a verb, means:
1. travel on water in a ship, yacht, etc. using *sails* or engine power :
They were *sailing* along the coast.

2. begin a voyage :
   When does the ship *sail*?
3. be able to control :
   She *sails* her own boat.

sale-n : (a) selling or being sold:
The money was raised by the *sale* of lottery tickets.
(b) act of selling sth :
He gets hundred rupees commission on each *sale*.
He has not made a *sale* all week.
(c) demand; desire to buy goods:
They found no sale for their goods.

4. SALLY/SULLY

sally-n : (a) sudden breaking out by troops who are surrounded by the enemy :
Our soldiers made a successful *sally*.
(b) lively or witty remark, as a good-humoured attack on sb / sth:
The laughter with which his *sallies* were greeted excited him.

sully-v : make sth dirty; stain; ruin or destroy (sb's reputation, etc.) :
I shall never *sully* my hands by accepting a bribe.
Don't *sully* your reputation by doing something wrong.

5. SALON/SALOON

salon-n : place where customers go to see a hairdresser, beauty consultant, etc :
He has gone to a hair-dressing *salon*.

saloon-n : (a) public room on a ship, in a hotel, etc :
I am going to the ship's dining *saloon*.
(b) public room or building for a specified purpose :
Do you visit a billiard *saloon*?

6. SATIRE/SATYR

satire-n : (a) attacking foolish or wicked behaviour by making fun of it :
Is there too much *satire* on T.V.?
The book contains exquisite touches of irony and *satire*.
That is a work of bitter *satire*.
(b) piece of writing, play, film, etc. that makes fun of foolish or wicked behaviour in this way:
Her novel is a *satire* on social snobbery.
It is a brilliant political *satire*.

satyr-n : (a) (in Greek and Roman myths) God of the woods, half man and half goat :
(b) man with very strong, sexual desire:
Is he a *satyr*?

7. SAVORY/SAVOURY

savory : herb of the mint family used in cooking :
Do you use *savory*?

savoury: (a) (of food) having a salty or sharp flavour, not a sweet one:
He is fond of *savoury* food dishes.
Do you want a *savoury* pancake?

(b) morally wholesome or respectable:
Her past life was not altogether *savoury*.

Note: *Savoury*, in the sense at above, is usually used in negative sentences.

8. SCARF/SCURF

scarf-n : piece of material worn for ornament or warmth round the neck, or (by women) over the shoulders or hair :
Where is your *scarf*?
The girl wrapped her woollen *scarf* tightly round her neck.

scurf-n : flakes of dead skin on the scalp; dandruff :
Clean your hair that is free of *scurf*.
Two monkeys were searching each other's fur for *scurf*.

9. SCENE/SCENERY

scene-n : (a) place of an actual or imagined event:
He visited the *scene* of the accident.
The *scene* of my novel is set in Kashmir.

(b) situation or incident in real life :
Did you see the horrific *scenes* after the earthquake?
There were hilarious *scenes* when a horse ran into the shop.

(c) outburst of emotion or anger:
There was quite a *scene* when she refused to pay.
Don't make a *scene*.

(d) sequence of continuous action in a play, film, etc :
The *scene* in the hospital was very moving.

(e) place represented on the stage of a theatre:
The first *scene* of the play is the Rashtrapati Bhawan.
The *scenes* were changed during the interval.

(f) view as seen by a spectator:
The boats in the Dal Lake, Srinagar, make a beautiful *scene*.

scenery-n: (a) general natural features of an area:
We stopped to admire the mountain *scenery*.

(b) furniture, woodwork, canvas, etc. used on a theatre stage to represent the place of action :
Who designed the *scenery*?

10. SCOOP/SCOPE

scoop-n : (a) deep shovel-like tool used for picking up and moving grain, flour, sugar, and other things :
The buckets on the dredger *scoop* up mud from the river bottom and dump it in a barge.

(b) piece of news made public by a newspaper, radio station, etc. before its rivals :
He got all the big *scoops* for the paper.

Note : *Scoop*, as a verb, means :

1. make (a hole, etc.) with, as if with, a *scoop*.
   He *scooped* a hole in the sand.
2. act before (a rival, etc.) to get a *scoop*:
   She *scooped* all the national newspapers to get the story.

scope-n : (a) opportunity to do or achieve sth :
He secured a job with a lot of *scope* for prospects.
This is a house with some *scope* for improvement.
(b) range of matters being dealt with, studied, etc :
This subject is outside the *scope* of our inquiry.

11. SCRAP/SCRAPE

scrap-n : (a) fragment; small piece :
He buys and sells *scraps* of paper, cloth, and so on.
Only a few *scraps* of news about the disaster have emerged.
(b) small amount of sth :
There is not a *scrap* of truth in her claim.
(c) items of left-over food :
Give the *scraps* to the beggar.

Note : 1. *Scrap*, in the sense at (b) above, is usually used in negative sentences.
2. *Scraps*, plural of scrap, must be used in the sense at (c) above.
3. *Scrap*, as a verb, means throwaway:
He scrapped an old car.
Lack of cash forced us to *scrap* plans for a new house.
4. There is another *scrap*, a noun, tomean fight; quarrel:
He got into a *scrap* with two strangers.
She had a *scrap* with her mother.
5. The *scrap* at 4 above is also used as a verb in the sense of fight; quarrel :
He was always *scrapping* at school.

scrape-v : make clean, level or smooth by drawing a sharp tool or sth rough across a surface, etc :
The maid *scraped* the floor with a stiff brush.
He *scraped* the walls clean.

Note : There is another *scrape*, a noun, used to mean:
(a) act or sound of *scraping*:
Did you hear the clink and *scrape* of knives and forks?
(b) awkward situation caused by foolish behaviour or by not thinking carefully:
She is always getting into *scrapes*.
Don't expect me to get you out of your *scrapes*.

12. SEAM/SEEM

seam-n : line along which two edges are joined or sewn together:
He was searching for a lost coin in the *seams* of his trousers.

seem-v : appear; or give the impression or appearance of being or doing sth:
She *seems* happy.
Do whatever *seems* best.
He *seems* to be right.

13. SEAR/SEER

sear-v : (a) scorch or burn a surface:
This is a cloth *seared* by the heat of the oven.
Sear the wound to prevent infection.

(b) affect sb with strong emotion :
His soul had been *seared* by injustice.
This novel is a *searing* indictment of abject poverty.

seer-n : person claiming to see into the future:
St. Aurobindo was a *seer*.

14. SEAT/SIT

seat-n : (a) thing made or used for sitting on :
She rose from her *seat* to welcome me.
(b) place where one pays to sit in a vehicle or in a theatre etc:
There are no *seats* left on the flight.
Book four seats for the concert.
(c) place where sth is based, or where an activity is carried on :
In India, Delhi is the *seat* of government.

Note : *Seat*, as a verb, denotes:
1. make sb/oneself sit:
I seated the girl next to her mother.
Ladies and gentlemen, please be seated.
I seated myself on the sofa.
2. have seats for (a specified number of people) :
This is a hall that *seats* 567 persons.

sit-v : (a) be in a position in which the body is upright and resting on the buttocks, either on a seat or on the ground :
Please *sit* on a chair.
(b) (of clothes) fit the body well:
The dress *sits* well on her.
The coat *sits* badly across the shoulders.
(c) be a candidate for (an examination) :
He will *sit* for a test tomorrow.

15. SECRET/SECRETE

secret-adj: (a) not known by other; kept or intended to be kept from the knowledge or view of others:
He escaped through a *secret* door.
That party was given *secret* financial support by some foreign backers.
(b) not openly declared or admitted :
He is a *secret* fan of soap operas on T.V.
(c) secluded or quiet :
I have a secret cottage in the rural area.

Note : *Secret* is also used as a noun in the sense of :
(a) fact, decision, etc. that is or must be kept *secret* :
Can you keep a *secret*?
I shall tell you a *secret*.
She has made no *secret* of the fact that she wants a job.
He made no *secret* of his dislike for me.
(b) method of doing sth or achieving sth that not many people know :
What is the *secret* of your tremendous success?
(c) anything not properly understood or difficult to understand; mystery:
Do you know the *secrets* of nature?

secrete-v: (a) (of an organ); produce either as waste material or for use within the body :
The kidneys *secrete* urine.
Saliva is *secreted* by glands in the mouth.
(b) put or keep sth in a secret place; hide:
He *secreted* money in a drawer.

16. SEED/CEDE : ***ALSO REFER TO P. 57.***

seed-n : part of a plant from which a new plant of the same kind can grow :
Sow a row of *seeds*.
He bought a packet of sunflower seeds.

cede-v : give up one's rights to, or possession of, sth :
A third of their territory was *ceded* to France.

17. SEEK/SICK

seek-v : (a) look for sth; try to find or obtain sth :
We *sought* long and hard but found no answer to the question.
They are *seeking* for solutions to the problems.
Let us *seek* shelter from the rain.
(b) try to reach; move towards sth :
The flood started and we had to *seek* higher ground.
Water *seeks* it own level.
(c) ask sb for sth:
She sought my advice.
You must *seek* permission from the manager.
(d) try; attempt to do sth :
Don't *seek* to mislead me.
Seek to bring the conflict to an end.

sick-adj : (a) ill; physically or mentally unwell :
She has been *sick* for over two weeks.
(b) likely to vomit; nauseous:
He is feeling *sick*.
He has a *sick* feeling in the stomach.
Flying always makes me feel *sick*.

Note : *Sick* is also used as a noun to mean:
1. vomit :
The basin was full of *sick*.
2. People who are ill :
He visited the *sick* in hospital.
All the *sick* and wounded have been sent to hospital.

18. SEEP/SIP

seep-v : flow slowly and in small quantities through a substance:
Water was *seeping* through the roof the house.
Oil is *seeping* out through a crack in the tank.

sip-v : drink sth, taking very small quantities each time :
Sip your coffee.
Have you *sipped* your tea?

19. SEIZE/SIEGE/CEASE

seize-v : (a) take told of sth suddenly and violently; grab :
He *seized* the money-bag and ran off.

(b) take stolen goods, illegal drugs, etc. away from sb :
A large quality of heroin was *seized* by the customs at the Delhi airport a few days ago.
(c) capture sth; take:
The army has *seized* power.
(d) see an opportunity, etc. and make use ofiteagerly and atonce :
He *seized* the chance the make some money.
(e) affect sb suddenly and overwhelmingly :
Panic seized us.

siege-n : (a) surrounding of a town, fortress, etc. by armed forces in order to capture it or force it to surrender:
By the time the *siege* ended, the citizens were nearly starving.
(b) surrounding by police, etc. of a building in which people are living or hiding:
The police began a *siege* of that big building.

cease-v : stop; come or bring sth to an end:
That department has *ceased* to exist.

20. SERF/SURF

serf-n : (a) person forced by a landowner to work on the land in a feudal system :
(b) worker treated harshly or like a slave:
In ancient times, a *serf* was forced to work on his lord's land, almost as a slave.

surf-n : waves breaking on the seashore:
They were splashing about in the *surf*.

21. SERGE/SURGE

serge-n : strong woollen cloth used for making suits :
He was wearing a suit made of *serge*.

surge-v : (a) move forward in or like waves :
The floods *surged* along the valley.
The crowd *surged* into the stadium.
(b) arise suddenly and intensely:
Anger *surged* within her.
Hope *surged* in him.

Note : Surge is also used as a noun to denote:
1. forward or upward movement:
Did you ever see the *surge* of the sea?
2. sudden occurrence or increase :
There is a *surge* in electricity demand at around 7 p.m.
She felt a *surge* of affection for me.
A *surge* of activity spread through the party.
There has been a *surge* in sale of our books.

22. SESSION/CESSION: ALSO REFER TO P. 57

session-n : (a) meeting or series of meetings or a Parliament, law court, etc. for discussing or deciding sth :
I shall not attend the autumn *session* of Parliament.
(b) school or college year:
(c) single continuous period spent in one activity :
He was present at the jazz *session*.

cession-n : action of ceding sth, especially land or rights :
We shall never agree the *cession* of even an inch of our territory.

23. SEVER/SEVERE

sever-n : (a) divide or break or separate sth by cutting :
Sever the rope, if you can't untie the knot.
His hand was *severed* from his arm.

(b) end; break off :
He has severed his connection with the firm.
Don't *sever* relations with her.

(c) break:
The rope severed under the strain.

severe-adj : (a) strict or harsh in attitude or treatment; imposing stern discipline:
The dacoit was awarded *severe*, punishment by the judge.
You should be severe with your children.
The magistrate was very *severe* on the thief.

(b) very bad, intense, difficult, etc :
He had a *severe* attack of toothache.

(c) demanding great skill, ability, patience, etc :
That was a *severe* test of the climbers' stamina.
There was a *severe* competition for admission to colleges.

(d) of style, appearance, clothing, etc :
His plain black dress was too *severe* for such a cheerful occasion.

24. SHAD/SHADE

sham-n : large edible fish:

shade-n : (a) comparative darkness caused by the cutting off of direct rays of light:
The trees give a pleasant *shade*.
Let us sit in the *shade* of the tree.

(b) slight difference in sth :
This is a word with many shades of meaning.
There are people with all shades of opinion.

Note : Shade, as a verb, denotes:

1. give *shade* to sb/sth:
She *shaded* her eyes from the Sun with her hand.
2. screen to reduce brightness:
Shade the bulb with a dark cloth.

25. SHAM/SHAME

sham-n : (a) person who pretends to be what he is not:
He claims to know all about computers but really he is a *sham*.

(b) thing, feeling, etc. that is not what one pretends it to be:
Her love was a *sham*; she really wanted his money.

(c) pretence:
What he says is all *sham*.

Note :
1. *Sham*, as a verb, means pretend sth; feign :
He *shammed* illness.
2. *Sham*, as an adjective, means pretended; not genuine:
He showed *sham* jewellery.

shame-n : (a) painful feeling caused by wrong, dishonourable, improper or ridiculous behaviour :
He felt *shame* at having told a lie.
You should hang your head in *shame*.
(b) ability to feel *shame*:
He is completely without shame.
(c) dishonour:
He brought *shame* on himself by doing something unworthy.
(d) person or thing that causes shame or is unworthy.
It is a *shame* to take money from those who can not afford it.

Note : *Shame*, as a verb, means :
(a) cause sb to feel *shame*:
He was *shamed* by how much more work the others had done.
(b) bring *shame* upon sb; dishonour :
You have *shamed* your family.
It is quite *shaming* that our society cares so little for the poor.

26. SHEAF/SHEEP/SHIP

sheaf-n : (a) bundle of stalks of corn, barley etc. tied together after reaping:
(b) bundle of papers, etc. laid lengthwise and often tied together:
Remove the *sheaves* of paper from here.

sheep-n : grass-eating animal with a thick fleecy coat, kept in flocks :
He has a flock of *sheep*.

ship-n : large vessel carrying people or goods by sea:
He boarded a *ship* for Bombay.
They were sent home by *ship*.

27. SHEAR/SHEER

Shear-v : (a) cut the wool off a sheep with *shears*:
It is the *sheep-shearing* time.
He *sheared* fifty *sheep*.
(b) become twisted or break under pressure :
The bolt *sheared* and the wheel came off.

sheer-adj : (a) complete; thorough; utter:
It was a *sheer* waste of time.
What you say is *sheer* nonsense.
Many of the audience walked out through *sheer* boredom.
(b) thin, light and almost transparent :
She was wearing clothes made of *sheer* nylon.

28. SHEEN/SHIN

sheen-n : shiny quality; gleaming brightness:
She has hair with a glossy, golden *sheen*.

shin-n : front part of the leg below the knee:
He got kicked on the *shin*.
She kicked my *shin*.

29. SHEET/SHIT

sheet-n : (a) large rectangular piece of cotton, linen, etc. usually used in pairs between which a person sleeps.
Put clean *sheets* on the bed.

(b) broad thin piece of any material:
Give me a *sheet* of glass.

(c) piece of paper for writing or printing on :
She gave me a *sheet* of plain paper.
Put a fresh *sheet* in the typewriter.

(d) wide expanse (of water, ice, snow, etc.) :
The rain came down in *sheets*.
After the heavy frost, the road was a *sheet* of ice.

Note : There is another sheet, a noun, used in the sense of rope or chain fastened to the lower comer of a sail to hold it and control the angle at which it is set :
Do you need a sheet?

shit-n : (a) stupid remarks or writing; nonsense :
You always talk a load of *shit*.

(b) contemptible person :
That little *shit* stole my money.

(c) waste matter from the bowels.

30. SHINGLE/SINGLE .

shingle-n : (a) small, flat, square or oblong piece of wood used as a covering on roofs and walls :

(b) small wooden signboard put up outside the office of doctor, dentist, etc :

Note : There is another *shingle*, a noun, used to mean small rounded pebbles on the sea-shore:
The beach is a mixture of sand and *shingle*.

single-adj: (a) one only; not in pair, group etc :
There is a single apple hanging from the tree.
We heard a *single* shot.
I just could not think of a single thing to say to her.

(b) separate; considered on its own:
What is the *single* most important event in the history of India since the middle of the year, 1975?
She removed every single thing from the box.

(c) not married:
Only *single* women are allowed to visit us.

(d) designed for; or used or done by one person:
Give me a *single* sheet.
Reserve one *single* and one double room.

31. SIGHT/SITE/CITE: ALSO REFER TO P. 61

sight-n : (a) ability to see; vision:
I have very good *sight*.

(b) action of seeing sb/sth:
We laughed at the *sight* of his strange clothes.

(c) range within which sb can see or sth can be seen:
The plane crashed out of our *sight*.
Get out of my *sight*.

site-n : (a) place where a building, town, etc. was, is, or will be situated:
This is the *site* for a hospital.

(b) place where sth has happened or will happen, or fora particular activity :
This is the *site* of the battle of Panipat.

cite-v : (a) mentionsth as an example or to support an argument; refer to :
Can you *cite* an example in support of your statement?
(b) speak or write; quote :
I *cited* a verse from a poem by Tennyson.

32. SIGN/SINE

sign-n : (a) mark, symbol, etc. used to represent sth :
These are mathematical *signs*.
(b) board, notice, etc. that directs sb towards sth, gives a warning, advertises a business, etc :
Look at the traffic *signs*.
Look out for a *sign* to the motorway.
(c) gesture or movement made with the hand, head, etc. to give informanation, a command, etc :
She gave us a *sign* to leave the room.
(d) thing that shows that sb/sth is present or exists, or that sth may happen :
There were *signs* of suffering on his face.
There are some *signs* of improvement in his work.
He shows no *sign* of being interested.

Note : There is another *sign*, a verb, used to mean :
1. write one's name on a document, etc :
He *signed* the document.
Sign your name here.
2. convey information or a request or an order by making a gesture:
The policeman *signed* them to stop.
She *signed* me to be quiet.

sine-n : (mathematics) (in a right-angled triangle) the ratio of the length of the side opposite one of the acute angles to the length of the hypotenuse:

33. SING/SINGE

sing-v: (a) make musical sounds with the voice:
Do you *sing* well?
Birds were *singing* away happily outside.
She *sang* me a very good song.
He *sang* the baby to sleep.
Will you *sing* a song for me?
(b) make a humming, buzzing or whistling sound:
The kettle was *singing* on the cooker.

singe-v: blacken sth by burning; scorch:
She did not notice that she had *singed* her gown.
The iron is too hot, you will *singe* the dress.

34. SLANDER/SLENDER

slander-n : false statement intended to damage sb's reputation:
I shall sue her for *slander*.

Note : *Slander* is also used as a verb in the sense of utter *slander* about somebody:
She *slandered* him behind his back.
Did you *slander* her?

slender-adj : (a) not very wide but comparatively long or high :
She has slender fingers.
Do you have a slender waist?
(b) slim:
Who is that *slender* girl?
She is a *slender*, graceful ballet-dancer.
(c) small in amount or size; inadequate; scanty :
I won the election by a *slender* margin.
He earns a *slender* income.
Those persons are of *slender* means.

35. SLAT/SLATE

slat-n : long thin narrow piece of wood, metal or plastic :

slate-n : (a) type of blue-grey rock that splits easily into thin flat layers:
Slate is ofen used for covering roofs.
(b) small sheet of *slate* in a wooden frame used by school children for writing on :
In rural areas slate is still used in schools.

Note : Slate is also used as a verb in the sense of :
1. propose sb (for an office, appointment, etc.) :
He is *slated* for the Presidency.
2. plan that sth will happen at a specified time:
The meeting is *slated* to take place on Friday.
I shall attend the meeting slated for Tuesday.
(c) criticize sb / sth severely:
They *slated* the film.
The proposal got *slated* by the committee.

36. SLEEK/SLICK

sleek-adj : (a) smooth and glossy: My sister has *sleek* hair.
(b) (of a person) looking well-fed and prosperous :
Who is that sleek man?
They were all fat and *sleek*, and too pleased with themselves.
(c) well-styled:
I have a *sleek*, shiny sports car.

slick-adj : (a) done smoothly and efficiently :
That was a *slick* translation of the story.
She gave a *slick* excuse for staying away from duty.
(b) doing things in a *slick* way :
He is a *slick* negotiator.
She is very *slick* but I don't believe a word she says.
(c) smooth and slippery:
The roads were *slick* with wet mud.

37. SLEEP/SLIP

sleep-n : (a) condition that occurs regularly in humans and animals in which the eyes are closed and the muscles, nervous system, etc. are relaxed :

He did not get much *sleep*.
How many hours' *sleep* do you need?
(b) substance that gathers in the comers of the eyes during sleep:
Wash the *sleep* out of your eyes.

slip-n : (a) false step; act of slipping:
One *slip* and you could fall off the cliff.
(b) minor error:
There were a few trivial *slips* in the translation.
(c) thin or small piece of paper:
Where in my salary *slip*?
I wrote her phone number on a *slip* of paper.

Note : *Slip* is also used as a verb to denote :
1. slide accidentally: lose balance and fall or nearly fall.
She *slipped* on the snow and broke her leg.
(b) slide accidently out of its proper position:
The razor *slipped* and cut my cheek.

38. SLEET/SLIT

sleet-n : falling snow or hail mixed with rain :
There were showers of *sleet* last evening.

slit-n : long narrow cut, tear or opening:
Put the letter through the *slit* of the letter-box.
There is a long *slit* in her saree.
Slit, as a verb, denotes make a *slit* in sth by cutting; open sth by slitting :
Dacoits *slit* his throat.
I *slit* the envelope open.
The tailor *slit* cloth into strips.

39. SLIM/SLIME

slim-adj: (a) slender; not fat or thick:
She is trying to get *slim*.
Do you have a *slim* waist?
I saw a tall, *slim* girl with long, straight hair.
(b) not as big as one would like or expect; small :
He has *slim* prospects of success.
He was condemned on the *slimmest* of evidence.

Note : Slim, as a verb, means eat less, take exercise, etc. in order to lose weight and become *slim*:
Try to get fit and *slim*.
I may be *slimming* but I have no intentions of starving myself.

slime-n : (a) thick soft slippery liquid substance, especially mud:
There was a coating of *slime* on the unwashed sink.
(b) sticky liquid produced by snails, slugs, etc :
Keep off the trail of *slime*.

40. SLOP/SLOPE

slop-v : (a) spill over the edge of a container :
I dropped the bucket, and water *slopped* out of it.
The tea *slopped* into the saucer.
(b) cause sth to spill :
She *slopped* the dirty water into the grass.

slope-n : (a) slanting line :
I rode up a grassy *slope*.
Can you run on the *slope* of the roof?
(b) area of rising or falling ground :
Let us go to the mountain *slopes*.
Note : *Slope*, as a verb, means have a *slope*; slant :
Does your handwriting *slope* forwards or backwards?
The fields *slopes* to the west.
The garden *slopes* towards the river.

41. SLOT/SLOTH

slot-n : (a) narrow opening through which sth can be put:
Put a 50 p coin in the *slot*.
(b) slit, groove or channel into which sth fits or along which sth slides:
The curtain hooks run along a *slot* in the curtain rail.
Ther is a *slot* on a dashboard for a car radio.
(c) position for sb/sth :
He found a *slot* for a talk on the political situation in the country.
sloth-n : laziness; idleness :
You must overcome your habitual *sloth*.

42. SNEAK/SNICK

sneak-adj: (a) (used by children) tell an adult about faults, wrongdoings, etc. of another child :
He sneaked on his best friend to the teacher.
(b) take sth secretly :
She *sneaked* my pen.
He *sneaked* a look at the Deepawali presents.
Note : Sneak, when used as a noun, means cowardly, deceitful person:
That man looks like a *sneak*.
snick-v : make a small cut or notch in sth :
I *snicked* my finger on the sharp knife.

43. SNIFF/SNIP

sniff-v : (a) draw air in through the nose, so that there is sound:
They all had colds and were *sniffing* and sneezing.
(b) draw air in through the nose to discover or enjoy the smell of sth :
He was *sniffing* at a rose.
Note : Sniff is also used as a noun in the sense of act or sound of sniffing; breath of air, etc :
He got a *sniff* fresh air.
She gave a bitter sniff.
"I am going," she said with a *sniff*.
One sniff of this is enough to kill you.
snip-v : (a) cut sth sharply in short quick strokes:
He *snipped* a stray lock of hair.
He *snipped* energetically at the hedge.
(b) remove sth with short quick strokes:
I *snipped* off a few loose threads.
Snip the corner of the carton of milk.

Note : *Snip*, as a noun, means:
1. cut made by *snipping*:
There is a *snip* in this cloth.
2. small piece cut off by *snipping*:
Many *snips* of material scattered over the floor.
3. act of *snipping*:
With a few quick *snips* of the shears, he pruned the bush.
4. surprisingly cheap article; bargain :
It is a *snip* at only five rupees.

44. SOAP/SOP

soap-n : substance used for washing and cleaning, made of fat or oil combined with an alkali :
Use plenty of *soap* and water.
thing offered to a displeased or troublesome person to calm him or win his favour :
I offered a new pen as a *sop* to her anger.
The child was given a prize as a *sop* to his disappointed parents.

45. SOAR/SORE/SOUR

soar-v : (a) go up high in the air quickly :
The jet *soared* into the air.
(b) rise rapidly:
Prices are *soaring*.

sore-adj : (a) aching; tender and painful; hunting when touched or used:
He has a *sore* throat.
My leg still very sore.
(b) irritated: hurt and angry:
I feel *sore* about not being invited to dinner.
She is still *sore* at me.
(c) serious; severe:
They are in *sore* need of financial help.

sour-adj : (a) having a sharp taste (like that of a lemon, etc.) :
This apple is really *sour*.
(b) tasting or smelling sharp and unpleasant; not fresh :
The milk has turned *sour*.
(c) having or *showing* a bad temper :
He is a *sour* and disillusioned man.
What a *sour* face she has?

Note: *Sour* is also used as a verb to denote cause sb/sth to become *sour* :
The hot weather *soured* the milk.
The old man has been *soured* by abject poverty.

46. SOLDER/SOLDIER

solder-n : soft mixture of metals used, when melted, for joining harder metals, wires, etc. together :
The solder thing is to use *solder* on them.

soldier-n : member of an army, especially one who is not an officer :
He is a *soldier* in the army.

47. SOLE/SOUL

sole-adj : (a) single; one and only :
They went with the *sole* purpose of making a nuisance of themselves.
What was the *sole* cause of the accident?
He is the *sale* survivor of the plane crash.

(b) not shared; belonging to or restricted to one person or group :
I have the *sole* responsibility for bringing up the child.
We have the *sole* right to sell this range of goods.
I acquired *sole* control of the newspaper last month.

Note : There is another *sole,* a noun, used to mean :

1. bottom surface of the human foot, the part on which one walks and stands.
2. part of a shoe, sock, etc. covering this :
There are holes in the *soles* of his socks.
The *soles* of his boots needed repairing.

soul-n : (a) spiritual or non-material part of a person, believed to exist after death :
I commend your *soul* to God, the Greatest.
Do you believe in the immortality of the *soul*?

(b) decency and honesty of feeling; emotional, moral and intellectual energy :
Are you a girl without a soul?
That was a very polished performance, but with-out soul.
This music has no *soul.*

(c) perfect example:
She is the *soul* of honour.

(d) person :
There was not a *soul* to be seen.
Don't tell a *soul.*

48. SOON/SWOON

soon-adv : (a) within a short time:
I shall *soon* be home.
They *soon* got there.
She will be here very *soon.*

(b) early; quickly :
How *soon* can you be ready?
He will be here *sooner* than your expect.
The sooner you begin, the *sooner* you will finish.
The sooner you leave, the *sooner* you will be home.

swoon-v : (a) faint; lose consciousness:
She *swooned* into my arms for joy.

(b) be emotionally affected by sb/sth:
All the girls are *swooning* over the new manager.

49. SOOT/SUIT/SUITE

soot-n : black powder in the smoke of wood, coal, etc :
Sweep the *soot* out of the chimney.
One small fire in the kitchen covered the whole house in *soot.*

suit-v : (a) look attractive on sb :
That colour does not *suit* your complexion.
Will this skirt *suit* her?
(b) be convenient for or acceptable to sb :
Will Friday *suit* you?
Would it *suit* you to come at five?
(c) be right or beneficial for sb/sth:
This climate does not *suit* me.
Very spicy food does not *suit* her stomach.

Note : There is another suit used as a noun in the sense of :
1. set of outer garments of the same material:
He was wearing a three piece suit.
He bought a business *suit*.
2. set of clothing for a particular activity :
Do you need a diving *suit*?

suite-n : (a) set of rooms in a hotel:
This is a honeymoon suite.
They always stayed in a *suite* at the Ashoka Hotel.
(b) set of matching pieces of furniture for a sitting room, etc :
He bought a three-piece *suite* for the lounge.
I need a dining room *suite*.

50. SOUP/SWOOP

soup-n : liquid food made by cooking vegetable, etc. in water:
Would you like to have tomato *soup*?
There is a range of tinned *soups* in the shop.

Note : The idiom in the *soup* means in trouble or difficulties.
If your wife finds out what you have done, you will really be in the *soup*.

swoop-v : (a) come down suddenly with a rushing movement :
The eagle *swooped* down on its prey.
The soldiers *swooped* down on the bandits.
Detectives *swooped* on the house at dawn.
(b) seize or match the whole of sth in one movement :
The robber *swooped* up the bank notes.

Note : *Swoop* is also used as a noun to denote sudden and unexpected attack :
The police made a dawn *swoop* on the den of thieves.

51. SPACIOUS/SPECIOUS

spacious-adj : having or providing much space; roomy :
It is a very *spacious* kitchen.
We have a *spacious* drawing room.

specious-adj : seeming right or true but actually wrong or false:
I don't agree with your *specious* argument.

52. SPAR/SPARE/SPUR

spar-v : (a) box sb using light blows for practice only :
(b) argue or dispute with sb in a friendly way :
Those two girls were *sparing* with each other.

spare-v : (a) refrain from hurting, harming or destroying sb/sth; show mercy to :
Dacoits killed the men but *spared* the children.
(b) refrain from using, giving, etc. sth; use as little as possible:
No trouble was *spared* to ensure our comfort.
(c) be able to afford to give:
Can you *spare* me hundred rupees?
She *spared* me a few minutes of her time.
Can you *spare* a cigarette for me?
(d) manage sb :
I cannot spare you for that job; you must finish this one first.

Note : There is another *spare,*an adjective, used to mean :
1. in addition to what is usually needed :
We have no *spare* room for a table.
Do you carry a *spare* wheel in your car?
I have no *spare* money this month.
2. free; unoccupied:
She is a busy woman with little *spare* time.
He paints in his *spare* time.
3. (of people) thin; lean:
He is a tall *spare* man.
4. small in quantity :
I am on a *spare* diet.
He had a *spare* meal.

Note : The idiom go *spare* means become very annoyed or upset ;
Your father will go *spare* if he finds out that you have lost two thousand rupees.

spur-n : (a) either of a pair of sharp-toothed wheels, worn on the heels of a rider's boots and used to make a horse go faster :
Where is the pair of *spurs*?
(b) incentive; thing that urges a person to greater activity :
What is the spur to greater efficiency?
International competition was a spur to modernisation.

Note : Spur is also used as a verb to denote :
1. strongly encourage sb/sth to do better, achieve more, etc.; incite or stimulate sb/sth :
I was spurred on by ambition.
2. make a horse go faster by prickling it with *spurs*:

53. SPAT/SPATE

spat-n : small or unimportant quarrel :
That was a *spat* between brother and sister.

spate-n : sudden fast rush (of business, etc.) :
There was a *spate* of orders for small cars.
The incident caused another *spate* of protests.

54. SPATIAL/SPECIAL

spatial-adj : concerning size, area or position :
What are the *spatial* qualities of the new concert hall?

special-adj : (a) not common, usual or general; of a particular or certain type:
She is a very *special* friend of mine.
What are your *special* interests?

He did it as a *special* favour.

(b) designed, reserved or arranged, etc. for a particular purpose :
You will need a *special* tool to do that.
She has her *special* way of doing things.
Newspapers send *special* correspondents to places where important events take place.

(c) exceptional in amount, degree, quality, etc :
Take special care of it.
He takes no *special* trouble with his work.
Why should I give you *special* treatment?

Note: *Special* is also used as a noun to denote person or thing that is not of the regular or usual type :
There was an all night television *special* on the election.
Specials were brought in to help the regular police force.

55. SPIN/SPINE

spin-v : (a) make sth turn round and round rapidly:
He *spun* the wheel of his bicycle.
Spin the ball.
They *spun* a coin to decide who should start.

(b) Move round and round rapidly :
The revolving sign was *spinning* round and round in the wind.
The collision sent the ear *spinning* across the road.

(c) make yam from wool, cotton, silk, etc:
She spins goat's hair into wool.
He spins wool from goat's hair.

spine-n : (a) row of bones along the back of humans and some animals; backbone :
He sustained an injury to his *spine* when he fell off his horse.

(b) back part of the cover of a book, where the pages are joined together.
The book has a large *spine*.

56. SPIT/SPITE

spit-v : (a) send out from the mouth:
He was *spitting* blood after being hit in the mouth.
The child took one sip of the tea and *spat* it out.

(b) send saliva from the mouth:
Don't *spit* in public.
He is inclined to *spit* when he talks quickly.

(c) send saliva from the mouth as a sign of anger or contempt:
She *spat* on his face.

(d) utter sth violently or forcefully:
She *spat* curses at him.

(e) make a noise like spitting to show anger:
He walked off *spitting* with fury.

(f) rain lightly :
It is not raining heavily any more, but it is still *spitting* a bit.

spite-n : desire to hurt, annoy or offend another person, ill will :
He said it out of *spite*.
She has a *spite* against me.

Note : *Spite,* as a verb, means annoy, offend or injure somebody because of *spite*:
He plays his radio loudly every evening just to *spite* us.
Don't do anything to *spite* your neighbours.

57. STAFF/STUFF

staff-n : (a) strong stick or pole used as a support when walking or as a symbol of authority or sign of office:
The old man leant on a long wooden *staff.*
(b) group of assistants working together in an office, a business, etc. responsible to a manager or person in authority :
We need more *staff* in the office.
I have a *staff* of forty.

Note: *Staff,* when used as a verb, means provide sth with *staff;* act as a *staff* for:
This is a *well-staffed* hotel.
There is nobody to staff the office today.
The school is *staffed* entirely by post-graduates.

stuff-n : (a) material of which sth is made:
We must find out what stuff he is made of.
Real life is the *stuff* of all good novels.
What *stuff* is this jacket made of?
(b) unnamed things, belongings, activities, subject matter, etc:
Leave your *stuff* in the hall.
That novel is really boring *stuff*

Note: *Stuff,* when used as a verb, means :
1. fill sth tightly with sth; cram sth with sth :
He *stuffed* a pillow with feathers.
Stuff up the hole with newspapers.
My nose is *stuffed* up.
2. put sth quickly and carelessly:
She *stuffed* the coins into her pocket.
He *stuffed* the letter through the door and hurried away.
3. fill sb/oneself with food; eat greedily:
I am *stuffed.*
He sat *stuffing* himself with biscuits.

58. STAMP/STUMP

stamp-n : (a) small piece of paper with an official design on it, stuck on an envelope or a document, etc :
This is a book of postage *stamps.*
He bought a 50 p *stamp.*
(b) instrument with which a design, mark, etc. is *stamped* on a surface:
Where is the rubber *stamp*?
(c) design, word/words, etc. made by *stamping* on a surface:
Have you got any stamps in your passport?
(d) act of sound of *stamping* with the foot:
He gave a *stamp* of impatience.
(e) characteristic mark or quality:
She bears the *stamp* of genius.

His face bears the *stamp* of suffering.
His story has the *stamp* of truth.

(f) kind; class; sort:
They are men of a different *stamps*.

Note: *Stamp*, as a verb, denotes:

1. put foot down heavily on the ground:
He *stamped* his foot in anger.
2. walk with loud heavy steps:
He *stamped* out of the room.
I *stamped* upstairs.
3. mark with an official seal, a design, etc :
They did not *stamp* my passport.
The librarian forgot to *stamp* my library books.
Stamp your name and address on the envelop.

stump-n : (a) part of a tree left in the ground after the rest has fallen or been cut down :

(b) anything similar that remains after the main part has been cut or broken off, worn down :
This is the *stump* of the cigar.

Note : Stump, as a verb, means :

1. walk stiffly or noisily :
He *stumped* out in fury.
They *stumped* up the stairs.
2. puzzle; be too difficult for sb :
I am *stumped* : I just do not know what to do.
Everybody was *stumped* by the problem.

59. STARE/STAIR

stare-v : (a) look with the eyes wide open in a fixed gaze :
Don't *stare* at old women.
They all *stared* in amazement.
Do you like being stared at?

(b) bring or force sb into a specified condition by staring :
I *stared* her into silence.

Note : Stare, as a noun, denotes long fixed gaze; *staring* look :
I gave him a rude stare.
We received a number of curious stares from the passers by.

stair-n : (a) anyone of a series of fixed steps from one floor of a building to another :
I passed her on the *stairs*.
The *stairs* need cleaning.

(b) anyone of these steps:
The child was sitting on the bottom *stair*.

60. STATIONARY/STATIONERY

stationary: (a) not moving :
The car collided with a *stationary* van.

(b) that cannot be moved or is not intended to be moved :
Where is the *stationary crane*?
The vehicle remained stationary.

stationery: writing materials, such as paper, pens, envelopes, etc :
He runs a *stationery* shop in a school.

61. STEAD/STEED

stead-n : instead of sb/sth :
I cannot attend the meeting but I shall send my assistant in my *stead.*

steed-n : horse : This is my trusty *steed.*

62. STEAL/STEEL/STILL

steal-v : (a) take sth dishonestly; take secretly without permission or legal right :
It is wrong to *steal.*
He stole from the rich to give to the poor.

(b) obtain sth quickly or steadily:
He *stole* a few minutes sleep.
I *stole* a kiss from her.
He *stole* a glance at the girl in the mirror.

(c) move secretly and quietly, or without being noticed:
She *stole* into my room.
A tear *stole* down her rosy cheek.

(a) strong, hard alloy of iron and carbon:
It is made of *steel.*

(b) industry that produces steel; production of *steel* :
Where are the steel mills?

Note : 1. The idiom of steel means of great strength :
He is a man of *steel.*

2. Steel, as a verb, means make oneself, one's heart, etc. hard or strong in preparation for sth :
I have bad news for you, so *steel* yourself.
He had to *steel* his heart against pity.
Steel yourself for a shock.

still-adj : (a) quiet and clam; without movement or sound :
Look at the *still* water of the pond.
Stand *still* while I take your photograph.

(b) without wind :
It was a *still* day after a stormy night.

Note : 1. *Still,* as a noun, means single photograph of a scene from a cinema or film :
These are *stills* from a new film.

2. Still, as a verb, denotes make or become calm or at rest :
The waves *stilled.*
He could not *still* his anxiety.

3. *Still,* as an adverb, means:

(i) up to and including the present time or the time mentioned:
He is still busy.
He still hopes for a letter from her.
Do you *still* live in Kolkata?
Will you *still* be here when I get back?

(ii) in spite of that; even so; nevertheless:
Although he felt ill, he *still* went to work.

(iii) in a greater amount or degree; even:
Ram is tall, but Shyam is taller *still.*

(iv) besides; in addition :

He came up with *still* more stories.

4. There is another *still*, a noun, used to denote apparatus for making alcoholic liquor by distilling :

63. STIFF/STEEP

stiff-adj : (a) not easily bent, folded, moved, changed in shape, etc :
Give me a sheet of *stiff* cardboard.

(b) not liquid; thick and hard to stir:
Stir the flour and milk to a stiff paste.

(c) difficult; hard to do :
That was a *stiff* test.

(d) formal in manner, behaviour, etc.; not friendly:
Their manner *was* rather stiff.
Her teller was stiff and formal.

(e) severe; tough:
Competition is very *stiff*.
The judge imposed a *stiff* sentence.

Note : Stiff is also used as an adverb in the sense of to an extreme degree; very much:
They were worried *stiff*.
The film bored him *stiff*.
We were scared stiff of meeting him.

steep-adj : (a) rising or falling sharply, not gradually :
He could not reach the steep roof of the house.
I always avoid a steep path.

(b) excessive; unreasonable; too much:
There is likely to be a steep increase in unemployment.
I shall not pay seventy thousand rupees for your old car, it is too steep.

Note : There is another steep, a verb, used to mean:

1. soak sth thoroughly in liquid in order to soften, clean or flavour:
   Steep onions in vinegar.
2. pervade or fill sth thoroughly with sth; give one-self/sb a thorough knowledge of sth :
   They are *steeped* in ignorance.
   It is a city *steeped* in history.
   She is an erudite scholar *steeped* in the literature of ancient India.

64. STOREY/STORY

storey-n : floor; section of a building with rooms all at the same level :
We have a house of two *storeys*.
She lives on the fourth *storey* of a block of flats.
He has a *five-storey* building.

story-n : (a) account of past events, incidents, etc :
These are the *stories* of ancient India.

(b) account of invented or imagined events, etc :
Tell me a fairy *story*.
The play is really a love *story*.

My mother always used to tell us bed time *stories*.
Can you narrate an adventure *story* for children?

(c) report of an item of news in a newspaper; article:
Did you like the front-page *story*?

(d) event, situation or material suitable for this :
That will make a good *story*.

(e) untrue statement, description, etc.
Don't tell *stories*.

65. STRAIGHT/STRAIT

Straight-adj :

(a) without a bend or curve; extending or moving continuously in one direction only:
Draw a *straight* line.

(b) tidy; correct; arrange in proper order :
It took hours to get the house straight.

(c) Properly *positioned*; level or upright; parallel to sth else:
Put the picture straight.

(d) honest; truthful:
Give a *straight* answer to a *straight* question.
I don't think you are being *straight* with me.
Let us have some *straight* talking.

(e) accurate and without additions; not modified or elaborate:
Tell me a *straight* story.

Note : 1. *Straight* is also used as a noun in the sense of :
(a) conventional person :
(b) heterosexual person :
Every human being is a *straight*.

2. There is another *straight*, an adverb. It means :
(a) honestly and frankly; in a straightforward manner:
I told him *straight* that I did not like him.
(b) by a direct route; without delay or hesitation :
Come *straight* home.
He went *straight* to Chennai, Without stopping in Hyderabad.
(c) directly; in a *straight* line.
Sit up *straight*.
Look *straight* ahead.
He was too weak to walk *straight*.

Strait-n : narrows passage of water connecting two seas or two large areas of water :
Where is the *Straits* of Gibraltar?

Note: 1. Strait is often used in the plural form with singular meaning :
2. The word *straits* is in the plural form. It means trouble; difficulty:
He is in financial *straits*.

66. SUPER/SUPPER

super-adj : excellent; splendid:
He was wearing a *super* dress.
I like her, she is *super*.

supper-n : last meal of the day:
I eat very little *supper*.
What will you like to have for *supper*?
Don't have a late *supper*.

67. SURELY/SURLY

surely-adv : (a) without doubt; certainly:
He will *surely* fail.
This will *surely* cause problems.
(b) certain of what one is saying, or to express surprise at sth:
This is *surely* her best play.
Surely, I have met you before somewhere.

surly-adj : bed-tempered and unfriendly:
Don't look so *surly*.
He is a *surly* person.

68. SYMBOL/CYMBAL : ALSO REFER TO P. 77

symbol-n : emblem; image, object, etc. tha t suggests or refers to sth else :
What is the *symbol* of courage?
What is a peace *symbol*?

cymbol-n : one of a pair of round grass plates struck together or hit with a stick to produce a clanging sound :

69. SYMMETRY/CEMETERY

symmetry-n : (a) exact match in size and shape between the two halves of sth :
Look at the perfect *symmetry* of the building.
(b) pleasingly regular way in which parts are arranged:
The *symmetry* of the Taj Mahal is immensely pleasing to the eyes.

cemetery-n : place where dead people are buried :

20

First Word of Each Group Beginning With-T

1. TAIL/TALE

tail-n : (a) movable part at the end of the body of a bird, an animal, a fish, etc :
Dogs wag their *tails* when they are pleased.
(b) thing like a *tail* in its shape or position:
Can you see the *tail* of the procession?
Look at the *tail* of the aircraft.
(c) buttocks :
I gave her a smack on the *tail.*
(d) person following or watching sb without being seen by him :
Put a *tail* on the suspicious-looking man.

tale-n : (a) narrative or story :
Tell me fairy *tales.*
He narrated a *tale* of adventure.
(b) report spread by gossip, often false or invented :
I have heard some old *tales* about her.
She is in the habit of telling all sorts of *tales.*

2. TALL/TOLL

tall-adj : (a) of more than average height; higher than surrounding objects :
She is *tall* for her age.
He is *taller* than me.
That is a *tall* tree.
(b) of a specified height :
Champa is six feet *tall.*

toll-n : (a) money paid for the use of a road, bridge, etc :
(b) loss or damage caused by sth :
The earthquake took a heavy *toll* of human life.

3. TAMPER/TEMPER

tamper-v : meddle of intefere with; alter sth without authority :
The records of the meeting had been *tampered* with.
Some one has been *tampering* with the lock.

temper-n : (a) state of the mind as regards anger of calmness :
She was in a bad *temper.*
(b) tendency to become angry easily :
He has a short *temper.*
Learn to control your *temper.*
He flew into a *temper.*
I slapped her in a fit of *temper.*

Note: *Temper* is also used as a verb to mean:

1. moderate or soften the effects of sth; mitigate sth :
   Judges should *temper* justice with mercy.
2. bring to the required degree of hardness and elasticity by heating and then cooling:
   Do you want *tempered* steel?

4. TAP/TAPE

tap-n : (a) device or controlling flow of liquid or gas out of a pipe, etc :
Do you have hot and cold *taps*?
Turn the *tap* on.
Don't leave the *taps* running.
He turned the *tap* off.

(b) act of *tapping* a telephone or connection for doing this:
The intelligence bureau put a tap on his telephone.

Note : 1. *Tap*, as a verb, denotes:

(i) extract or obtain sth from sth/ sb :
Vast mineral wealth is waiting to be *tapped*.
Find out new ways of *tapping* the skills of young people.

(ii) fit a listening device to (a telophone line) :
I think my phone is being *tapped*.

2. (i) There is another *tap*, a noun, used to mean sound of a quick light blow :
She gave gentle *taps* on my shoulder.
I heard a *tap* on the door.

(ii) *Tap*, as a verb, means :

(a) knock gently on sb/sth :
I *tapped* her on the shoulder.

(b) strike sth lightly with sth :
He was *tapping* his fingers on the table.

tape-n : (a) piece of a narrow strip of material used for tying, fastening or labelling things :
The parcel was tied up the *tape*.
He bought four metres of linen *tape*.
The seat covers are held in place by *tapes*.

(b) strip of paper of other flexible material coated with adhesive for fastening packages, etc :
Where is the sticky *tape*?

(c) reel of magnetic *tape*; reading made on this :
Make a *tape* of her conversation.

5. TAR/TARE

tar-n : thick black sticky liquid, hard when cold, obtained from coal, etc. and used in making roads, to preserve timber, etc :

tare-n : (a) weight of the container in which goods are packed, or of the vehicle carrying them:

(b) allowance made for this when goods are weighed together with their container or vehicle :

6. TARN/TURN

tarn-n : small mountain lake:

turn-n : (a) act of turning; *turning* movement :
Give a few *turns* of the handle.
(b) change of direction:
There are sudden *turns* in the road.
He was frustrated at every *turn.*
(c) change in condition:
His illness took a *turn* for the worse.
(d) occasion or opportunity for doing sth :
It is your *turn* to speak now.

Note: There is another *turn,* a verb. It means :
1. move round a point :
The Earth *turns* round the sun.
He *turned* his back on me.
She *turned* to look at me.
This tap *turns* easily.
2. change in nature, quality, condition, etc :
Frost *turns* water into ice.
His hair has *turned* grey.
3. reach and pass :
She has *turned* twenty.
It has just *turned* two.

7. TARRY/TERRY

tarry-v : delay in coming to, or going from, a place; linger :
Let us *tarry* a few days at her place.

terry-n : cotton fabric used for towels, etc. with raised loops of thread left uncut :
Tomels are made of *terry*-cloth.

8. TASTE/TEST

taste-n : (a) sensation caused in the tongue by things placed on it :
Sugar has a sweet *taste.*
(b) small quantity of food or drink taken as a sample :
Just have a *taste* of this cheese.
(c) preference or liking :
Have you a *taste* for foreign travel?
(d) ability to perceive and enjoy what is beautiful or harmonious :
I have an excellent *taste* in clothes.

Note: There is another *taste,* a verb. It means :
1. be able to perceive flavours:
Can you *taste* the garlic in this stew?
2. have a certain flavour :
It *tastes* bitter.
It *tastes* strongly of mint.
3. taste the flavour of sth :
She *tasted* the soup to see if she had put enough salt in it.
4. eat or drink :
They had not *tasted* hot food for over a week.
That is the best food I have ever *tasted.*

test-n : (a) examination or trial of qualities, etc :
That was an endurance *test*.
She left her purse on the table as a *test* of the child's honesty.
(b) examination of a person's ability or knowledge in a particular area:
I gave them a *test* in history.

Note: *Test*, as a verb, means :
1. examine and measure qualities, etc. of sb/sth :
I had my eyesight *tested*.
The long climb *tested* our powers of endurance.
2. test sb's knowledge and ability in a particular area:
I *tested* the whole class on irregular verbs.

9. TEAK/TIC/TICK

teak-n : strong hard wood of a tall evergeen tree, used for making furniture, ship-building, etc :
The *teak* tree grows in tropical forests.

tic-n : occasional involuntary twitching of the muscles, especially of the face :
He has a nervous *tic*.

tick-n : (a) light and regularly repeated sound, especially of a clock or watch :
If you can hear your watch *tick* you know it is going.
(b) moment :
Just wait a *tick*.
(c) mark put beside an item in a list to show that it has been checked or done or is correct :

Note: 1. *Tick* is also used as a verb to denote :
(i) make a series of *ticks* :
His watch does not *tick* because it is electric.
(ii) put a *tick* beside an item, etc :
Tick off the names of those present.
The jobs that are done have been *ticked* off.
2. There is another *tick*, a noun. It means credit:
He buys goods on *tick*.

10. TEAL/TILL

teal-n : small wild duck living near rivers or lakes :

till-n: drawer in which money is kept behind the counter in a shop, bank, etc :
A shopkeeper puts the money he takes in a *till*.

Note: 1. There is another *till*, a verb, used in the sense of prepare and use land for growing crops :
The farmers were *tilling* the land.
2. Another *till* is used as a conjunction and as a preposition :
(i) *Till*, as a conjunction, means up to the time when:
Wait *till* the rain stops.
Don't leave *till* I arrive.
Continue in this direction *till* you see a sign.
(ii) *Till*, as a preposition, denotes :
(a) up to a specified time :

It may last *till* Friday.
Nothing happened *till* 5 O'clock.
Till now I have always lived alone.
(b) up to the time of a specified event :
Don't open it *till* your birthday.
The secret was never told *till* after the old man's death.

11. TEAM/TEEM

team-n : (a) group of players forming one side in certain games and sports :
Which *team* do you play for?
(b) group of people working together :
Those young men are a sales *team*.
He is a good *team* worker.

Note: *Team*, as a verb, denotes work together with sb for a common purpose :
The two companies have *teamed* to develop a new racing car.

teem-v : (a) have sth in great numbers :
The river was *teeming* with fish.
His mind is *teeming* with bright ideas.
(b) be present in geat numbers :
Fish *teem* in these waters.

Note: There is another *teem*, a verb. It means (if water, rain, etc.) fall heavily; pour :
It was *teeming* with rain.
The rain was *teeming* down.

12. TEAT/TIT

teat-n : (a) animal's nipple :
(b) rubber mouth-piece on a child's feeding-bottle, through which the contents are sucked :

tit-n : (a) woman's breast :
(b) nipple :

Note : 1. The idiom *tit* for tat means blow, injury, insult, etc. given in return for one received :
He hit me, so I hit him back-It was *tit* for tat.
2. There is another *tit*, a noun. It means any of various types of small birds, often with a dark spot on the head :
That is a blue *tit*.

13. TENNER/TENOR

tenner-n : note worth ten rupees :
I shall give you a *tenner* for this towel.

tenor-n : (a) general routine or course of sth :
Don't disrupt the even *tenor* of her life.
(b) general meaning or drift of sth :
I know enough of the language to grasp the *tenor* of what is being said.

Note : There is another *tenor*, a noun. It means :
1. highest, normal adult male voice :
2. singer with such a voice :
Are you a *tenor*?

14. THRASH/THRESH

thrash-v : (a) beat with a stick or whip :
We were *thrashed* a lot at school.
(b) hit sth with repeated blows :
The whale *thrashed* the water with its tail.
(c) defeat sb thoroughly in a contest :
We had challenged and *thrashed* the enemy's navy.
(d) make violent or convulsive movement :
Swimmers were *thrashing* about in the water.
(e) discuss sth thoroughly and frankly:
Call a meeting to *thrash* out the problem.
(f) produce sth by discussion :
After much argument, we *thrashed* out a plan.

thresh-v : beat out or separate grain from husks of wheat, etc. using a machine or an implement held in the hand :

15. TIFF/TIP

tiff-n : slight quarrel between friends or acquaintance :
Did you have a *tiff* with your girl-friend?

tip-n : (a) small sum of money given to a waiter, taxi-driver, etc. as personal reward for their services :
He left a *tip* under his plate.
(b) small but useful piece of practical advice :
Here is a handly *tip* for removing stains from clothing.
(c) private or special piece of information :
Take a *tip* from me and buy these shares now.

Note : *Tip*, as a verb, means :
1. give a small sum of money to waiter, etc :
He *tipped* the postman five rupees.
2. give advice or an opinion about sb/sth :
He has been widely *tipped* as the President's successor.
3. touch or strike sth lightly :
The ball just *tipped* the edge of his racket.

Note: 1. (i) There is another *tip*, a verb, used to mean :
(a) caused sth to lean, rise or tilt on one side or at one end :
Tip the box up and empty it.
(b) pour out by tilting :
Tip the dirty water out of the bowl into the sink.
(ii) *Tip*, as a noun, denotes :
(a) place where rubbish may be tipped :
Take the broken chair to the *tip*.
(b) dirty or untidy place :
Your house is an absolute *tip*.
2. There is another *tip*, a noun, used to mean :
(i) pointed or this end of sth :
She was walking on the *tips* of her toes.
He was hanging by his finger *tips* from a window frame.
(ii) small part or piece fitted to the end of sth :
This is a cane with a rubber *tip*.
These are shoes with metal *tips*.

16. TIRE/TYRE

tire-v : (a) make or become weary :
Old people *tire* easily.
The long walk *tired* me.
She has got so much energy–she never seems to *tire*.
(b) become uninterested in doing sth :
After a week he *tired* of eating rice.
He never *tires* of the sound of his voice.

tyre-n : covering fitted round the rim of a wheel to absorb shocks :
He bought a bicycle *tyre*.
Your *tyres* are badly worn.

17. TOFF/TOP

toff-n : rich or well-dressed person of high social class :

top-n : (a) highest part or point :
My office is at the *top* of the building.
(b) upper surface :
Polish the *top* of the table.
Put the luggage on *top* of the car.
(c) highest or most important rank or position :
I am at the *top* of my profession.
We have got a lot of things to do, but packing is *top* of the list.
(d) thing forming or covering the upper part of sth :
She took off the *top* of her bikini. (bikini = scanty two-piece costume worn by woman for swimming and sun-bathing.)
(e) (especially woman's) garment covering the upper part of the body :
She needs a *top* to go with her slacks.

Note: *Top* is also used as an adjective in the sense of highest in position, rank or degree :
There are two rooms on the *top* floor.
He is one of India's *top* scientists.
Don't travel at *top* speed.

18. TOT/TOTE

tot-n : (a) small child :
There is a T.V. programme for tiny *tots*.
I have known her since she was a *tot*.
(b) small glass of alcoholic drink :
He is eager to have a *tot* of whisky.

Note : There is another *tot*, a verb, used to denote add up :
Let us *tot* up our expenses.
I was *totting* up the number of photographs.

tote-v: carry sth :
He has been *toting* this bag round all day.

19. TRACK/TREK

track-n : (a) line or series of marks left by a moving vehicle, person, animal, and so on :
We followed his *tracks* through the snow.

(b) path or rough road :
There is a muddy *track* through forest.

trek-n : long hard journey, especially on foot :

Note : *Trek*, as a verb, means make long hard journey :
They were *trekking* for days across the desert.

20. TRANCE/TRENCH

trance-n : (a) sleep-like state :
He fell into a *trance*.
She came out of a *trance*.

(b) dreamy state in which one concentrates on one's thoughts, and does not notice what is happening around one :
She has been in a *trance* all day-I think she is in love.

trench-n : ditch dug in the ground :
They dug a *trench* for the new water-pipe.

21. TROOP/TROUPE

troop-n : large group of people or animals, especially when moving :
I saw a *troop* of school children going to school.

Note : The word *troops* means soldiers :
They demanded the withdrawal of foreign *troops*.

troupe-n : group of actors, singers or dancers who work together :
That is a dance *troupe*.

21

First Word of Each Group Beginning With-U

1. UNWANTED/UNWONTED

unwanted-adj : not wanted :
Do you feel *unwanted* ?

unwonted-adj : not customary or usual :
Your *unwonted* intrusion annoyed her.

2. URBAN/URBANE

urban-adj : of, situated in or living in a city or town :
Adequate steps should be taken to solve *urban* unemployment.
What is the *urban* population of Delhi?

urbane-adj : having or showing refined manners, smooth elegance and sophistication :
Are you an *urbane* person?
She was composed, *urbane* and affable.

3. URGENT/ARGENT

urgent-adj : (a) needing immediate attention, action or decesion :
I have an *urgent* message for you.
My car is in *urgent* need of repair.

(b) showing that sth is urgent; persistent in one's demands :
She spoke in an *urgent* whisper.
I spoke to him in a low and *urgent* voice.

argent-n : silver :

Note : *Argent* is also used as an adjective to mean silvery.
He has *argent* hair.

4. URN/EARN

urn-n : (a) tall vase, usually with a stem and a base, especially one used for holding the ashes of a cremated person :

(b) large metal container with a tap, in which tea, coffee, etc. is made, or from which it is served :
Do you have a tea *urn*?

(a) get money by working :
She *earned* her living by singing in a night club.
How much do you *earn* a month?

(b) get money as a return on a loan or investement :
Money *earns* more in a high interest account.

(c) gain sth deserved in return for one's achievements, behaviour, etc :
Her honesty *earned* her great respect.
His bad manners *earned* him a sharp rebuke.
You have certainly *earned* your retirement.

22

First Word of Each Group Beginning With-V

1. VAIN/VEIN

vain-adj : (a) having too high an opinion of one's looks, abilities, etc; conceited :
He is a *vain* young aristocrat.
She is *vain* of her beauty.
(b) having no value of significance :
He always makes *vain* promises.
(c) useless or futile :
He did his best in the *vain* hope of winning her friendship.
He made a *vain* attempt to steal her car.

Note : The idiom in *vain* means:
1. with no result; uselessly :
I tried in *vain* to sleep.
They tried in *vain* to discover what had happened.
2. useless or fruitless :
All our work was in *vain*.

vein-n : (a) any of the tubes carrying blood from all parts of the body to the heart :
Royal blood ran in his *veins*.
(b) distinctive feature or quality; streak :
He has a *vein* of melancholy in his character.
Her stories revealed rich *vein* of humour.
(c) mood; manner or style :
She talked to me in a sad *vein*.
The complaints continued in the same *vein*.
His letter continued in this *vein* for ten pages.

2. VALENEIL

vale-n : valley :
Let us visit a rich, lush *vale* of meadows and blossoms.

veil-n : (a) covering of fine net or other material worn, especially by women, to protect or hide the face, or as part of a head-dress :
Don't raise you *veil*.
Where is the bridal *veil*?
(b) thing that hides or disguises :
There was a *veil* of mist over the hills.
They hatched a plot under the *veil* of secrecy.

Note : *Veil*, as a verb, means :
1. put a *veil* over sb/sth :
Who is that *veiled* woman?

2. hide or disguise sth :
   He could hardly *veil* his contempt at your ignorance.
   He held out a thinly *veiled* threat.

3. VALET/BALLET: ALSO REFER TOP. 20

valet-n : (a) man's personal servant who looks after his clothes, serves his meals, and so forth :
Who is your *valet*?
(b) hotel employee with similar duties :

ballet-n : (a) style of dancing used to tell a story in a dramatic performance with music, but without speech or singing :
Did you enjoy the classical *ballet*?
(b) story performed in this way :
I had not seen this *ballet* before.
(c) group of dancers who regularly perform *ballet* together :
They are the members of the Kolkata *Ballet*.

4. VALLEY/BELLY: ALSO REFER TOP. 31

valley-n : stretch of land between hills or mountains, often with a river flowing through it :

belly-a : (a) part of the body below the chest, containing the stomach, bowels and digestive organs; abdomen :
One should not go out with an empty *belly*.
(b) bulging or rounded part of sth :
What is he doing in the *belly* of the ship?

5. VALOUR/VELOUR

valour-n : bravery :
I displayed great *valour*.
Many soldiers were decorated for *valour*.

velour-n : woven fabric like velvet or felt :
He was wearing a *velour* hat.
Where are the *velour* chair-covers?

6. VAN/VANE

van-n : (a) covered vehicle, with no side windows, for transporting goods or people :
Where is the police *van*?
(b) closed railway carriage for luggage, mail or goods, or for use of the guard :
That is the luggage *van*.

vane-n: arrow or pointer on the top of a building, turned by the wind so as to show its direction :
On the top of the building is a weather *vane* to show which way the wind is blowing.

7. VARY/VERY

vary-v : (a) be different in size, volume, strength, etc :
Opinions *vary* on this point.
The results of the experiment *varied* wildly.
(b) change :
Our routine never *varies*.
Prices *vary* with the seasons.
He works with *varying* degrees of enthusiasm.

(c) make sth different by introducing changes :
Do you *vary* the speed at which you work?

very-adv : (a) in a high degree :
I am *very* busy.
(b) In the fullest sense :
He was the *very* first to arrive.
You should call on her at six o'clock at the *very* latest.
(c) exactly :
He was sitting on the *very* same seat.

Note: *Very* is also used an an adjective in the sense of :
1. actual; truly such; itself, himself, etc. and no other :
This is the *very* book I want.
At that *very* moment, the phone rang.
You are the *very* lady I want to see.
2. extreme:
What did he say at the *very* beginning.
3. used to emphasise a noun :
The *very* idea of going abroad delighted me.

8. VASE/BASE

vase-n : vessel without handles, usually made of glass, china, etc. and used for holding cut flowers or as an ornament :

base-n : (a) lowest part of sth :
Look at the *base* of the pillar.
(b) starting point; underlying principle :
His arguments had a sound economic *base*.
She used her family's history as a *base* for her novel.
(c) place at which armed forces, expeditions, etc. have their stores :
There is a college near the naval *base*.

Note : 1. Another *base*, a verb, is used to mean :
1. use sth as grounds, evidence, etc. for sth else :
My novel is *based* on historical facts.
Direct taxation is usually based on income.
2. place sb in (a place from which to work and travel) :
Most of our staff are *based* in Tokyo.

2. There is another *base*, an adjective. It means :
1. dishonourable; despicable :
He was acting from *base* motives.
2. not pure :
This is a *base* coin.
3. low in value :
We do not need *base* metal.

9. VASSAL/VESSEL/BASAL

vassal-n : (a) (in the Middle Ages) man promising to fight for and be loyal to a king or lord in return for the right to hold land :
A *vassal* state is one having to take hours from a more important state.
(b) person or nation dependent on another :
Russia is not a *vassal* state.

vessel-n : (a) ship, or boat, especially a large one :
Where are the cargo *vessels* ?

(b) any hollow container for holding liquids :
Cups, basins, pots, bottles, casks, etc., are *vessels* that hold liquids.
(c) tube-like structure in the body of an animal or a plant, conveying or holding blood or other fluid :
Can you tell me something about blood *vessels*?

basal-adj : fundamental; of, at, or forming the base :
The citizens of India enjoy many *basal* rights enshrined in the Constitution of India.

10. VAST/BUST: *ALSO REFER TOP. 47*

vast-adj : (a) immense; very large in area, size, quantity or degree :
I am responsible for running a *vast* organisation.
He incurred a *vast* expense in constructing a house of his own.
(b) very great :
There is a *vast* difference between this book and any other on the subject available in the market all over the country :

bust-n : (a) sculpture of a person's head, shoulders and chest :
(b) woman's breasts; bosom :
(c) measurement round a woman's chest and back :
What is your *bust* size, please?

Note: There is another *bust* used as a verb to mean :
1. smash; break sth :
She dropped her alarm clock on the pavement and *bust* it.
2. raid a house or arrest sb :
Had you been *busted* for heroin?

11. VAT/BAT/BET: *ALSO REFER TOP. 19*

vat-n : tank or large container for holding liquids, etc. in distilling, brewing, dyeing and tanning :

bat-n : small mouse-like animal that flies at night and feeds on fruit and insects :

Note : Another *bat*, a noun, is used to mean :
Implement of a specified size and shape, and with a handle, used for hitting the ball in games such as cricket, baseball and table tennis :

bet-v : risk money on a race or on some other event of which the result is doubtful :
He spends all his money *betting* on horses.
I don't enjoy *betting*.

Note: *Bet* is also used as a noun to denote:
1. arrangement to risk money, etc. on an event of which the result is doubtful :
He made a *bet* on the football match.
2. opinion; prediction :
I *bet* he has got held up in the traffic.

12. VEER/BEER: *ALSO REFER TOP. 30 AND 31*

veer-v : (a) change course or direction :
The plane *veered* wildly.
(b) of conversation, behaviour or opinion of sb :
The debate *veered* away from politics and round to philosophy.

beer-n : alcoholic drink made from malt and flavoured with hops etc : Make it a point never to drink *beer*.

13. VERB/VERVE : *ALSO REFER TO P. 23*

verb-n : word or phrase indicating an action, an event or a state : Bring me a glass of cold water.

verve-n: enthusiasm, spirit or vigour, especially in artistic or literary work : I always write with *verve*.

14. VERGE/BARGE

verge-n : (a) edge; border :
Sita is on the *verge* of tears (almost crying).
(b) grass edging along a path or round a flower-bed :
We began walking together along the grass *verge*.

Note: 1. The idiom ***on/to the verge of sth*** means at or close to the point where sth new begins or takes place :
People are living on the *verge* of starvation.
The two countries were on the *verge* of war.
His financial distress brought him to the *verge* of tears.
She was brought to the *verge* of bursting into tears.
2. *Verge* is also used as a verb in a phrase, verge on/ upon sth. It means be very close or similar to sth; be approaching sth :
Such ideas *verge* on foolhardiness.
I had a feeling of distrust *verging* on panic.
Don't take a direct action *verging* on violence.

barge-n : (a) large flat-bottomed boat for carrying goods and people on rivers, canals, and so on :
I never travelled in a *barge*.
(b) large ornamental rowing-boat for ceremonial occasion :
Does he know how to row a *barge* ?

Note : 1. There is another *barge*, a verb. It means rush or bump heavily and clumsily :
He *barged* past me in the queue.
2. The phrase, barge in/into sth, denotes enter or interrupt sth rudely or clumsily :
He tried to stop her coming through the door but she just *barged* in.
Don't *barge* into our conversation.

15. VEST/BEST: *ALSO REFER TOP. 32 ADN 33*

vest-n : (a) garment worn under a shirt, etc. next to the skin :
He wears cotton *vests*.
(b) special garment covering the upper part of the body:
He was wearing a bullet-proof *vest*.

Note : There is another *vest*, a verb, used in the sense of giving sth as a firm or legal right to sb/sth; confer sth on sb/sth :
It must be borne in mind that authority is *vested* in the people.
Parliament is *vested* with the power of making laws.

best-adj : of the most excellent, desirable, suitable, etc., kind :
She is my *best* friend.
That was the *best* party I have ever had.
He is the *best* man for the job.

Note : 1. *Best*, as an adverb, means :

(a) in the most excellent manner :
He works *best* in the morning.
Who is the *best* dressed politician?

(b) most; to the greatest degree :
He is the *best*-known lawyer.
I enjoyed her first novel *best* of all.

2. Best, as a noun, denotes :

(a) that which is *best*; the outstanding thing or person among several.
I was acting from the *best* of motives.
He is the *best* of the bunch.

(b) most important advantage or aspect of sth :
That is the *best* of having a video set.
The *best* we can hope for is that nobody gets hurt.

16. VILE/BILE

vile-adj : **(a)** extremly disgusting :
Don't use *vile* language.
The curry has a *vile* smell.

(b) corrupt; despicable on moral grounds :
It goes without saying that bribery is a *vile* practice.

(c) extremely bad :
Don't go out in the *vile* weather.
As he was in a *vile* mood, I did not talk to him.

bile-n : (a) bitter yellowish liquid produced by the lever to help the body to digest fats :

(b) bad temper; irritability :
I detest his *bile*.
Do you best to get rid of your *bile*.

17. VIM/BEAM: *ALSO REFER TOP. 29*

vim-n : energy or vigour :
She is full of *vim*.
You should put more *vim* into your work.

beam-n : (a) long thick bar of wood, metal or concrete used to support the roof of a building :

(b) bright and happy look or smile :
She talked to me with a *beam* of delight.

Note: *Beam* is also used as a verb to mean :

1. (of the sun) send out light and warmth :
2. smile happily and cheerfully :
The player *beamed* with satisfaction.

18. VOL T/BOL T : *ALSO REFER TOP. 38*

volt-n : unit of electrical force :

bolt-n : (a) long metal objects which screws into a nut and is used to fasten things together :
The *bolts* are all very tight.

(b) metal bar that slides into a socket to lock a door, window, etc :

(c) quantity of cloth, etc. wound in a roll :

23

First Word of Each Group Beginning With-W

1. WAD/WADE

wad-n : (a) quantity of documents or banknotes folded, rolled or held together :
He pulled a *wad* of ₹ 100/- notes out of his pocket.
(b) lump or bundle of soft material used for keeping things apart or in place, or to block a hole, etc :
The noise was so loud that he put *wads* of cotton wool in her ears.
(c) sandwich or bun :
Would you like to have a cup of tea and a *wad*?

wade-v : walk with an effort (through mud, water, etc. that makes walking difficult) :
I cannot *wade* in these boots.
They had to *wade* knee-deep through mud and debris to reach the earthquake victims.
They *waded* across the canal.

2. WAIST/WASTE

waist-n : (a) part of the body between the ribs and the hips :
She measures 25 inches round her *waist*.
He has a 30-inch *waist*.
The workmen were stripped to the *waist*.
(b) part of a garment that goes round the *waist* :
If the skirt is too big, you can take in the *waist*.
The *waist* is too tight for me.
He wears trousers with 30-inch *waist*.

waste-v : (a) use sth extravagantly, needlessly or without an adequate result :
Don't *waste* time.
All our efforts were *wasted*.
She has *wasted* her money on things she does not need.
(b) not make full use of (a person or his abilities) :
He has *wasted* in his present job.
(c) make or become weaker and thinner :
His body was *wasted* by long illness.

Note : 1. Another *waste*, a noun, is used to mean :
(i) material, food, etc. that is no longer needed and is thrown away: refuse:
Dustbins are used for household *waste*.
(ii) *wasting* or being *wasted* :

The waste of public money on the project was severely criticised.
It is a *waste* of time doing that.

(iii) large area of land that is not or cannot be inhabited or cultivated; desert :
Tell me something about the arid *wastes* of the Sahara.

2. There is another *waste*, an adjective, used to mean :
 (i) not fit to be used; not cultivated; not inhabited :
 That is an area of *waste* ground.
 (ii) no longer useful and to be thrown away :
 Don't accumulate *waste* matter produced by the manufacturing process.

3. WAIT/WEIGHT

wait-v : (a) stay where one is, delay acting, etc :
They are *waiting* for the rain to stop.
Tell her I cannot see her now, she will have to *wait*.

(b) await; wait and watch for sth :
You will just have to *wait* your turn.

(c) be postponed; not be dealt with immediately :
The matter can *wait* until the next meeting; it is not urgent.

Note : There is another *wait*, a noun, used to mean act or time of *waiting* :
They had a long *wait* for the bus.

weight-n : (a) The heaviness of something, especially as measured by a certain system :
What is the *weight* of this sack?

(b) a piece of metal that has a known heaviness and can be balanced against something else :
Please give me a one-kilo *weight*.

(c) (something with) a large amount of weight :
He's got a bad back so he can't lift *weights*.

(d) something that causes a feeling of worry or anxiety :
The loss of the money has been a *weight* on my mind.

(e) the value, importance or influence that Someone or something has :
I don't attach any *weight* to these rumours.

Note : Weight, as a verb, means to put a weight on or add something heavy to :
Fishing nets are *weighted*.

4. WAIVE/WAVE

waive-n : not insist on sth in a particular case; forego:
Don't *waive* the relevant rules.
We have decided case. to *waive* the age-limit for applicants in her

wave-v : (a) move regularly and loosely or to and fro or up and down :
A flag is *waving* in the breeze.
Branches are *waving* in the wind.

(b) move one's hand to and fro or up and down, in order to attract sb's attention :
She *waved* to me when she saw me.
They *waved* at us from across the room.

(c) cause to move up and down or to and fro, in order to make a signal or give a greeting :
He *waved* a hand at me.
He came out *waving* the document at the crowd.
They *waved* to us to stay where we were.

(d) give a greeting by *waving* one's hand :
I *waved* her goodbye.
They *waved* goodbye to us.

(e) form a series of curves :
Her hair *waves* beautifully.

(f) cause sth to form curves :
She has had her hair *waved.*

Note : There is another wave, a noun, used to mean :

1. ridge of water :
The storm whipped up huge *waves.*
2. act or gesture of *waving* :
She greeted me with a *wave.*
The magician made the rabbit disappear with a *wave* of his hand.
3. sudden, temporary increase and spread of sth :
A mounting *wave* of anger and dislike rose within me.
There was a crime *wave* in certain parts of the city.
There was a heat *wave* in the recent past.

5. WAN/WANE

wan-adj : pale and looking ill or tired; pallid :
She looked *wan* and fragile.
He talked to us with a *wan* smile.

wane-v : (a) (of the moon) show a gradually decreasing area of brightness after being full :
The moon began to *wane.*

(b) gradually lose power or importance; become smaller or weaker or less impressive :
My enthusiasm for her has begun to wane.
The influence of this group *waned* considerably.

Note : 1. The idiom wax and *wane* means increase and then decrease in strength or importance :
Throughout history, empires have waxed and *waned.*
The popularity of most of our leaders waxed and *waned.*

2. The idiom on the *wane* means gradully decreasing; waning :
The authority of the dictator is on the *wane.*
Is your popularity on the *wane* ?

6. WANDER/WONDER

wander-v : (a) roam :
She was *wandering* aimlessly up and down the road.
We *wandered* around for hours looking for the house.
He *wandered* out into the darkness.
His thoughts *wandered* back to his youth.

(b) move aimlessly around in a place :
The child was found *wandering* the streets alone.

(c) be inattentive or confused :
He realised his audience's attention was beginning to *wander*.

Note : *Wander* is also used as a noun to mean act of wandering :
He went for a little *wander* round the park.

wonder-n : feeling of surprise mixed with admiration, be wilderment or disbelief :
They were filled with *wonder* at the sight.

Note : *Wonder* is also used as a verb to denote :

(a) feel great surprise, admiration, etc.; marvel :
We *wondered* at the speed with which it arrived.
I *wonder* that he was not killed in the accident.

(b) feel curious :
There has been no news for a week and he is beginning to *wonder*.

(c) ask oneself :
I *wonder* whether they will arrive on time.

7. WANT/WONT

want-v : (a) wish for; have a desire for sth :
What do you *want* ?
She *wants* me to go with her.
I don't *want* you arriving late.
They *want* you as their leader.

(b) require or need sth :
We shall *want* more staff for the new office.
Let me know how many copies you *want*.
The plant *want* to be watered daily.

(c) should or ought to do sth:
You *want* to be more careful.

(d) lack; not have enough of sth ;
He *wants* the courage to speak the truth.

(e) need; require sb to be present :
You are *wanted* by the police.
He is *wanted* immediately in the director's office.

(f) fall short by sth :
It still *wants* half an hour till midnight.

Note : 1. There is another *want*, a noun, used to denote :

(i) requirement; desire for sth :
I am a man of few *wants*.
This book meets a long-felt *want*.

(ii) thing desired :
All their *wants* were provided by their host.

(iii) lack or insufficiency of sth :
The refugees are suffering for *want* of food and medical supplies.
The plant died from *want* of water.
She decided to accept the offer for *want* of any thing better.

(iv) state of being poor or in need; poverty :
He lived in *want* for many a year.
Their health had suffered from years of *want*.
This is a policy aimed at fighting *want* and deprivation.

2. The idiom in want of sth denotes needing sth :
His house is in *want* of repair.

wont-n: custom; habit :
She went for a walk after breakfast, as was her *wont*.

Note : *Wont* is also used as an adjective to denote in the habit of doing sth; accustomed to doing sth :
He was *wont* to give length speeches.

8. WARD/WORD

ward-n : (a) separate part or room for a particular group of patients :
He went to visit a patient in the surgical *ward*.
(b) division of a town, etc. that elects and is represented by a councillor in local government :
There are four candidates standing for election in this *ward*.
(c) person who is under the care of a guardian or the protection of a lawcourt :
The child was made a *ward* of court.
He invested the money on behalf of her *ward*.

word-n : (a) sound or combination of sounds that expresses a meaning and forms an independent unit of the grammar or vocabulary of a language :
The story is told in words and pictures.
I have not *words* to express my gratitude to her.
(b) remark or statement; anything said :
I don't believe a *word* of your story.
He did not say a *word* about it.
Did you say a few *words* of sympathy to him?
(c) message; piece of news :
Please send me *word* of your safe arrival.
Word came that I was needed at home.

Note : *Word*, when used in the sense at (c) above, must not be preceded by a or the :

(d) rumour :
The *word* is that she has left her husband.

Note : *Word*, when used in the sense at (d) above, must be preceded by the definite article, the.

(e) spoken command or signal :
Stay hidden until I give the *word*.
Their *word* is law.

Note : Word is also used as a verb to denote express sth in particular words; phrase sth :
The advice was not very tactfully *worded*.
Send a carefully *worded* reminder.

9. WARM/WORM

warm-adj : (a) of or at a fairly high temperature, between cool and hot :
Food for a baby should be *warm*, not hot.
The weather is a bit *warmer* today.
(b) having the normal body temperature :
The patient must be kept *warm*.
(c) hearty; showing enthusiasm :

She gave me a *warm* welcome.

(d) affectionate or sympathetic :
He has a *warm* heart.
He showed *warm* feelings of love and gratitude.

Note : There is another *warm*, a verb, used to denote make or become *warm* or *warmer* :
The milk is *warming* up on the stove.
Warm up the milk.
Warm yourself by the fire.

worm-n : (a) small long thin creeping animal with a soft rounded or flattened body and no backbone or limbs :
There are a lot of *worms* in the soil.

(b) person considered weak and insignificant, and who is not respected by others :
She says you are a *worm*.

10. WEAK/WEEK/WICK

weak-adj (a) lacking strength or power; easily broken, bent or defeated :
She was still *weak* after her illness.
He is too *weak* to walk even fifty metres.
I am so *weak* that I cannot walk far.
She felt *weak* in the legs.

(b) not functioning properly; deficient :
He has a *weak* heart.
Do you have *weak* eyes ?

(c) not forceful or convincing :
Your *weak* arguments are not acceptable.
Know it for certain that *weak* evidence will not help you.

(d) deficient; not achieving a high standard :
She is *weak* at Biology.
Are you *weak* in English grammar?
That book is *weak* on the medieval period.

Note : The expression the *weak* is used as a noun in the sense of people who are poor, sick or powerless, and are therefore easily exploited, infected, etc :
It is the role of the government to protect the *weak*.
The weak should struggle against their oppressors.

week-n : (a) period of seven days :
Sunday is the first day of the *week*.
She comes to see me once a *week*.
What day of the *week* was the 2nd July last year?

(b) the six days apart from Sunday:
During the *week*, the road is very busy but there is very little traffic on Sunday :

(c) The five days other than Saturday and Sunday :
They live in Patna during the *week* and go to their village at the *weekend*.

wick-n : (a) length of thread in the centre of a candle, the top end of which is lit and burns as the wax melts :

(b) flat or rounded length of woven material by which oil is drawn up to be burnt, in oil-lamps, oil-stoves, etc :

Trim the *wick* of the lamp.

Note : The idiom, get on sb's *wick*, means irritate sb continually: Don't get on my *wick*.

11. WEAN/WIN

wean-v : gradually stop feeding a baby with its mother's milk and start feeding it with solid food :

Note : The phrasal verb, *wean* sb away from sth/doing sth, means cause sb to stop doing sth, gradually :
You should *wean* him away from drugs.

win-v: (a) be victorious in; do best :
Did you *win* the bet?
(b) obtain or achieve sth as the result of :
He *won* first prize in the raffle.
(c) obtain or reach sth as a result of hard work or perseverance :
We are trying to *win* support for our proposal.
(d) cause sb to achieve sth :
Her performance *won* her much acclaim.

12. WHEAT/WHIT/WIT

wheat-n : (a) grain from which flour is made :
He bought a tonne of *wheat*.
(b) plant that produces this :
This is a field of *wheat*.

whit-n : the smallest amount :
I don't care a *whit* whether she stays or not :
I have read the report but I am no *whit* the wiser.

wit-n : (a) ability to combine words, ideas, etc. so as to produce a clever type of humour :
He has a ready *wit*.
This is a literary style full of elegance and *wit*.
She is a journalist much admired for her *wit*.
(b) witty person :
He is a well-known *wit* and raconteur.
(c) intelligence; quick understanding :
He had not the *wit* enough to realise the danger.

Note : The idiom, at one's *wits* end, means not knowing what to do or say because of worry or desperation :
I am at my *wits*' end worrying about how to pay the bills.

13. WHOLE/HOLE

whole-adj : (a) entire; complete :
The *whole* country mourned the death of the king.
She told me the *whole* truth.
(b) intact; not broken, damaged or injured :
After the function, there was not a glass left *whole*.

Note : *Whole* is also used as a noun to denote :
1. thing that is complete in itself :
Four quarters make a *whole*.
2. all that there is of sth :
She spent the *whole* of the year in hospital.

hole-n : (a) cavity; sunken or hollow place in a solid mass or surface :
That road is full of *holes.*
(b) gap; opening through sth :
He escaped through a *hole* in the wall.
(c) animal's burrow :
That is a mouse *hole.*
(d) difficult of awkward situation :
Do you find yourself in a *hole*?
Note : *Hole* is also used as a verb to mean :
1. make a *hole* in sth :
The ship was *holed* by an iceberg.
2. hide oneself :
The gang was *holed* up in the mountains somewhere.

14. WHOOP/HOOF/HOOP

whoop-n : (a) loud cry, expressing joy or excitement :
He opened the parcel with *whoops* of delight.
(b) harsh gasping sound made by sb with *whooping* cough :
hoof-n : horny part of the foot of a horse, an ox or a deer :
Note : The idiom, hoof it, means go on foot :
As the last bus had gone, I had to *hoof* it home.
hoop-n : (a) circular band of wood, metal, etc :
This is a barrel bound with iron *hoops.*
(b) large ring used at a circus for riders or animals to jump through.

15. WIFE/WIPE

wife-n : married woman, when considered in relation to her husband :
She is the doctor's wife.
She was a good wife and mother.
wipe-v : clean or dry sth by rubbing its surface with a cloth, etc :
Wipe the dishes.
Wipe your hands on the towel.

24

First Word of Each Group Beginning With-Y

1. YACK/YAK

yack-v : talk continuously and often noisily :
He kept *yacking* about his marriage.
Stop *yacking* about your riches.

Note : Yack is also used as a noun to denote persistent or trivial conversation; chatter :
She is having a good old *yack* with the neighbours.

yak-n : wild or domesticated ox of Central Asia, with long horns and hair :

2. YARN/YEARN/EARN : ***ALSO REFER TO P. 90***

3. YAWL/YELL

yawl-n : (a) seating boat with two masts :
(b) type of small fishing boat :
(c) ship's boat with four or six oars :
Do you have a *yawl* ?

yell-v : (a) utter a loud, sharp cry or cries as of pain, excitement, etc :
He *yelled* with fear.
She *yelled* at her mischievous child.
(b) speak or say in a yelling voice :
She *yelled* at her husband about his constant drunkeness.
The crowd *yelled* encouragement at the players.

Note : *Yell* is also used as a noun to denote loud, sharp cry of pain, excitement, etc :
He let out an ear-splitting *yell*.
That seemed to be a *yell* of terror.

25

First Word of Each Group Beginning With-Z

1. ZEALOUS/JEALOUS: *ALSO REFER TO P. 122*

zealous-adj : full of zeal; eager :
people are *zealous* for freedom and liberty.
I am *zealous* to succeed at work.

jealous-adj :
(a) feeling or showing fear or resentment of possible rivals in love or affection:
He was *jealous* of his wife and suspected her of adultery.
(b) feeling or showing resentment of sb's advantages, achievements, etc; envious:
She is *jealous* of my success in examination.
(c) possessive; anxiously protective of one's rights, belongings, etc:
He keeps a *jealous* eye on his property.

2. ZEST/JEST

zest-n: (a) gusto; great enjoyment or excitement:
I entered into her plans with tremendous *zest*.
My *zest* for life is as great as ever.
The children were full of life and *zest*.
(b) quality of having added interest, charm, flavour, and so on :
He felt that some of the *zest* had gone out of his life.
(c) outer skin of oranges, lemons, etc. when used as a flavouring in cooking :
Do you use *zest* in cooking?

jest-n : thing said or done to cause amusement; joke:
I dislike your *jests*.

Note: 1. The idiom, *in jest*, means *in fun*; not seriously:
It was said in *jest*.
Bear in mind that many a true word is spoken in *jest*.
2. *Jest* is also used as a verb to mean jokes; speak or act without seriousness :
Don't *jest* about religious matters.
Stop *jesting*, and be serious for a minute.

3. ZIP/JEEP: *ALSO REFER TO P. 122*

zip-n : (a) device for bringing together or separating two rows of metal of plastic teeth, used for fastening clothing, baggage, etc :
The *zip* on my anorak has not stuck.
(b) vigour; energy :

INDEX

INTERESTING STORIES OF SOME WORDS

Hello

The word 'hello' is probably used more often than any other one in the English language. Almost everbody, even in India, uses the word again and again, every day of the week.

The first thing you hear when you pick up the phone is 'hello.'

Where did the word come from? There are all sorts of beliefs. Some say it came from the French, 'ho' and 'la'-'Ho, there!' This greeting may have arrived in England during the Norman Conquest in the year 1066.

'Ho, there' slowly became something that sounded like 'hallow' (accent last syllable), often heard in the 1300's, during the days of English poet, Geoffrey Chaucer.

Two hundred years later, in Shakespeare's time, 'hallow' had become 'halloo.'

And later, sound like 'halloa,' 'halloo,' and 'hollo' were often used by sailors and huntsmen. 'Halloo,' is still used today by fox hunters.

As time passed, 'halloo' and 'halloa' changed into 'hullo', and during the 1800's, this was how people greeted each other in America.

The American inventor, Thomas Alva Edison, is believed to be the first person to use 'hello' in the late 1800's, soon after the invention of the telephone.

At first, people had greeted each other on the telephone with 'Are you there?'

They were not sure the new instrument could really carry voices. Tom Edison, however, was a man of few words. He wasted no time. The first time he picked up the phone, he did not ask if anyone was there. He was sure someone was, and simply said, 'Hello.'

From that time only about 100 years ago the 'hullo' became 'hello,' as it is heard today.

GREETING BONANZA

The independent London, once documented an exhaustive list of greetings, ways of saying 'hello' and 'goodbye'. Here it goes!

Hello
Hi
How're you doing
What's up, then?
How's tricks?
How's yourself?
How do you do?
Pleased to meet you
I've heard a lot about you
I've heard all about you ...

Hello there
Good morning campers
Rise and shine
Let's be having you
Wakey wakey
Up and doing
Hello, handsome
Hello, chief
Greetings, white man

Top of the morning to you
And a very good morning to you, too
What's so good about it?
Which side of the bed did you get out of this morning, then?
Be like that, then

See if I care

Hello, stranger
Hail fellow, well met
All hail
Ave
Fraternal greetings from the people's
Take that!
Touche!
Geronimo!
Hello; what's nice girl like you doing in ...?

Republic
Ciao, baby
Hey, man
Groovy
Unbelievable
Crucial
Of whom do I have the honour?
You have the advantage of me
We haven't been introduced
You don't know me from Adam
Haven't we met somewhere before?
I know the face, but…
I say
Steady on
Pardon me
Do you mind?
Is this seat taken?
Any chance you could squeeze up?
Room for one more?
Would you mind very much if I……?
Oops
Excuse me
I'm so sorry
Allow me
I'm sure it will come off
What are the washing instructions?
I think you're meant to sprinkle salt on it
To welcome a stranger
Don't be like that...
You would, would you?
Engrade
Have at you !
Well well well
Well I never did!
Surprise surprise!
Would you believe it?

Look, do you remember someone
called Rosemary who left you in 1969
to go to Australia and you haven't heard
from her since? Well, She's my mother
and I'm her daughter Carly and I've
come to say hellow, oh, and can you
lend me 60,000?
I think this calls for a drink
Evening, landlord

What's your pleasure, squire?
How about your good self?
'Ello, 'ello, 'ello, what have we got here '
Some kind of a comedian, are we?
On our way to a fire are we?
Thinking of driving in that condition, sir?

Excuse me, would you mind switching
off your engine and pulling onto the
side of the road?
Well!
Well well

Lord save us
Lord love a duck
Holy Moses
Heavens above
Hell's bell
I'll be damned
Fancy seeing you here
Look who the cat dragged in!
Look who just crawled
out from under a stone!

My sainted aunt Fanny!
Gordon Bennett!
There you go
It's been nice
Hello and goodbye
Have a nice day
Be good
Take care
So long
Over
Out

Okay

The word 'okay' is known and used by millions of people all over the world. Still, language experts do not agree on where it came from.

Some say it came from the Red Indian people of America. When Europeans first came to the America, they heard hundreds of different Red Indian languages. Many were well developed.

One tribe especially had a well developed language. This was the Chocktaw tribe. They were farmers and fishermen who lived in the rich Mississippi valley in what is now the State Of Alabama. When problems arose, Chocktaw leaders discussed them with the tribal chief. They sat in a circle and listened to the wisdom of the chief.

He heard the different proposals, often raising and lowering his head in agreement, and saying, 'Okeh,' meaning 'It is so.'

Nevertheless, there are many who dispute the idea that 'Okay' came from the Red Indians. Some say that President Andrew Jackson of America first used the word 'okay.' Others claim the word was invented by John Jacob Astor, a fur trader of the late 1700's who became one of the world's richest men. Still others say a poor railroad clerk made up this word. His name was Obadiah Kelly and he put his initials O.K. on each package people gave him to ship by train.

So it goes, each story sounds reasonable and official.

But, perhaps the most believable explanation is that the word 'okay' was invented by a political organization in the 1800s.

Martin Van Buren was running for President of America. A group of people organized a club to support him. They called their political organisation the 'Okay Club'. The letters 'O' and 'K' were taken from the name of Van Buren's home town, the place where he was born, Old Kinderhook, New York.

There is one thing about 'Okay' that the experts do agree on: that the word is pure American and that it has spread to almost every country on Earth.

There is something about the word that appeals to people of every language. In recent times, 'okay' has been given an official place in the English language.

Bogus

No one is sure where the word came from. The first time it appeared in print was in 1827 in Ohio, U.S.A. At that time, police found a group of men who were coining fake money. A large crowd gathered around to look at the strange machine that was used to make the counterfeit money. Someone in the crowd said that the machine looked like a 'bogus'. The next day the local newspaper used the word and it became part of the language.

The machine used by counterfeiters was called a 'bogus press', and counterfeit or false money was soon called 'bogus money'. As the years passed, any article that was not the real thing was called 'bogus'.

But that is only one story about the birth of 'bogus'. The Boston Courier, a newspaper that died a long time ago, said that the word came from a famous swindler with the Italian name of Borghese.

Borghese, the newspaper became famous by writing bad cheques, cashing them at banks and stores, then leaving town in a hurry. In 1837, 'Borghese' was known throughout the South and the West for his worthless cheques, bills of exchange and notes. In time, the newspaper said, the name 'Borghese' was shortened to "bogus."

Today we have bogus money, bogus mines, bogus hair, bogus diamonds and so on.

Bears and Bulls

The bull was a sacred creature in the religion and folklore of the ancient world.

His power was worshipped by ancient people.

Therefore, is not surprising, that the financial markets of Western Europe should be moved by those ancient legends about the creative power of the bull. The stock market speculators translated that power into money and made it as a part of the speech of financial investors.

The bull's back was strong enough to carry the gambler's greed for money.

There were some who bought stock because they expected it would rise in price and give them a good profit. This kind of speculator was soon called 'a bull.'

On the other side of the coin was the 'bear.' Instead of buying a stock, then selling it, the bear did the opposite. He sold a stock first, then bought it back at what he hoped would be a lower price.

There is hard evidence that 'bull' was stock market slang in Europe in the middle 1700s.

Such evidence can be found in the works of several 18th century British dramatists. The famous Colley Cibber, for example, describes a man who boasts of the money he has been making on the London Exchange. "Every shilling," he says, "out of stocks, bulls, bears and bubbles!"

Samuel Foote calls one of his characters 'a mere bull and bear booby - the patron of lame ducks, brokers and fraudulent foot bankrupts!'

Still, it is generally believed that 'bear' became part of stock market slang long before 'bull' did so. The use of 'bear,' we are told, comes from a very old and well known fable.

This is the story of a man who sold the skin of a bear even before he caught the animal, just as some speculators sold stocks that they had not yet bought.

English financiers of the 17th century made fun of such traders and called them 'bearskin jobbers.' As an English dictionary of the time, explained: 'To sell a bear is to sell what one hath not.'

The financial history of the past 200 years, both in America and Europe, tells some wild stories about the bears and bulls and their efforts to influence the stock market. Some of their dishonest deals, trades and speculations have given writers and dramatists much material for their plays, novels and satires.

Happily in recent times, the bears and the bulls have been brought under control. Laws have been passed to keep dishonest traders from the exchanges.

The bears and the bulls in their time have had their fun and their profits.

They certainly were a wild breed in their more dramatic and destructive days, bringing ruin to the exchanges and economies of nations.

They make colourful, exciting reading. But, they are part of the past. Today, thank God, the bears and bulls have been tamed. They now act like house pets as seen in the words of a modem American poet, 'I play with the bulls and the bears.'

Animal Vocabulary

ANIMAL ALPHABETS

Alligator, beetle, porcupine, whale,
Bobolink, panther, dragon-fly, snail,
Crocodile, monkey, buffalo, hare,
Dromedary, leopard, mud-turtle, bear,
Elephant, badger, pelican, ox,
Flying-fish, reindeer, anaconda, fox,
Guinea-pig, dolphin, antelope, goose,

Humming-bird, weasel, pickerel,
moose, Ibex, rhinoceros, owl,
kangaroo, Jackal, opossum, toad,
cockatoo, Kingfisher, peacock,
anteater, bat, Lizard, ichneumon,
honey-bee, rat, Mocking-bird, camel,
grasshopper, mouse.

Nightingale, spider, cuttle fish, grouse,
Ocelot, pheasant, wolverine, auk,
Periwinkle, ermine, katydid, hawk,
Quail, hippopotamus, armadillo,
moth, Rattlesnake, lion, woodpecker,
sloth, Salamander, goldfinch,
angleworm, dog,

Tiger, flamingo, scorpion, frog, Unicorn,
ostrich, nautilus, mole, Viper, gorilla,
basilisk, sole, Whippoorwill, beaver,
centipede, fawn, Xantho, canary,
polliwog, swan, Yellowhammer,
eagle, hyena, lark, Zebra, chameleon,
butterfly, shark.

ANIMAL NOISE

The cry of a cat is a meow,
And an oink is the meow of a hog;
And a moo is the oink of a cow,
And a bark is the moo of a dog;
And a neigh is the bark of a horse,
And a sound an elephant's trumpet;
And the sound of lions are roars,
And the sound of a donkey's a hee hao;
And the sound of a duck is a quack,

And the sound of a snake is a hiss;
And if that doesn't take you a back,
You may be confounded by this;
The sound of a sheep is a baa,
And a hyena's baa is a laugh;
And the laugh of a babe is a waah,
And the waah of a, say, a giraffe
Is so small
It is nothing
Nothing at all.

ANIMAL OFFSPRINGS

A cow has a calf, but the calf of a mare
Is a foal, *and a cub is the foal* of a bear;
A fawn is the cub of a deer, while the fawn
Of a beaver's a kitten and carrying on,
The kit of a sheep is a lamb and the lamb
Of a wolf is a whelp, while the whelp of Madame
Is a babe and the babe of a dog is a pup,
And I though for a while this would wind the thing up,
But the pup of a goat is a kid and Mon Dieu!
A joey's kid is a kang kangaroo.

* orcolt

QUIZZES

A C CHANGE

There is one a c in the passage below; it requires many. Put a c before each capitalised word except those that begin the sentences and the passage will clear up. Mark on the space provided.

The_____Optic_____Reed has a_____Haste_____Harm. It_____Hose, one assumes, not to be_____Lever; it neither_____Heats the-Ripple, nor_____Hides and_____Razed sinner for his_____Rude-Rime; it is not_____Old. Then_____Leave to it; ere thy grave_____Loses, thou mayst find here the_____Hart to the_____Rest thou_____Ravest to_____Limb.

ALTERNATES FOR DEMOCRACY

Here are ten forms of government. From the list below, choose the correct word for each type of rule. Write your answers in the space provided.

1. rule by riffraff or gangsters ....
2. government by the worst people ....
3. rule of the majority ....
4. government by the military ....
5. government by workers ....
6. rule by harlots ....
7. government by aged persons ....
8. government by the wealthy ....
9. rule of gold ....
10. government by upstarts ....

LIST

aristocracy	ergatocracy	kakistocracy	oligocracy
arithmocracy	gerontocracy	monocracy	plutocracy
autocracy	hagiocracy	neocracy	pornocracy
chrysocracy	hierocracy	ochlocracy	stratocracy

WHO'S IN CHARGE?

Here are ten different leaders. From the list below, choose the correct word for each V.I.P. Write your answers in the space provided.

1. Chief of a clan ....
2. Ruler of a church ....
3. Head of an unorthodox sect ....
4. Chief magistrate of a modem Greek province ....
5. Toastmaster ....
6. Leader of a revolt ....
7. One of the few who have the power ....
8. Chief of a sacred order ....
9. Commander of a thousand men ....
10. Governor, viceroy ....

LIST

anarch	heresiarch	nomarch	polemarch
chiliarch	hierarch	oligarch	scholarch
ecclesiarch	matriarch	patriarch	symposiarch
exarch	monarch	phylarch	tetrarch

SPECIALITIES

Here are ten fields in which people specialize. From the list below, choose the correct word for each of the studies, arts or sciences. Write your answers in the space provided.

1. Science of kissing ....
2. Study of birds's nests ....
3. Art of engraving on precious stones ....
4. Study of molluscs ....
5. Scientific study of ants ....
6. Obstetrician's field ....
7. Study of mosses ....
8. Catalogue of saints ....
9. Art of treating fractures ....
10. Bellringer's art ....

LIST

agmatology	cytology	glyptology	myrmecology
areology	dendrology	hagiology	oenology
caliology	enigmatology	malacology	philematology
campanology	gerontology	muscology	tocology

MENTAL MENU

In each of the words clued below, whether at the beginning, at the end, or in between, you should be able to find something edible. Write your answers in the space provided.

1. Alms seeker ....
2. Outer garments ....
3. Sailing vessel ....
4. Width ....
5. Gravity ....
6. Smooth ....
7. Tool ....
8. Satisfy ....
9. Sharp-pointed weapon ....
10. Mottled ....
11. Parti-coloured ....
12. Fixer of fixtures ....
13. Capriciousness ....
14. Move in haste ....
15. Irritate; annoy ....
16. Loud cry ....

WORDS FROM PEOPLE

Identify the people from whose names or nicknames the following words are derived. Write your answers on the space provided.

1. Sandwich ....
2. Boycott ....
3. Volt ....
4. Chauvinism ....
5. Silhouette ....
6. Guillotine ....
7. Rog ....
8. Masochism ....
9. Belisha beacon ....
10. Dunce ....
11. Shrapnel ....
12. Forsythia ....
13. Lynch ....
14. Curium ....
15. Maverick ....

ACRONYMS

Acronyms are pronounceable words formed from the initial letters (and sometimes other letters) of a series of words or names. How were the following examples formed, and what do they mean? Write your answers on the space provided.

1. Laser ....
....
....

2. Derv ....
....
....

3. BASIC ....
....
....

4. Quango ....
....
....

5. Radar ....
....
....

6. MASH ....
....
....

7. Asdic ....
....
....

8. Quasar ....
....
....

9. NATO ....
....
....

10. NOIDA ....
....
....

11. FIDO ....
....
....

12. Scuba ....
....
....

13. POSH ....
....
....

14. NASA ....
....
....

15. STAR ....
....
....

SYMMETRICAL LETTERS AND WORDS

I. Some capital letters, such as Y, are the same when you read them back to front (for instance, from the otherside of a glass door). From the definitions given, identify these words made up of such vertically symmetrical letters. Write your answers on the space provided.

1. The noise of a flute ....
2. A small bird ....
3. A cry of triumph ....
4. A cry of excitement ....
5. A parent ....
6. A toddler ....

II. Capital letters can also be horizontally symmetrical i.e. they will read the same in a mirror if you hold the page upside down. Which of the following words are made up of such letters? Tick in the space provided.

1. BIKE	☐	2. SAWN	☐
3. HOCK	☐	4. IBEX	☐
5. TRUMP	☐	6. GRAVY	☐
7. CHIDE	☐	8. FLUTE	☐
9. CHOICE	☐	10. COOKBOOK	☐

PALINDROMES

A palindrome is a word (such as toot) or phrase (such as never odd or even) which reads the same backwards and forwards. Identify the palindromic words defined as follows and write your answers on the space provided.

1. Even ....
2. The middle of the day ....
3. An enclosed super structure at the stern of a ship ....
4. A revolving part in a machine ....
5. An action ....
6. Made into a God ....
7. Glance ....
8. A doctrine ....
9. An electronic tracking device ....
10. Someone or something separating again ....
11. A stupid mistake ....
12. Language spoken in Kerala ....

BEGINNINGS

Add the same three letters to the beginning of each set of four words to make four new words (e.g. armhole/let/our/pit). Write your answers on the space provided.

1. Rot, bide, ton, away ....
2. Riot, rolling, ten, tern ....
3. End, ace, late, lower ....
4. Bate, claim, create, verb ....
5. Pant, part, shackle, sons ....
6. And, edition, end, lode ....
7. Cot, sage, ted, tiff ....
8. Ill, imp, ink, off ....
9. Ion, amount, kin, atonic ....
10. Line, oil, over, yangle ....
11. Low, lop, king, let ....
12. Low, grim, chard, lory ....

ODD-ONE-OUT-ORIGINS

In each set, all the words (or pairs of words) except one are of related origin, i.e. have been borrowed into English from the same language or have been formed by the same linguistic process. Which is the odd one out? Write your answers on the space provided.

1. Alcohol, alcove, algebra, algorithm, alkali, altitude ....
2. Chocolate, diamond, hammock, hurricane, tapioca, tomato ....
   ....
3. Begonia, freesia, fuchsia, lobelia, magnolia, petunia ....
4. Candidate, candle, candour, candy, incandescent, incense ......
5. Adder, aitchbone, amulet, apron, auger, umpire ....
6. Abyss, atom, ignore, immense, negotiate, nonagenarian ....
7. Hydrate, otter, river, urine, vodka, water ....
8. Chopsuey, kaolin, kowtow, sampan, taboo, tea ....
9. Beef, lamb, mutton, pork, veal, venison ....
10. Albino/album, captain/chieftain, car/chariot, envious/invidious, legal/ loyal, parade/ paradise ....

FOREIGN PHRASES

Match the meaning of these foreign phrases which are now familiar in England and say which languages they come from. Tick matching answers in the boxes provide and write the name of language of origin in the space provided.

1.	a la carte	☐	A.	If God is willing
	....			
2.	ad nauseam	☐	B.	Arranged for this specific purpose
	....			
3.	eureka	☐	C.	According to the bill of fare
	....			
4.	raison dêtre	☐	D.	When the necessary changes have been made
	....			
5.	ad hoc	☐	E.	The reason for (a thing's or person's existence; justification)
	....			

6.	mañana	[ ]	F.	Among the family
7.	Kinder, Kirche, Kuche	[ ]	G.	That's what all (women) do
8.	tête-a-tête	[ ]	H.	To the point of disgust
9.	inshallah	[ ]	I.	Tomorrow; some time in the future
10.	cosi fan tutte	[ ]	J.	Children, church, kitchen
11.	en famille	[ ]	K.	A private chat
12.	mutatis mutandis	[ ]	L.	I have found it.

COINED WORDS

Which authors were apparently responsible for forming or introducing the following words and what do they mean? Write your answers on the space provided.

1. Serendipity ....
2. Esemplastic ....
3. International ....
4. Sharawaggi ....
5. Synonymous ....
6. Blatant ....
7. Witticism ....
8. Agnostic ....
9. Galumph ....
10. Robot ....
11. Parp ....
12. Runcible ....

PHOBIAS

If you suffer from the following phobias, what are you frightened of? Write your answers on the space provided.

1. Aerophobia ....
2. Ailurophobia ....
3. Acrophobia ....
4. Claustrophobia ....
5. Agoraphobia..............
6. Ergophobia..............
7. Gallophobia ....
8. Nyctophobia ....
9. Necrophobia ....
10. Xenophobia ....
11. Cynophobia ....
12. Ochlophobia ....
13. Pyrophobia ....
14. Erythrophobia..............
15. Triskaidekaphobia ....

ANSWERS

A C CHANGE

The coptic creed has a chaste charm. It chose, one assumes, not to be cleverly: it neither cheats the cripple, nor chides the crazed sinner for his crude crime; it is not cold. Then cleave to it; ere thy grave closes, thou mayst find here the chart to the crest thou cravest to climb.

ALTERNATES FOR DEMOCRACY

1. ochlocracy
2. kakistocracy
3. arithomocracy
4. stratocracy
5. ergatocracy
6. pornocracy
7. gerontocracy
8. plutocracy
9. chrysocracy
10. neocracy

WHO'S IN CHARGE?

1. phylarch
2. ecclesiarch
3. heresiarch
4. nomarch
5. symposiarch
6. anarch
7. oligarch
8. hierarch
9. chiliarch
10. exarch

SPECIALITIES

1. philematology
2. caliology
3. glyptology
4. malacology
5. murmecology
6. tocology
7. muscology
8. hagiology
9. agmatology
10. campanology

MENTAL MENU

1. Beggar, egg
2. Coats, oats
3. Windjammer, jam
4. Breadth, bread
5. Sobriety, brie
6. Sleek, leek
7. Hammer, ham
8. Appease, pears
9. Spear, pear
10. Dapple, apple
11. Pied, pie
12 Plumber, plum
13. Caprice, rice
14. Scurry, curry
15. Tease, tea
16. Scream, cream

WORDS FROM PEOPLE

1. John Montagu, 4th Earl of *Sandwich* (1718-1792), a diplomat and notorious gambler who reputedly invented the Sandwich as a meal he could eat without leaving the gaming-table.
2. Captain Charles *Boycott* (1832-1897), a land agent in Ireland who was ostracized for refusing to reduce rents.
3. Count Alessandro *Volta* (1745-1827), an Italian physicist.
4. Nicolas *Chauvin* (flourished 1815), a French soldier famed for his excessive patriotism and blind devotion to Napoleon.
5. Etienne de *Silhouette* (1709-1767), French controller-general of finances. The reason why he gave his name to the Silhouette is uncertain.
6. Joseph *Guillotin* (1738-1814), French physician. He did not invent the machine, but advocated its introduction on humanitarian and egalitarian grounds.
7. Admiral Edward Vernon (1684-1757), nicknamed 'Old Grog' because of his habit of wearing a cloak made of the material grogram; who diluted the British navy's issue of rum.
8. Leopold Von Sacher-*Masoch* (1836-1895), Austrian novelist whose works feature scenes of flagellation, humiliation, etc.
9. Leslie Hore-*Belisha* (1893-1957), British Minister of Transport.
10. John *Duns* Scotus, 13th century British scholastic philosopher whose works were unjustly ridiculed in the 16th century.
11. Henry *Shrapnel* (1761-1842), English artillery officer and inventor.
12. William *Forsyth* (1737-1804), superintendent of the royal gardens at St. James and Kensington in London.
13. Captain William *Lynch* (1742-1820), who organised unofficial judicial tribunals in Virginia.
14. Marie Curie (1867-1934) and her husband Pierre (1859-1906), the discoverers of radium.
15. Samuel *Maverick* (1803-1870), a Texan whose cattle were unbranded and allowed to stray. Hence, a *Maverick* was originally an unbranded cow; the meaning was later extended to mean a wandering or independent person.'

ACRONYMS

1. Light amplification by stimulated emission of radiation i.e. a device that generates an intense beam of coherent light or other electromagnetic radiation.
2. Diesel-engined road vehicle: fuel oil for diesel engines.
3. Beginner's All purpose Symbolic Instruction Code, a computer programming language.
4. Quasi-Autonomous Non-Governmental Organization, or Quasi Non-Governmental Organisation, or QUasi-Autonomous National Governmental Organisation (the exact origin is disputed): an independent body setup by the government and having statutory powers in a specified field.

5. Radio Detection and Ranging: an electronic device for locating objects by means of radio waves.
6. Mobile Army Surgical Hospital : a field hospital in the US army.
7. Anti-Submarine Detection Investigation Committee : sonar, a device for detecting underwater objects by means of sound waves.
8. Quasi-Stell AR radio source : a very bright and distant star, like celestial body.
9. North Atlantic Treaty Organisation : a military alliance of the USA, Canada, Britain, Germany, and other nations.
10. New Okhla Industrial Development Agency : now known as a Township.
11. Fog Investigation Dispersal Operation : a system of dispersing fog over airfields by burning petrol in troughs beside the runway.
12. Self-Contained Underwater Breathing Apparatus: an aqualung.
13. Port-out Starboard Home : very comfortable cabins in a ocean liner; now synonym of first class.
14. National Aeronautics and Space Administration : the US government body responsible for space flights.
15. Satellite Television Asia Region : T.V. channel network.

SYMMETRICAL LETTERS AND WORDS

I.	II.
1. TOOT	2. TIT
3. AHA	4. WOW
5. MUM	6. TOT
7. BIKE	8. HOCK
9. IBEX	10. CHIDE
11. CHOICE	12. COOKBOOK

PALINDROMES

1. level
2. noon
3. poop
4. rotor
5. deed
6. deified
7. peep
8. tenet
9. radar
10. redivider
11. boob
12. Malayalam

BEGINNINGS

1. car
2. pat
3. def
4. pro
5. ram
6. exp
7. mas
8. shr
9. cat
10. rec
11. wal
12. pil

ODD-ONE-OUT -ORIGINS

1. *altitude*. All the others are ultimately from Arabic, where *al* is the definite article. *Altitude* derives from Latin *altus* 'high'.
2. *diamond*. All the others come from South American Indian languages. *Diamond* dervies from the Greek (and hence Latin) word *adamas, adamant,* originally meaning, a very hard metal from which the English word *adamant* also comes.
3. *Petunia*. All the others are based on the names of people (Michel Begon, F.H.T. Freese, Leonhard Fuchs, Matthias de Lobel, Pierre Magnol). *Petunia* comes from *petyn*, the word for Tobacco in Tupi, a South American Indian language.
4. *candy*. All the others are ultimately from the Latin verb *candere*, meaning 'to glow' or 'to be white'. In ancient Rome, a *candidate* for office was dressed in a white toga. *Candy* is from Arabic *qand* 'cane sugar'.
5. *amulet*. All the others have lost the initial letter *n* they originally had in English, because of confusion when preceded by the indefinite article. Thus, a *napron* was mistakenly taken as *an apron*, and *a nauger as an auger*. *Amulet* is simply borrowed from Latin *amuletum*.
6. *nonagenarian*. All the others contain a Greek or Latin element meaning 'not' (e.g. negotiate is from Latin *negotium* 'business', from neg- 'not' + *otium* 'leisure'). *Nonagenarian* is based on Latin nonaginta 'ninety', and has nothing to do with the negative element non.
7. *river*. All the others are distantly related by common descent from the assumed Proto-Indo-European root *wod-*, *wed-*, or *ud-*, meaning 'water'. *River* comes, *via* French from Latin *ripa* 'bank'.
8. *taboo*. All the others come from Chinese. *Taboo* is from Tongan.
9. *lamb*. This is a Germanic word, as are our other words for live domestic animals (cow, pig, deer, etc). Most words for the edible flesh of animals came into English from French after the Norman conquest.
10. *parade* and *paradise*. Both words in all the other pairs are of the same ultimate origin (e.g. *albino* and *album* both descend from Latin *albus* 'white' and *captain* and *chieftain* both from Latin *caput* 'head'). Parade and *paradise* are unrelated.

FOREIGN PHRASES

1 + C (French) A *la carte* is often found on restaurant menus in opposition to *table d' hôte*. This literally means host's table and refers to a set meal at a fixed price.

2 + H (Latin)

3 + L (Greek) This was the exclamation allegedly made by the Greek scientist Archimedes (287-212 BC), when on stepping into his bath, he conceived the principle that 'when immersed, a body displaces its own bulk of liquid'.

4 + E (French)

5 + B (Latin)

6 + I (Spanish)

7 + J (German) The phrase is associated with the Nazi era in Germany and encapsulates what were considered to be women's main concerns and priorities.

8 + K (French) The phrase literally means 'head to head'.

9 + A (Arabic)

10 + G (Italian) This is familiar as the title of an opera by Wolfgang Amadeus Mozart.

11 + F (French)

12 + D (Latin)

COINED WORDS

1. Horace Walpole (1717-1797) : The faculty of making happy accidental discoveries.
2. S.T. Coleridge (1772-1834) : Shaping disparate things into a unified whole.
3. Jeremy Bentham (1748-1832) : Between nations.
4. Sir William Temple (1628-1699) : The beauty of studied irregularity.
5. John Donne (1572-1631) : Having the same or a similar meaning.
6. Edmund Spenser (1552-1599) : Used by Spenser with uncertain meaning; now used to mean noisy obtrusive.
7. John Dryden (1631-1700) : A witty remark.
8. T.H. Huxley (1825-1895) : A person believing that God and ultimate reality are not, and cannot be, known.
9. Lewis Carroll (C.L. Dodgson) (1832-1898) : To move with a heavy clumsy tread.
10. Karel Capek (1890-1938) : A human like machine.
11. Enid Blyton (1897-1968) : The noise of a car horn.
12. Edward Lear (1812-1888) : Used by Lear with uncertain meaning; now used in *runcible spoon*, a sharp-edged fork with three broad curved prongs.

PHOBIAS

1. fresh air (from Greek *aer* 'air')
2. cats (from Greek *ailuros* 'cat')
3. heights (from Greek *akros* 'topmost, extreme')
4. open spaces (from Greek *agora* 'meeting-place, assembly')
5. enclosed spaces (from Latin *claustrum* 'bolt, bar')
6. work (from Greek *ergon* 'work')
7. the French (from Latin *Gallus* 'a Gaul')
8. the dark (from Greek *nykt-nyx* 'night')
9. corpses (from Greek *nekros* 'corpse')
10. foreigners (from Greek *xenos* 'a stranger')
11. dogs (from Greek *kyn-kyon* 'dog')
12. crowds (from Greek *ochlos* 'crowd, mob')
13. fire (from Greek *pyr* 'fire')
14. blushing (from Greek *erythros* 'red')
15. the number 13 (from Greek *triskaideka* 'thirteen')

APPENDIX

Foreign Words and Phrases

a fortiori

In Latin, for *from yet firmer ground or with stronger reason*. It is a term from logic and is used to introduce a fact that, if already accepted as true, must then be double true :

She could not have been cured in a month, a *fortiori* not in a day.

With the exception of very formal writing, it is better to find an english equivalent for this term.

agent provocateur (plural : agents provocateurs)

In French, for *describing a person who is employed to lead others-* by pretending to be an accomplice - into acts for which they will be discovered and punished :

Communist guerrillas have been arrested after being betrayed by *agenets provocateurs* employed by the government.

al fresco (also often alfresco)

In Italian, for *in the open air*. It is used only to describe eating in the open air; you do not swim al fresco or go to an al fresco theatre :

One of the delights of an evening's opera at Glyndeboume is the *al fresco* in that perfect garden setting.

alibi

In Latin, for *elsewhere*. In informal speech it has come to be used generally, but formally it is a legal term.

He denied being at the scene of the crime, giving as his *alibi* the fact that he was in hospital.

alma mater

In Latin, for *bounteous mother*. It is used by graduates to refer to the university where they studied :

amanuensis (plural : amanuenses)

In Latin, for someone *who writes from dictation*. The term is usually reserved to describe the personal and private secretary of an elderly individual :

As well as her housekeeper, Miss Armitage now employed *amanuensis* for her sight was fading and her fingers stiffening with arthritis.

ambience/ambiance

In French, for *surroundings* and is useful to describe a general atmosphere : The club's *ambience* was dark and romantic.

amour propre

Means *self-love* or *self-esteem* in French :

A writer's *amour propre* is dependent on the success of his books.

aplomb

A useful French word for describing certain actions that are performed in a self-possessed and spirited way :

He played a difficult piece on the piano with great *aplomb*.

a priori

In Latin, for *from the previous*. To argue *a priori* is to argue from assumed premises, not from experience :

There is no a *priori* reason for our failure; we must have made some mistake.

a propos (also often apropos)

French for *with reference* to. Do not use it in formal writing :

A *propos* (of) our conversation yesterday ...

bete moire (plural : betes noires)

In French, for *black beast*. In English, it is used to mean *pet hate* i.e. something which a person particularly dislikes :

Our English teacher's *bete moire* was the split infinitive; he was always pointing them out.

billet-doux (plural: billets-doux)

In French, for *love letter*. It is usually used in humorous sense :

He had hidden a *billet-doux* under her pillow.

blase

In French, for *surfeited with pleasure* (and with the senses dulled as a result) :

Living in Oxford had made him *blase* about the beauties of the city.

bona fide

In Latin, for *good faith, genuine*. The adjectival use is the more proper, and to be preferred to a substantive form which is sometimes seen (his bona fides-i.e. his genuineness impressed us) :

As a *bona* fide unmarried mother, she got a council flat immediately.

bourgeois

Means *middle class* in French. It is commonly used in a deprecating sense :

He was every thing a *bourgeois* stood for-concerned only for his respectability.

carte blanche (plural : cartes blances)

In French, for a *white paper*, used to mean a free hand or full permission :

As the consultant brought in by the firm, she had *create blanche* to suggest improvements.

chacun a son gout

In French, *Each man* to his taste :

'So you like pigs' brains?' he asked. '*Chacun a son gout.*'

charge d'affaires (plural : charges d'affaires)

In French, for a person responsible for affairs of state abroad, often an acting ambassador :

We regret that there is no ambassador for Brazil at present, only a *charged'* affaires.

chez

In French, for *at the house of.* It always takes the name of a person or persons after it :

The party is *chez* Paul.

chic

A French word for smart, stylish clothes :

She looked very *chic* in her pink beret and blue suit.

contretemps (plural : contretemps)

In French, for a *misunderstanding* and *awkward mishap* :

arriving early led to the unfortunate *contretemps* of finding my hosts in the middle of an argument.

coup de foudre (plural : coups de foudre)

The literal French meaning is *thunderbolt.* This is used to describe a subden and unexpected event or love at first sight :

It was a *coup de foudre* - they were married in two months.

coup de grace (plural : coups de grace)

In French, for *finishing stroke* :

I put the dying animal out of its pain by one swift *coup de grace.*

curriculum vitae (plural : curricula vitae)

In Latin, for an account of one's life. It is often abbreviated to C.V., and is used only in job advertisements :

Applicants must send a full *curriculum vitae.*

de facto, de jure

In Latin, de facto means *in fact or in reality.* It is a legal term, contrasting with the parallel phrase *de jure.* A de facto leader does not rule on a legal basis, but simply because he has won his position. He may gain official status later if he becomes a *de jure* ruler - if his position becomes legally regularised :

An army colonel overthrew the country's President and was its *de facto* leader until elections were held.

de rigueur

The literal French meaning is of *strictness*. In English, it is used (often slightly humorously) to mean *required by convention or fashion* :

Mini-skirts were *de rigueur* in the 1960s.

deus ex machina

In Latin, for *the God from the machine*. The term is taken from Greek drama, where a complicated plot would be resolved by the sudden appearance of a God. It can describe situation other than the plots of plays and films :

My aunts arrived, like a *deus ex machina*, and normalty was miraculously restored.

dilettante (plural: dilettanti or dilettantes)

The Italian word for one who dabbles in the arts or sciences but does not pursue them seriously :

He played the piono in a *dilettante* fashion, never practising.

double entendre

In French, for the double meaning there might be in puns and innuendoes; In the after-dinner speech he made any *double entendres* which set the *guests* laughing.

ennui

Describes a state of languor and boredom in French :

Ennui was a 19th century disease among rich people who had nothing to do.

entente cordiale

In French, for a complete and cordial understanding between two sovereign powers :

All *entente cordiale* between France and Britain has meant that the channel tunnel will now go ahead.

esprit de corps

In French, for a spirit of solidarity and unity with one's peers :

The *esprit de corps* of the rebels gave them the courage to bring down the dictatorship.

ex officio

In Latin, for *by virtue of his office*, in general; used only to describe the position of committee members :

As the secretary of the society, he will be an *ex officio* member of all the sub-committees.

faux pas (plural : faux pas)

Means *false step* in French. It is usually used to describe tactless mistakes :

She made a terrible faux pas when she congratulated my mother on her success, which was supposed to be a secret.

graffiti

Italian for scribbling or drawing on walls :

The schools walls were covered in *graffiti*.

hors de combat

Literally, in French, *out of the fight*. It is used to mean *injured* or in some way unable to do something :

I'm afraid i'm *hors de combat* : I've sprained my ankle and can't play tennis today.

infra dignitatem

In Latin, for *below one's dignity*. It is usually abbreviated in colloquial use to infra dig :

As, professional musician, she considered it *infra dignitaten* to play duets with her sister.

in loco parentis

In Latin, for *in the place of a parent*. A legal term, defining the relations of a principal to his pupils :

While his parents were abroad, the headmaster acted *in loco parentis*.

insouciance

In French, for *unconcern*, carelessness :

His *insouciance* about the risks he was taking was remarkable.

Jeu d' esprit

Means *witticism* in French :

He greeted my late arrival with a sardonic *jeu d'esprit*.

kudos

A greek word meaning *glory*, use in the sense of fame and prestige :

This obscure sportsman now enjoys great *kudos*, having won the championships.

laissez faire

In French, for *leave be*. The terms is usually used to describe government policy when events are allowed to take their course :

During the 18th century, the government had a policy of *laissez faire* for international trade.

louche

In French, for ambiguous, disreputable, shifty :

His attitude towards the affairs was very *louche*.

memento mori

Means *reminder of death* in Latin. It is the term which describes traditional death emblems :

Often you find a skull in the comer of the painting, a conventional *memento mori* reminding the viewer of his end.

milieu (plural: milieus of milieux)

In French, for *environment*, setting :

This is not the right *milieu* for thinking creatively.

nee

In French, for *born*. It is used in public notices of marriages and deaths to indicate a woman's maiden name :

Mrs. Sarah Cobbett (*nee* Latham) died on Tuesday.

non compos mentis

In Latin, for *not in control of one's mind* :

He was so drunk, he was *non compos mentis*.

non sequitur

In Latin, for *it does not follow* :

The idea that you can tell what the summer weather will be by where frogs lay their spawn is a *non sequitur*.

nouveau riche (plural : nouveaux riches)

In French, for one who has recently acquired wealth and who usually displays it ostentatiously :

He was a *nouveau riche* who took pride in buying a new carin every six months

obiter dictum (plural : obiter dicta)

A latin term used in legal language. It describes the opinion made by a judge when arguing a point of giving judgement, which is without binding authority, for it is not essential to his decision. Out of a legal context, it can therefore mean an incidental remark :

He intended his remark to be an *obiter dictum* which would not affect the decision.

Pace

In Latin, for *with all due respect* to the opinion of someone, notwithstanding the opinion of someone :

Pace the doctor's opinion, I am determined to run the race.

parvenu

In French, for *an upstart*, for someone who was newly risen into wealth, power or notice :

He was a *parvenue* in politics, quickly becoming unpopular with other politicians and the press.

patois

In French, for *regional dialect* or jargon :
Few of us could understand the *patois* he deliberately used.

persona grata/persona non grata [plural: personac (non) gratae]

Persona grata (In Latin: a person in favour) usually refers to someone who is diplomatically in favour with a foreign government. *Persona non grata* means the opposite :

The foreign minister was *persona non grata* in the country and his visit was shorter than had been arranged.

piece de resistance

In French, for the *principal course* or *item :*

The piece *de resistance* of the dinner was the salmon en croute.

post mortem

Means *after death* in Latin. It refers to the medical examination of a corpse to discover the cause of death :

The results of the *post mortem* showed that he died from natural causes.

prima facie

Literally, In Latin, for *at first face*. In English, *on first impression* :

This seems *prima facie,* the answer we are looking for.

pro rata

Means *in proportion* in Latin :

The salary will be *pro rata* age and experience.

pro tempore

In Latin, for the *time being*. It is usually shortended to *pro tempore* in coversation :

I will be responsible for the book-keeping *pro tempore.*

raison d'etre

In French, for a reason for *existence* :
His *raison d'etre* seems to be exploiting people.

rapport

In French, feeling a sympathy and understanding for someone else :
I felt an instant *rapport* with her.

savior-faire

In French, for *skill, know how :*

She showed great *savoir-faire* in persuading people to do things they didn't want to do.

soi-disant

In French, for *self styled* :

He was a *soi-disant* writer whose prose was incomprehensible.

status quo

Means *the state in which* in Latin, used to mean as things are or were. It is a legal term used in official language :

Now the management have revoked their decision, the *status quo* has been restored.

tableau (plural: tableaux or tableaus)

In French, for *picture or sight*, used in english to mean a living picture - a representation of a picture by people in costume :

When the children went to the gallery, they dressed up and created a *tableau* of one of the painting.

tete-a-tete

Literally, in French, *head to head*. In English usage, it means an intimate conversation between two people :

Come for coffee, and we'll have a *tete-a-tete* about it.

tour de force (plural: tours de force)

In French, for a feat of strength or a distinguished performance :

The stunts m the film really were a *tour de force.*

vice versa

In Latin, for the *other way round* :

If the price of apples goes down, people buy more and *vice versa.*

virtuoso (plural: virtuosos or virtuosi)

In Italian, for *an artist* (originally a musician) of the highest skill :

Kathleen ferrier was *virtuoso* singer.

vis-a-vis

In French, for *face to face*. In English use, it is a somewhat clumsy and pompous expression, better replaced by *about*, but since you will hear and see if you should be familiar with its meaning :

What do you think *vis-a-vis* the new proposals?

TEST YOUR KNOWLEDGE

Use a foreign word, instead of some of the words in these sentences :

1. He dabbled in many hobbies in an amateurish way.
2. When he became rich, he started to take luxuries for granted.
3. Please send details of your education, work experience, interests, etc.
4. He had suddenly become rich and famous and was letting the whole world know.
5. Are you in favour with the director?
6. Felt an instant understanding and sympathy with her.
7. It was an incredible performance. He is a brilliant comedian.
8. After he died, a medical examination revealed that he had been on drugs.
9. With all due respect to Mr. Huber's view, I still think, I am right.
10. He now leads the country, but not because he has gained this position lawfully.

Answers :

1. He dabbled in many hobbies, like a dilettante.
2. When he became rich, he started to be blase about luxuries.
3. Please send your curriculum vitae.
4. He was parvenu who, was letting the whole world know who he was.
5. Are you the director's persona grata?
6. I felt an instant rapport with her.
7. It was tour de force. He is a brilliant comedian.
8. A post mortem revealed that he had been on drugs.
9. Pace Mr. Hubert's view, I still think, I am right.
10. He is now the de facto leader of the country.